VERNON HINKLE

A Man Would Not Be a Good
American Citizen if He Did Not Know
of Atlantic City.
(Theodore Roosevelt)

BY THE
BEAUTIFUL SEA

BY THE BEAUTIFUL SEA

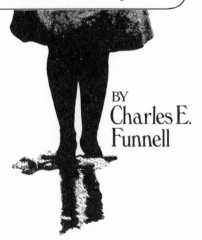

The Rise and High
Times of That Great
American Resort,
Atlantic City

BY
Charles E.
Funnell

NEW YORK   ALFRED A. KNOPF   1975

THIS IS A BORZOI BOOK
PUBLISHED BY ALFRED A. KNOPF, INC.

Copyright © 1975 by Charles E. Funnell
All rights reserved under
International and Pan-American Copyright
Conventions. Published in the United States
by Alfred A. Knopf, Inc., New York,
and simultaneously in Canada by Random House
of Canada Limited. Toronto. Distributed
by Random House, Inc., New York.

Library of Congress Cataloging in
Publication Data
Funnell, Charles E
By the beautiful sea.
Bibliography: p.
Includes index.
1. Atlantic City—Social conditions.
2. Atlantic City—Economic conditions.
3. Seaside resorts—United States.
I. Title.
HN80.A83F85 309.1′749′85 75–8219
ISBN 0–394–49175–0

Manufactured in the United States of America
First Edition

This history is dedicated to
Our Lady of the Jersey Meadows.

Contents

Preface

ONE FINE summer day, while pursuing a brief acquaintance with a charming if somewhat loony young lady whose taste ran to sleazy resorts, I found myself in Atlantic City. I was immediately taken with the gaudy whirl, the energetic vulgarity, the brazenly cheerful tastelessness of the place. Like all Americans, I assume in my viscera that the world began with Howard Johnson's, but a newspaper clipping in a taffy-shop window enlightened me. Atlantic City, it said, was some hundred and twenty years old, as old as the pyramids for American purposes. Suddenly, I scented mysteries on the Boardwalk. Some months later, having grudgingly taken a responsible and dull dissertation topic to wife, I happened to be at a party for graduate student historians. My consciousness elevated by a quantity of those cheaper wines to which graduate students are forced to resort, Atlantic City suddenly popped to the surface. Next day I drafted a new proposal; this book is the result.

By the Beautiful Sea attempts to construct a pattern of social history for the greatest popular Victorian American resort, using the themes of the Machine and the City, Nature, Morality, and Pleasure. I admit to some embarrassment for rendering these as proper nouns, but they occupied such a prominent place in the public mind at the end of the nineteenth century that I believe I am justified. The themes arrange themselves into two major alignments—namely, the Machine and the City versus Nature, and Morality versus Pleasure. The less tangible relationship between the two alignments emerges near the conclusion of the book. *By the Beautiful Sea* focuses on the 1890's, and nearly all of its data come from the years 1890 to 1908. This is the *fin de siècle* period, which witnessed the waning of Victorian society and its peculiar ambiance of social problems, moral values, and political and economic phenomena.

The term "Victorian" is not meant to be an idle borrowing. Queen Victoria, who ruled England for the immensely long time of sixty-five years, gave her name to the age. "Victorian" has many associations for English culture, but I will mention only those which impel me to apply it to American culture as displayed at Atlantic City in the 1890's.

Urban vigor and squalor, masses of humanity and a new popular culture, florid but charming sentimentality, sinister but inventive criminality, optimism and bad taste, ingenuity and eccentricity—these were Victorian America, as well as Victorian England. We shall see them all at Atlantic City.

Atlantic City was not entirely unique in this era. Unless a specific contrary claim appears, the reader may assume that much of what is true of this resort is also true of many of the other seaside towns of the Jersey coast at the turn of the century. In fact, while gathering data for my study, I occasionally examined material such as pamphlets promoting Cape May and Asbury Park, which were quite like those that extolled Atlantic City. This is all to the good as I see it, since a social history should attempt to deal with a culture's widely shared experiences rather than what is peculiar and exceptional. Nevertheless, Atlantic City's magnitude endows it with representative cultural importance lacking in smaller resorts.

I want to add two things here. The first is a declaration. I do not imagine myself to be above my subject. Anyone who has seen me taking the All-American Treat (burger-fries-shake) at the various franchise food pavilions I help support, riffling through stacks of 1930's girlie magazines at Philadelphia flea markets (*Stocking Parade*; *Zippy*, "Illustrated Breezy Fiction"), or affectionately musing over my lithographed tin Douglas "World Air Line" made in postwar Japan, will know how preposterous it would be to suggest that I gaze upon Atlantic City from an elitist pedestal. I find my own tastes as curious as the next man's. Nevertheless, I have sometimes been harsh and often sarcastic in dealing with my topic. I can only say that my apparent animosity is really disguised affection. I attribute a certain sourness in my temperament to too many solitary walks on deserted beaches as a child and the cannibalisms of modern life. Let me say flatly that—on the whole—I regard Atlantic City as a warm and appealing story, and I wish the contemporary resort long life and health.

The second thing I want to add is a question and its answer. What is Atlantic City of the 1890's about? I believe it is about the sadness of being merely human, the limitations of desire, and the compassion one feels in retracing the aspirations of dead people. For me, however improbable it may seem from what I write, history is a sacrament of compassion. Humans in large groups imply the need for mercy.

Of my personal and intellectual sources of inspiration for this book I will make brief mention. I was born on the wrong side of the elms in a patrician resort, Southampton, Long Island (now on the bourgeois skids). When I was very young, my father took me on trips to New

York City, and certain memories were given me forever: fresh deep-green paint on a subway entrance, a storm of ticker tape for a home-coming general, hot English mustard on a ham sandwich at the Hotel Commodore lunch counter, the sound of the word "Idlewild," and the stained copper of the Statue of Liberty. Much later, I came to love the view from the Pennsylvania Railroad as the train crosses the marshes in northeastern New Jersey. Here you can see the Empire State Build-ing over the crown of a rocky mound, beneath which the tracks plunge as they lead to Manhattan. And finally there were books—Alan Trach-tenberg's *Brooklyn Bridge*, Leo Marx's *Machine in the Garden*, and Theodore Dreiser's *Sister Carrie* come to mind.

The progress of *By the Beautiful Sea* from dissertation to book was facilitated by the Muse of Unemployment, the gracious companion of today's doctors of philosophy. Those cheaper wines to which graduate students resort are now a fond memory for wineless days. Neverthe-less, the slum-green interior in the district office of the Commonwealth of Pennsylvania Bureau of Employment Security has a meditative serenity which is rather attractive, and fruitful of scholarship.

I wish to thank the New Jersey Historical Commission and its Asso-ciate Director, William C. Wright, for a grant to defray my expenses of travel and research. Richard Sweeney, director of the Atlantic City Public Library, and Leslie Randall, supervisor of its local history collec-tion, kindly made the library's resources available to me. The respective staffs of the Historical Society of Pennsylvania, the Atlantic County Historical Society (particularly Mrs. Russell Andrew), the Free Library of Philadelphia, and the Division of Prints and Photographs of the Li-brary of Congress provided me with data and photographs in profusion, and Mr. William McMahon of Atlantic City graciously contributed several photographs from his personal collection. I am indebted to Pro-fessors Neil Leonard and Charles Rosenberg for criticism of my manu-script. My gratitude to Professor Michael Zuckerman could not be greater. His sharp criticism of the study's errors was exceeded only by his generous praise of its modest virtues. Messrs. Charles Elliott and David Bain of Alfred A. Knopf, Inc., were similarly encouraging in the latter stages of my effort. Finally, I want to thank my mother and father (a historian before me) for waiting patiently for the results.

BY THE BEAUTIFUL SEA

HARPER'S WEEKLY.

JOURNAL OF CIVILIZATION.

Vol. XXXIV.—No. 1755.
Copyright, 1890, by Harper & Brothers.
All Rights Reserved.

NEW YORK, SATURDAY, AUGUST 9, 1890.

TEN CENTS A COPY,
INCLUDING SUPPLEMENT.

Watching the tide come in at Atlantic City.

The Great Democracy Claims a Washbasin

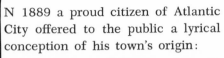

N 1889 a proud citizen of Atlantic City offered to the public a lyrical conception of his town's origin:

To the inquiry, "Whence came Atlantic City?" we reply: It is a refuge thrown up by the continent building sea. Fashion took a caprice and shook it out of a fold of her flounce. A railroad laid a wager to find the shortest distance from Penn's treaty elm to the Atlantic Ocean; it dashed into the water and a city emerged from its train as a consequence of the manoeuvre.

Several decades mellow one's vision. In truth, the critical moment in Atlantic City's creation came on a day in 1852 when Richard B. Osborne—a civil engineer from Philadelphia and a man of very practical instincts—led a group of timid local capitalists to the shore of forlorn Absecon Island on the Jersey coast. He wanted them to get the whiff of dollars in the breezes that skirled about the untrodden sands. His guests, city dwellers at heart, didn't care a fig for the wild beauty of the coast, but Osborne was made of stern stuff, and was not to be put off by the cautions of jerkwater capitalists. He had been in on the ground floor of the building of Chicago, *the* city of nineteenth-century America, and had acquired the arts of town-booming in the West. He told his companions that raw landscape was just the thing to carve fortunes from, and when they still quailed at the feasibility of a railroad across the bays and marshes to the island, he assured them that such technical problems could safely be left to him. He observed that if Cape May, the sedate little resort at the southern tip of the Jersey coast, could pull in 120,000 customers in 1851, they would be duffers indeed if they could not scare up 20,000 passengers in the first year of operation of a railroad to Absecon beach. He also whetted their appetite with a vision of the railroad's "rich reward to its enterprising promoters."

Engineer Osborne had been enlisted in the project by Dr. Jonathan Pitney, a resident of Absecon village on the mainland across from the island. Pitney had been a resident of Atlantic County since 1820, and was an important citizen, for he had represented his county at the

state constitutional convention in 1844 and had run for Congress in 1848. For two decades he had pondered the possibility of a railroad to the coast and the development of the beach. He met general discouragement. There were only seven houses on Absecon beach, and the people of the surrounding area cared little whether they received the blessings of urbanization or not. Besides, it seemed that Cape May had already monopolized tourism on the coast. Pitney knew better: Cape May was too far south to compete with a resort located next door to Philadelphia. The idea intrigued him for years, and he cast about for support. He assembled a group of moneyed backers who combined land and manufacturing interests in southeastern Jersey. These men included Thomas and Samuel Richards, glass manufacturers near Hammonton; Joseph Porter, glass manufacturer and landowner at Waterford; William Coffin and Andrew Hay, glass manufacturers and landowners at Winslow; William Fleming, owner of 60,000 acres at Atsion; Stephen Colwell, pipe manufacturer and owner of 100,000 acres at Weymouth; General Enoch Doughty, lumber manufacturer and owner of 30,000 acres at Absecon; and Jesse Richards, glass and iron manufacturer and owner of 50,000 acres at Batsto. His associates stood to gain at least two ways from a rail connection to the coast, and since Pitney himself owned 500 acres he would not be left out in the cold. After some difficulty, the doctor elicited a charter for a railroad from the New Jersey legislature in March 1852. With the help of Osborne, he persuaded his backers that the risk was reasonable, and a railroad company was formed. In June 1852 ten thousand shares of stock were sold in one day in Philadelphia to thirty-eight subscribers.

Osborne suggested the kind of resort he had in mind. It was not going to be another Newport. "The work-worn artisan shut up in the close and debilitating shops of the city, whose limited means prevent a long absence from his calling, will find here the rest and recreation he cannot now obtain." He was possessed of a homely vision of the town as the future "lungs of Philadelphia." Samuel Richards fancied that it might also become the winter port for Philadelphia, a rather idle speculation, since that city is not commonly icebound. In any case, it didn't take clairvoyance to see that the projected resort's main chance lay with the urban masses.

The railroad was built with such relative ease that it furnished no epics for future local histories, though it cost more than anticipated. Wharves and a station were built at Camden to receive the visitors from across the Delaware. The next goal was to buy up as much land as possible on Absecon Island to reap the profits that the new transportation facilities would provide. Only ten miles in length and quite narrow, the island presented attractive possibilities for monopolization. At the fiftieth anniversary of the founding of the resort in 1904, John Gardner, a congressman from New Jersey, claimed that "Atlantic City was in no sense a speculative venture. There was no purpose to develop the island with the object of increasing values." This is belied by the facts. The Camden and Atlantic Railroad started by buying up two hundred acres on the island at $17 per acre, and continued to buy land in such quantities that the New Jersey legislature eventually passed an act prohibiting further purchasing. But this posed no problem for the directors and stockholders of the railroad. They organized a Camden and Atlantic Land Company and continued to gobble up beach acreage. This avatar of Pitney and his friends issued a pamphlet to subscribers of railroad stock pointing out that the Land Company was a favorable venture: "You will be satisfied that your investment has been a good one, independent of the Land Company; the stock of which you cannot fail to see will be lucrative." The Land Company acquired a thousand acres at an average price of $10 per acre, and sales were made of the same land, after the railroad was put through, at $100 to $300 an acre. By 1900 this land was selling for $500 to $800 a front-foot. In 1884 an old resident of the resort recalled the lush times that had prevailed: "The people who lived here made just as much money then as now, because there weren't so many of them after the pennies. With a capital of $1000 one could become a land speculator and clear a good round sum without waiting very long." If Atlantic City was not a speculative venture, it made plenty of money all the same.

It was a happy arrangement: the railroad would increase the value of the Land Company's holdings, and the sale of land would bring customers for the railroad. But there was a further step. By building an excursion house, provision could profitably be made for the reception and entertainment of the railroad's customers. The same men, therefore, formed the Surf House Association, which erected a two-story block-long structure in 1854. The Surf House not only made money itself; its facilities further encouraged travel on the railroad and increased the value of the surrounding land.

The last task was to survey the area and to bring the town into being. Various names were advanced for the resort: "Ocean City," "Seabeach," "Surfing," "Strand," and "Bath." They were bland, imitative, or insufficiently pretentious. Once again Richard Osborne took a firm hand, for he knew what was required. When he unrolled his map of the town survey for the directors, "Atlantic City" appeared emblazoned across breaking waves. The directors enthusiastically assented. Thus was begun a significant theme in the resort's development, the claim to cultural symbolism. Twenty-five years later, when the town was beginning to enjoy flush times, Osborne recalled: "I have ever claimed, and do so now, that this name created in the minds of men throughout the Union a certain interest in the city, and this interest it was sought to further secure by giving to each state its own avenue." Samuel Richards is credited with the optimistic street nomenclature. The city was laid out with broad avenues parallel to the ocean: Pacific, Atlantic, Arctic, Baltic, Mediterranean, Adriatic. The right-angle streets were given the names of the states. It was a rigid grid plan, ideal for maximum profit from land sale, if boring in effect. Still, the land was flat as a pancake and had few topographical features. The city clung to the ocean and was thin and long. On March 3, 1854, the governor of New Jersey approved the City Charter, and on May 1, 1855, the city was officially incorporated. The first train to Atlantic City arrived on July 1, 1854, loaded with newspapermen and notables selected to help promote the town. The great Victorian American resort had been launched.

Why was Atlantic City placed where it was? Observers gave feeble answers, such as the proximity of the Gulf Stream, the angle of the beach to the prevailing winds, and the surrounding ring of water which allegedly made the island free of malaria (though there were mosquitoes aplenty). The only convincing explanation is that the resort lies in a straight line from Philadelphia to the Atlantic Ocean.

About the time of the resort's founding, industrialization had emerged as the dominant force in a hitherto basically agrarian society. The "country" and the "city" had formerly been distinct places, and there were genuinely pastoral sections free from urban influence. But technology was liquidating the barriers between urban and rural styles of life, radiating out from the cities as a great centrifugal force that was permanently changing the character of the countryside. In 1852 it was the Jersey shore's turn to feel this great change. In later decades the inhabitants of Atlantic City liked to imagine that unusual foresight and dynamism characterized the founding of their town, but the truth is that the Jersey shore could not escape the forces that were reaching out into the country everywhere. Lying only sixty miles from Philadelphia, it was predestined to come within the orbit of the city.

It is fitting that a city created inevitably by the outreaching forces of urbanization and industrialization should have no peculiar advantages. The expanding city had merely bumped into the ocean here first. A local history published in 1899—like the others, really a promotional history—admitted this frankly: "A casual study of the map of Central New Jersey affords no special hint of the advantage of this peculiar stretch of shore above that either to the north or south of it for many miles, save that here only it was possible to build a railroad direct to the beach. . . ." Following this the author added a couple of the slender "special advantages" mentioned above. A letter to the *Philadelphia Daily Times* prophesied that the new resort would be close enough to Philadelphia to permit daily commuting, whereby "one of the great drawbacks of Cape May is remedied." A magazine article of 1873 ascribed Atlantic City's leadership as a shore attraction to its accessibility: "The Camden and Atlantic Railroad . . . has simply drawn a straight line to the coast, which may be reached in an hour and three-quarters from Vine street wharf." The true provenance of the resort was somewhat embarrassing to the city's promoters at the turn of the century, for they liked to imagine that their town was the heroic creation of supermen; but they could take comfort from the fact that it was part of the march of destiny instead. Thus Alfred M. Heston, town eulogist, explained: "The attractions here do not depend on any special conditions. Atlantic City seems to have been marked out by nature as a point where all the forces needed for the constitution of a complete resort should centralize."

To say that compelling forces determined the location and shaped the role of Atlantic City is not to belittle the initiative of the founding fathers. In comfortable retrospect, history may appear to be a matter of unfolding certainties; in the midst of experience, however, it is not so easy to discern the pattern of events. The resort's builders knew not only hard work, but considerable anxiety as well, as they groped toward successful business formulas and dealt with the many variables of an entertainment economy.

Because Atlantic City was created by Philadelphia, it was also a satellite of Philadelphia. But one may validly call the city a "national resort," for by 1880 it enjoyed a sizable clientele from around the country. In the same year, the first reference to the "American Brighton" appeared. Nevertheless, the bulk of the town's trade came from Philadelphia, and while the national clientele gave it color and reputation, it could not have survived without the nearby city. This dependence touched every aspect of the resort's life. Philadelphia and Atlantic City were near enough to allow would-be visitors to react to bad weather and stay away, and if there was too much bad weather, the summer was a disaster. Much of the resort's food and building supplies, as well as its liquor and entertainment, came from the city. Even its crime was tied in with the great city.

This satellite relationship—which posed problems for resort businessmen, politicians, and all who depended directly or indirectly on tourist revenue—is well illustrated in Atlantic City's dependence on Philadelphia's newspapers. They were the principal source of free advertising, and their ill will could have most unhappy consequences. Local papers were a pale reflection of the big-time press, and they knew it. The first editor of the *Atlantic City Review* confessed that "while never aspiring to any great heights" for his publication, "owing to the proximity of Philadelphia and the facilities for bringing the journals of that city here in the early morning," he had simply hoped to "meet the demand for a reliable and popular home newspaper." The local newspapers could bluster about unfavorable statements in the city press, but they could do nothing about it. On the other hand, the city press could do plenty about the resort's newspapers and the resort itself. Their good or bad opinion spread far and wide.

The resort was in an awkward position, and it is hard not to have some sympathy for it. Regardless of right or wrong, the big city held all the aces and on occasion could relish its superiority. A vivid example occurred on August 30, 1891, when a *Philadelphia Inquirer* columnist smirked, "The season has been a failure!" Financial trouble and weather were partly responsible, he said, but there was more:

> There is a further explanation, however, and one which few have knowledge of. I tell it with regret. At the beginning of the season the correspondent of the Inquirer was told plainly and without a desire to withhold the thought that Atlantic City could do "without Philadelphia," that the metropolis had to come here anyhow, and that they, the hotel keepers, proposed hereafter to court the trade of Pittsburgh, and the West, Washington and the South. These schemers had as assistants a line of malcontents that were opposed to Philadelphia newspapers for reasons which they assigned, and to the Atlantic City Journalist Club in particular. They refrained from looking to the Philadelphia papers for help until the first of August, then they came begging for support. They urged that the old stories of wonderful success be told; that the old weapons of cajolement be brought out; that the old system of writing of the grand triumphs of this and that event be put in cold type. . . .
>
> A few newspaper men resolved to teach these nondescripts a lesson. . . .
>
> Have I sent you a line since that said the season was a prosperous one? Has any other correspondent said that there were 100,000 people here when there were only 35,000? Has any one told you that the places of amusement were jammed when they were virtually [deserted]? These newspaper men were representatives of the newspapers that sent them there, and they were refuting the idea that Atlantic City could do without Philadelphia.

The resort's hostility to Philadelphia newspapers in 1891 was probably due to a great exposé of seaside vice and corruption which the *Bulletin* had featured the previous summer. The Atlantic City Journalist Club was a gathering place in the resort for visiting newsmen, and its annual banquet was a reunion for men of the trade. The columnist went on to say that if the club was disbanded, newspapermen "would seek the pleasures and refinements of summer life in other quarters." Such a pointed warning was well calculated to remind Atlantic City of its satellite status in relation to Philadelphia—a status that affected many areas of its daily life.

Population figures reveal the development of Atlantic City. Of course, summer population was always much greater than the permanent population, but since the year-round population was directly related to summer use and residence (other sources of income were trivial for the town as a whole), permanent population accurately reflects growth:

(*estimated*) 1855	250	1890	13,037
(*census begins*) 1860	687	1895	18,329
1865	746	1900	27,838
1870	1,043	1905	37,593
1875	2,009	1910	46,150
1880	5,477	1920	50,707
1885	7,962		

It can be seen from the above that the resort began to come to life after the Civil War. From 1875 to 1910 it boomed, particularly during the 1890's. By 1910, the years of expansion were practically over, the town having reached its zenith with nearly fifty thousand permanent residents.

Times were indeed hard in the early years. The coming of the Civil War retarded the resort's growth and blighted its hopes: "Those who went away in '61 and returned in '65 found the landscape little changed." In 1871 the first report of the board of directors of the Camden and Atlantic Railroad mentioned the "days of darkness and depression" which it hoped had been left behind. The railroad's troubles ranged from flooding of its tracks to shaky financing, and the company took to offering dollar round-trip excursions to lure riders.

A visitor to the City by the Sea in its infancy found a bigger dose of nature awaiting him than the urban pretensions of the resort had led him to expect. His tribulations began with the train ride:

> *The dust was something fierce. The cars had canvas curtains*
> *hung from the sills on the sides on iron frames to within a short*
> *distance of the rails, which helped to keep down some of the*

dust. Everybody wore a linen or alpaca duster, a very necessary adjunct when traveling in those days. Any passenger that reached Atlantic City without getting his or her eyes full of cinders was looked upon as a curiosity.

When he arrived, the visitor discovered that the "city" was still a village. High tides occasionally flooded the streets, and until 1864 cattle were allowed to run at large. And the mosquitoes! Greenhead flies were bad every year, and in 1858 they appeared in such swarms that the complaints of visitors reverberated all the way to Philadelphia. The island abounded with hundreds of wet places where flies could breed, and the city had to fill them in or cover them with coal oil. The problem diminished in time, but as late as 1876 the flies were still an annoyance. Sir Charles West Cope, president of the Royal Academy of England and official portrait painter to Edward VII, exclaimed: "They were the largest I had ever seen, and would bite through thick hairy trousers. The knee, while sitting, was a favourite point of attack."

From 1852 to 1870 the beach was not highly developed. The bathhouses were crude structures that were carried down to the water in the summer and dragged into the dunes in the winter, and it was customary for anyone who owned property in the city to regard himself as entitled to a bathhouse on the sand. Permanent structures on the beach and exclusive property rights down to the high-water line had not yet appeared. There were, however, a number of hotels, the most important and prestigious being the United States, built in 1854 for the railroad but quickly sold to private interests. There were about a dozen others of importance, such as Schaufler's and Congress Hall and of course the Surf House. But in 1870 the resort still had a rather Dogpatch-like atmosphere. According to one visitor: "I could not help wishing that the city was a little nearer to the sea, or that there was less sand between them. It was deep in the street, it was in the gardens, over the fences, heaped up in drifts like snow, and as white, glaring insufferably in the sunlight . . ." Atlantic City was shortly to remedy this kind of complaint for all time.

In 1870 the first boardwalk was built. A skimpy affair eight feet in width and made in sections so as to be portable, it was all the same a milestone in the urbanization of the beach. Extending from Absecon Lighthouse to the Seaview Excursion House, it turned "tiresome areas of mosquito marsh and soft sand" into a bustling thoroughfare of tourists who preferred comfortable walking to pristine nature. This popular aversion to unmodified wilderness was manifested in the

market for hot and cold sea-water baths, a convenience introduced about this time at the Island House Hotel. The number of hotels proliferated, and about forty boardinghouses sprang up in their wake. Mule-powered streetcars began to operate in 1865, and by 1875 the town had acquired a city hall and a fire department. In the late 1870's, while the winter population was only around 5,000, the summer population was reaching 34,000. The village was acquiring the appearance of a city, as the retired first mayor noted. President Grant, that good man who nevertheless lent his prestige so well to private interests, gave the resort a boost by staying at the United States Hotel in 1874. "It was the turning point in the prosperity of the city," said a local newspaper. In spite of that, the Centennial year of 1876 was "dull and disappointing." Atlantic City suffered from the competition of the great exhibition in Philadelphia, its only compensation being the State of Michigan Pavilion, which was moved to the resort in sections to be used as a private residence.

But the trend of things could only be interrupted, not blocked. Now occurred events which were to push the city toward bigness and national status. In 1876 the president of the Camden and Atlantic, Samuel Richards, and two of its directors withdrew to organize a rival, the Philadelphia and Atlantic City Railway. A narrow-gauge line designed to be constructed cheaply, its entrance into Atlantic City divided the town politically and was hotly and unsuccessfully contested by the older line. Most residents were probably glad to get a monopoly off their backs. The narrow-gauge line did not prosper, and was sold in 1883 to the Philadelphia and Reading Railroad, which changed it to a double-tracked standard-gauge route. Thereafter it was a critical part of the resort's prosperity, greatly stimulating travel by the lower middle and lower classes. Meantime, in 1880 the Pennsylvania Railroad extended its West Jersey Division to the city, providing the first direct rail connection with New York City. The Pennsylvania proceeded to buy up the Camden and Atlantic in 1883, reducing the competing rail interests once more to two. Travel time from Philadelphia now was a very reasonable hour and a half, fully realizing Atlantic City's potential as an excursion center. While the local population resented the stranglehold the railroads held, they recognized that their prosperity depended upon excellent transportation.

Building proceeded apace. Besides the Seaview Excursion House, built to meet "the claims of the great democracy to a wash-basin," there appeared the Narrow Gauge Excursion House in 1877 and the West Jersey Excursion House in 1880. A second boardwalk, fourteen feet in width, replaced the first in the same year, while Colonel George W. Howard constructed the first public amusement pier in 1882, inaugurating a building form that not only was to be one of the chief appeals of the resort but would also threaten to obliterate the waterfront. John R. Applegate followed with a second pier in 1884, which at 625 feet was slightly shorter than Howard's. It had a large pavilion suspended over the water for dances, shows, and contests. In 1887 a pier of iron 1,000 feet long was begun, as competition encouraged more lengthy structures to hog the visitor's attention. By this time no one could mistake the coast of Absecon Island for wilderness. George F. Lee's Park Bath House, two-storied with 116 dressing rooms, was the commercial successor to the simple bathhouses of the old days; here the vacationer or excursionist could rent bathing suits and rooms by the day, week, or season. Lee owned the Brighton Hotel, now as esteemed as the older United States. Beer gardens and popular opera houses sprung up to entertain the visitors, and in 1888 at least 506 hotels and boardinghouses met the huge demand for accommodations. There were hotels for most pocketbooks and most tastes, too. An advertisement for the Windsor emphasized that there was *"no bar."* For Bedford House an advertisement featured the traditional pointing-hand symbol with the message: "N.B.—First class Bar and Restaurant attached." Of more importance to the lower middle class were the legions of boardinghouses that dotted the city. Lacking the elegance of the showy hotels, they were still part of the lifeblood of the resort.

The city acquired an important citizen in 1884 when Alfred M. Heston took over the editorship of the *Atlantic City Review* from A. L. English. Educated in Philadelphia's Central High School and the editorial offices of several New Jersey newspapers, he was a slightly built, vinegarish man much inclined to antiquarian studies and progressive Republican politics. He distinguished himself as the author of volumes on South Jersey lore, the creator of an annual handbook widely popularizing Atlantic City, a zealous booster of the resort's interests, and City Comptroller from 1895 to 1912. During his tenure in office, he demonstrated how wholly unsuited he was to urban politics by honestly auditing city accounts, earning for himself the cordial hatred of the Republican machine and eventual ouster from the comptrollership. Thus he coined the memorable line "I would rather be right than be Comptroller of Atlantic City." Nevertheless, Heston's participation in the *Review* lasted but three years, and thereafter—in the 1890's—that journal pursued a cozily sympathetic relationship with entrenched city powers. This encouraged the opposition of the *Daily Union,* a second

newspaper founded by John F. Hall in 1888. Democratic in sympathy, it was not averse to intelligent criticism of the resort's shortcomings.

In the twistings of the sapling could be discerned the configuration of the adult tree. It promised to be vigorous, but crazy-grained, a pepperidge rather than a pine. Already the resort offered a variety of loony but arresting entertainments, such as the ones to be found about the railroad excursion houses: "We have there all kinds of catchpenny shows, the wonderful women snake charmers, the man with the iron jaws, the learned pigs, the Johnny go rounds. . . . It is a real Vanity Fair." Some amusements had an exotic flavor, like the performances of one "prestidigitateur" who executed feats styled "The Egyptian Miser" and "The Eastern Magic Outdone," together with the more homely "Wonderful Bird, Dick." Crowds of excursionists poured into town to sample these enticements and to refresh themselves from the labors of working life. The niceties of religious observation did not inhibit them:

> There was no Sunday; that is, so that you would notice it. Bar rooms, billiard rooms, shuffle boards, bowling alleys all wide open and almost every place near the Inlet one would see a barrel of beer set up under a shed and crowds around drinking.

Gaudy and impious, the young Atlantic City also had a markedly unsavory streak that was to mature as fully as its other characteristics. One old inhabitant recalled that "the nearest building to my own was a shanty where the gamblers used to make rendezvous. . . . It was quite a notorious resort until Mayor Lewis Reed [1859–62] broke it up." But not all crimes in the town lacked victims, for eager and guileful eyes pursued the gullible tourist as he enjoyed his unwary recreations. As early as 1882, police were trying to drive "policy men" away from the city. Moreover, the city fathers did not emerge with unimpeached dignity from the first decades; in 1883 a group of taxpayers charged the city government with corruption in its expenditures. The annals of municipal skulduggery were to have many a later entry.

Two factors essential to the success of a mass resort were provided during the early development of Atlantic City. The first was a large work force to fill the hundreds of service positions which the operation of a resort demanded. Atlantic City found that blacks were the answer to a substantial part of its labor requirements. Far ahead of most northern cities, the resort acquired a significant black minority among its population. The 1,220 blacks in 1885 represented 15 percent of the town's residents, virtually all of them having come since 1870. By 1895 the number had increased to 3,893, or 21 percent of the population. The white community grew quickly, but the black community grew still more quickly, for in 1905 the total was 8,846, amounting to 23.5 percent of the population. The large number of blacks concentrated in Atlantic City presented a stark contrast to the adjoining areas on the mainland, where there were very few blacks. Moreover, only 1.6 percent of the population of New York City was black in 1890, and even by 1910 the figures were 6.4 percent for Camden, 2.2 percent for Jersey City, 3 percent for Newark, and 2.7 percent for Trenton. Thus Atlantic City, though hardly comparable to these large cities, nevertheless had to deal as a community with appreciable racial differences and the accompanying tensions, at an early date.

The curse of Atlantic City's laboring force was "seasonal" unemployment for most of the year. Brief opulence yielded to long months of the narrowest kind of living with nothing to do. Large numbers of blacks came because of the town's reputation, only to find that work was a short-range proposition. Stranded, with no livelihood and no means to return whence they came, they sought the paltry handouts supplied by the office of the Overseer of the Poor. Blacks were housed in squalid shacks huddled at the rear of hotels and crammed into back alleys. Dark, damp, with meager sanitary facilities, such homes contributed to the high mortality rate that prevailed for black children. Since the parents spent long hours at work, the situation was still worse: "Colored people came here for the purpose of doing laundry work and waiting, and their children are bottle-fed and neglected. The mortality is therefore very great among them in consequence." This apparently did not trouble the whites overmuch. Heston advances this explanation of black mortality to show that Atlantic City's death rate, low as he claimed it to be, was still lower for whites.

Blacks were in a poor position to resist economic exploitation. In 1877, when the narrow-gauge railway was being built, one landowner refused to allow construction across his land. The railway surreptitiously hired a hundred blacks for the illegal task of pushing the line across the disputed land one dark evening. Shortage of work forced blacks into cutthroat competition that made unionization impossible. At the Hotel Windsor in 1893 one waiter balked at the help's food and ordered a restaurant dinner from the head steward. The management informed him that workers were fed only in the employees' kitchen. Apparently the rest of the waiters did not find their meals palatable either, for that night they approached the steward.

He was notified the waiters were out on strike. He coolly told them to strike out for another job and summoned all the chamber maids attired in their nobby white caps and aprons to wait at

supper and the next morning he had a new force of colored waiters.

Although racial hostility did not lead to violence—the newspapers, at any rate, did not report any violence—there is plenty of evidence of tension. When blacks dared to reach for political power, the whites became vituperative. The press faithfully reported black criminality, sometimes in derogatory terms: "James Jones, colored, charged with attempting to set fire last night to the Seaview Excursion House, was before Recorder Leedom this morning. He is a half-witted coon." The schools were officially integrated in the 1890's, but mixed couples were vigorously discouraged. In 1893 the *Philadelphia Inquirer* claimed that the large number of blacks in the resort posed a severe "problem" for white visitors, prompting the *Philadelphia Weekly Tribune*, a black publication, to send a correspondent to find out what the trouble was. The *Daily Union* reported his observations, which certainly represented the wishful thinking of the resort, though they may or may not be what the correspondent thought:

> *He found no serious "problem" agitating the public. His people were here in great numbers because they were needed and had been sent for as servants. As a rule, they kept in their places becomingly, and did not intrude to offend those who were over-sensitive as to race prejudice. The colored people are natural born servants, taking bossing more meekly and gracefully, than white help, and are for these and other good reasons, generally preferred.*

Besides an abundant supply of labor, the second fundamental requirement of the resort was advertising. This was provided on many levels. The railroads played a leading role, particularly by bringing excursions of influential bankers, politicians, and the like to the city. There the town government saw that they had carriages at their disposal, fine food and lodging, and entertainment. The Camden and Atlantic encouraged the building of the first boardwalk in 1870, foreseeing that its popularity would stimulate rail travel. The railroads printed up large batches of pamphlets touting the resort, sometimes stretching the truth a good deal. Absecon Island suffered from a lack of sweet water, and only a few of the deepest wells were not brackish. Rainwater was collected in cisterns until 1882, when a pipeline was completed to the mainland. One Camden and Atlantic brochure turned shortcoming to advantage and puffed the resort's cisterns as superior to the shallow wells of other seaside towns, conveniently neglecting Atlantic City's lack of an alternative. With a cavalier regard for fact, a Pennsylvania Railroad pamphlet described the town in terms more suitable to the Riviera than the chilly winter coast of Jersey:

There is an out-of-doorness about the place that does not prevail at any other point in the same latitude. Even in mid-winter, when the Northern world is housed up in overheated quarters in order to secure some measure of comfort, sojourners at Atlantic City are lolling on the sands, revelling in glorious sunlight, and drinking in deep draughts of the strength-creating air. Long lines of these sun-bathers, snugly ensconced under flaming red umbrellas, form not only a picturesque but an exceedingly attractive feature of the city's daily life.

Surely Philadelphians could not be fooled by such buncombe, but distant travelers who swallowed the pamphlet must have discovered on arrival that descriptions including "flaming red umbrellas" were mercenary fantasies. Perhaps more persuasive was the endorsement the Camden and Atlantic obtained in 1878 from "eminent" Philadelphia physicians testifying to the salubrity of the resort; this endorsement was printed up and broadcast throughout the country. Exaggerated health claims were part of the arsenal of Atlantic City's seductions for decades.

The city was eager to encourage the convention trade, which became a permanent source of revenue and a means of attracting more guests. "The convention element is usually composed of intelligent and substantial people of the middle classes. They are well worth looking after as they are sure to go home and spread the fame of Atlantic City's greatness far and wide." The innumerable gatherings of what became a convention mill included such groups as the Elks, glass manufacturers, and rabbinical conventions (in 1894) and the American Medical Association convocation (in 1897). This was the kind of free advertising the resort favored, and it also included such windfalls as President Grant's visit in 1874 and the trip the Centennial Committee took there in 1876. The city tried hard to persuade President Benjamin Harrison to favor them in 1891, but he eluded the boosters' grasp. Over the years, however, many other notables succumbed.

Besides all the brochures and souvenir photograph albums the city cranked out, there were Heston's handbooks. Heston first published his guide to the resort in 1887, and continued it past the turn of the century. It was a sampler of romantic vignettes, hotel listings, things to do, merchants and services, sentimental poetry and engravings, and information on travel. The author used his newspaper connections to have the book reviewed and publicized in New York, Boston, Baltimore, Philadelphia, and St. Augustine, Florida. It was sold by the Reading News Company on its stands and on the Reading Railroad system, and by the Union News Company on the Pennsylvania system. The handbooks were full of the booster spirit, presenting a uniformly

sunny picture of the resort. Heston clearly enunciated the philosophy of boosterism in the 1887 edition: "It is a very easy matter to judge who are the public-spirited men of any town. It is those who help along every enterprise designed to further the interests of the place."

Magazine articles were a welcome source of publicity. Most of them were uncritical, and disseminated booster pap with the tone of informed journalism, thereby helping the resort manufacture its desired image in the public mind. And at least some magazines were not above a practical understanding with local interests. In 1894 the *Daily Union* reported that a representative of the *North American Review* was in town canvassing for an article: "One hundred subscribers for this popular magazine secures two or three pages of space of great value as an advertisement." Then there were the out-of-town newspapers, though they could provide negative as well as positive publicity. Nevertheless, their regular seasonal reporting of seaside life was a principal means of keeping Atlantic City in the limelight. Moreover, in 1900 hotelkeepers raised $16,000 for advertising in sixty newspapers in twenty cities, opened a travel bureau in New York City, and set up part-time offices in Chicago, St. Louis, Toronto, and Montreal. Picture postcards became exceedingly popular in the first decade of the twentieth century, affording the resort an inexpensive means of encouraging new visitors. With vivacious scenes of boardwalk and beach, often charmingly tinted, they passed direct impressions of resort life to friends and relatives ("Tillie—This Hotel is a little too classy for me, but I am right there with the goods alright." "Phila. is all right but Atlantic goes it one better.—Ed." "Dear Mrs. Compton—Am down in this wicked place today. Aren't you ashamed of the Gold Dust Twin." "Gee it is great to be foolish." "Dear Sis—Miss Knox is my room mate. She is a Presbyterian girl and good company. Send me a clipping from the V. which tells of the Barn dance.—Mallie").

Windfall advertising occurred in such forms as "Why Don't You Try, or the Rolling Chair Song" (1905). Appearing in sheet-music form with a colored illustration of the boardwalk on the cover, it combined traditional Victorian sentimentality with a chilling strain of Darwinian pragmatism:

> *Did you ever see a maiden in a little rolling chair,*
> *Room for two, Sue and you*
> *Hear the salty breezes whistle through her curly locks of hair,*
> *Oceans blue, so are you*
> *For another lucky fellow is attending by her side,*
> *There to stay, if he may*
> *And she whispers in his ear,*
> *Don't be quite so distant dear,*

Tho' we first met yesterday.

(Chorus) *Do you think you'd like me better*
                    If you thought that I liked you,
          Do you think that I'd be angry
                    If you stole a kiss or two,
          Do you think that you could love me
                    In the sweet, sweet bye and bye,
          If you think that you could learn to,
                    Why don't you try, why don't you try.

Just another season later in another rolling chair,
          There is Sue, so are you
But you don't remember Susan and her curly locks of hair,
          Nor does Sue think of you
So at last you get acquainted and you think you've made a hit,
          But you're wrong all a-long
For there'll be another year,
And there'll be another dear,
          Who will hear the same old song.

The "Rolling Chair Song" must have brought back many pleasant memories to parlor gatherings on dour February evenings and stirred anticipation of the coming summer season.

Beyond all the direct advertising, there was the factor of momentum. It was hard to get a resort rolling at first, because travelers had to be coaxed away from rival places, had to learn how to get to the new town, and had to be sold on its attractions. But once its reputation was made, Atlantic City rolled along under its own steam. Its superior location and its highly developed facilities discouraged new efforts to start shore resorts in the area. Moreover, the city's special emphasis on grandiose display, colossal turnover, and kaleidoscopic materialism forged a unique image for the urban masses of the period. Atlantic City was "in." This was the advantage of being a cultural symbol: For millions the resort was not to be criticized. It was a part of the definition of happiness, and hence contained no sadness or disappointment —an American Dream, a Victorian Disneyland for adults.

By 1890 the City by the Sea had made good on its name. It was a fairyland of wood, an epic of the jigsaw:

> *The architecture is varied and beautiful. There are nearly five-thousand structures, and it is difficult to find two alike; and where two are alike in contour they differ in coloring. Nearly all the buildings are frame, which affords the widest scope for architects and painters.*

Of course, some complained of the "distressingly ornate . . . yellow paint" and "planing-mill gingerbread," and Heston felt obliged to apologize that "the town lacks a few pretty curves and graces." Charles Dudley Warner, who with Mark Twain wrote a famous portrait of the times, *The Gilded Age*, chortled, "What will you have? Shall vulgarity be left vulgar, and have no apotheosis and glorification?" Atlantic City, he said, was the stylistic deification of the common man:

> *If the town had been made to order and sawed out by one man, it could not be more beautifully regular and more satisfactorily monotonous. There is nothing about it to give the most common- place mind in the world a throb of disturbance. The hotels, the cheap shops, the cottages, are all of wood, and, with three or four exceptions in the thousands, they are all practically alike, all ornamented with scroll-work, as if cut out by the jig-saw, all vividly painted, all appealing to a primitive taste just awakening to the appreciation of the gaudy chrome and the illuminating and consoling household motto.*

Nevertheless, to most lower-middle-class visitors Atlantic City was a secular heaven, and if its architecture was garish, it related to their taste and aspiration in a way that today's aluminum and poured concrete perhaps do not. True, it was a flammable city. One official begged loyal citizens to be careful about going overboard during Fourth of July celebrations for the Columbian year of 1893, lest the town not be standing on the morrow. At regular intervals, in fact, parts of it disappeared in a twinkling. But wood was cheap and new buildings could be constructed quickly, and capital was plentiful in a city which promised heady profits. There were many disappointments, but no real tragedies.

At the beginning of the 1890's, the Mauve Decade, Atlantic City regularly drew the trade of the eastern cities, and had weekly patron- age from Pittsburgh, Cincinnati, St. Louis, Chicago, and more distant places. It had decisively won the struggle for Philadelphia, with Asbury Park relegated to an unthreatening second. Cape May might be more high-toned, but it had experienced its zenith and was no longer a serious competitor. The *Cape May Star* flattered itself that its town was free from "the gross immoralities" that prevailed at the City by the Sea, but that was just sour grapes. "More doctors, more ministers, more statesmen, more millionaires, more family, cottage people [*sic*] come to Atlantic City in one year than go to Cape May in five," sneered the *Daily Union*. Though the visitors may have been incorrectly identi- fied, numerically the newspaper was right. Atlantic City rang the bells of profit louder than any other resort on the Jersey coast; it was a cathedral town of the capitalist faith. Travel time from Philadelphia had declined from ninety to sixty-eight minutes, and in a couple of years the "Royal Reading Route" would reduce it to a stunning fifty minutes. As a result, the transient population was mammoth. In addition to the huge accommodation industry, there was a gargantuan entertainment industry of great and small elements: light opera and musicals, vaudeville, variety, popular music, mechanical rides, spectacles, "auction" houses, sand "sculptures," and other amusements in endless variety. The boardwalk had passed through a third to a fourth incarnation, a formidable steel-framed wooden boulevard crammed with shops, eager to have front footage on the new social and economic artery of the town.

A typical trip to Atlantic City might begin on a July day in 1891. Philadelphia, an old, dignified, and cultivated city, is nevertheless

cursed with a summer climate not comprehended in the term "temperate." Hundreds of blocks of chocolate-colored homes melt in the sun, and miles of red-brick row houses swelter in the velvet atmosphere. The streets are fouled with swill from vendors' carts and stalls, horse manure, refuse of shops and homes, and impacted layers of anonymous filth. The humid, smoky air leaves an oily film on the body, making starched shirts stick to armpits and dresses to backsides. The Schuylkill and Delaware rivers offer no relief to the eye or to the skin, save to the children of the poorest families who dare to dive from cluttered banks into fetid water.

On this ordinary Philadelphia summer day, passengers board a ferry at 9:15 a.m. for Federal Street in Camden. In ten minutes they are seated on the Camden and Atlantic Railroad's Atlantic Express, Train No. 277, nonstop to Atlantic City. For the first dozen miles, the train passes through early traces of suburban growth, with fledgling developments at Collingswood, Westmont, Haddonfield, and Lindenwold. Hurtling through the Kirkwood station, the passengers glimpse Lakeside Park, a picnic grove and amusement park which the Camden and Atlantic runs for city people. But in 1891 a healthy Philadelphia has not yet yielded the despairing exhalation of regional suburbia, and after Lindenwold patches of pine forest appear and become progressively denser, broken by the orchards and charcoal works of Berlin. The track winds in shallow curves past creeks, marl pits, and cranberry bogs, and by the time the vicinity of Atco is reached, the solemnity of the landscape contrasts vividly with the city but twenty miles behind.

Ahead stretch the pine barrens, somber and mysterious, but to the Victorian eye an ellipsis of civilization. Pitch pine and scrub oak dominate the view, blueberries grow in the underbrush, and druidical white cedars preside over gulfs of sepia-colored swamp water. Even from the onrushing train, the fiery-orange butterfly weed and molten goldenrod are visible in the fields, and pungent yarrow, fragrant purple horsemint, loosestrife, pitcher plant, Queen Anne's lace, and mullein grow in the thickets, swamp edges, and tracksides.

Atco is a modest glass-making village, Chesilhurst is hardly larger than a hamlet, and Waterford is a half-deserted mill town with boarded-up homes and a burnt-out factory. Dense forest brackets the right-of-way, nearly overwhelming the tiny new settlement at Ancora, and past Winslow Junction the tracks plunge dead straight through the wilderness toward the coast. Hammonton is a large fruit-growing town, but Elwood is a sandy waste platted by speculators into a paper city of nonexistent parks, avenues, squares, and lots. The train continues past creeks and swampland to the Italian and German wine-making settlement of Egg Harbor City (neither a harbor nor a city) and onward through Germania, Pomona, and Doughty's, tiny islands of habitation in a forlorn sea. At Absecon, the salt marshes announce the last stage of the journey, as pine-barren vegetation yields to saw grass and sea lavender and the air is tinged with salt. The train turns hard right to skirt Absecon Bay and runs out over a marshy neck of land.

Atlantic City suddenly unfolds to view, perched like a mirage across four miles of briny flats, the Atlantic Ocean winking electric azure between the great hotels which stand as a huge dike before the sea. In a couple of minutes the train lurches across the drawbridge over the Beach Thorofare into the city itself. At 10:45, amidst a hiss of steam and the frantic squabbling of hotel touts, the passengers descend. To the asphyxiating heat, drabness, and familiarity of Philadelphia, to the morose emptiness of central New Jersey, the resort opposes a prismatic wonderland of new paint, brightly colored confections, best clothing, cool sea breezes, music, and motion—a fantasy island of laughter, novelty, display, prosperity, and optimism. Life as it is lies sixty miles back down the tracks; life as it should be is a two-block walk from the station. For the crowd which Train No. 277 disgorges at the Atlantic City station, and for hundreds of other trainloads which endlessly arrive, there is no desire to glance behind.

The city had attained the national resort status it desired, and could claim to be "the Brighton of Philadelphia, as Brighton is now the Atlantic City of London." The resort was unselfconscious and confident of its national popularity. As "the verdict of the people," it unblushingly built things, professed things, and showed things which gave the place a surreal atmosphere, larger than life. One cultivated observer exclaimed: "Atlantic City is an eighth wonder of the world. It is over-whelming in its crudeness—barbaric, hideous and magnificent. There is something colossal about its vulgarity." But multitudes of less sophis-ticated Americans felt simply that it was an eighth wonder.

2

Newport of the Nouveaux Bourgeois

ANY different kinds of people patronized Atlantic City in the turn-of-the-century period, but the ambiance of the resort was lower middle class. From this class came the greatest number of visitors and the largest part of the city's revenue, and accordingly the atmosphere of Atlantic City was a product of lower-middle-class preferences and aspirations. Many people today believe, and some at the time asserted, that the city was then an upper-class resort. Articles appearing recently in popular magazines have offered a casual sketch of the gentility and elegance of the Victorian resort, its swell tone and distinguished patronage. We will speculate on the causes of this attitude in the last chapter, but here we must consider why it is basically erroneous. Bedizened, gauche, extravagant, conniving, ingenuous— Atlantic City from the start depended on the lower middle class for its success, and was the charming preposterous artifact of its customers' tastes.

Before beginning, it is necessary to consider the class structure applied here. The most useful divisions for the town's history are upper class, upper middle class, lower middle class, lower class, blacks, and bums. The upper class is divided into "society," defined strictly as individuals listed in the *Social Register* for Philadelphia, and the nouveaux riches, those enjoying wealth but not yet accepted by the traditional upper class. The upper middle class consists mainly of professional people, substantial businessmen, executives, and the like. Also, and importantly, newspaper editors. To the lower middle class belong lesser white-collar workers of all varieties, including the many different kinds of clerks staffing the commerce and retail trade of Philadelphia. Many of these are women, employed in growing numbers as salesgirls. The lower class consists of factory workers, male and female, and other laborers engaged in heavy, tedious, and generally unremunerative work. Blacks include residents of Atlantic City and visitors from Philadelphia, and are properly considered apart from all classes of whites, in a period which witnessed the acme of racial sentiment in American society. Economically trivial but socially interesting, bums are the *Lumpenproletariat* of unemployed drifters and down-and-outs.

Many observers of Atlantic City believed, or liked to believe, that it was an expression of high society. A Pennsylvania Railroad pamphlet of 1889 spoke of the "representatives of the best society" which frequented the resort. In 1897 a member of the Atlantic City Hotel Men's Association, expansively describing the future of the town in the twentieth century to a Philadelphia businessmen's group, predicted that a bicycle path recently built between the city and its resort would be improved to a broad highway for the wealthy: "A modern Appian way, upon which the rich and pleasure-loving people, blessed with fine horses, can drive down from Philadelphia in their carriages." John F. Hall, editor of the *Daily Union*, boasted that "there is hardly a family of any prominence residing within a thousand miles of this favored region that has not at one time or another occupied, as host or guest, one of the beautiful homes which form the crowning glory of the town." The resort's Easter Parade, one of the annual highlights, drew great crowds to promenade the Boardwalk. *Harper's Weekly* said of it in 1908: "Practically all of the Easter guests here are people of wealth and fashion. . . . Seventy-five per cent of their names figure in the social registers of their home cities."

Such claims, of course, are immediately suspect. If they are to be believed, Atlantic City was hot on the trail of Newport for the patronage of the Four Hundred. Was the resort in fact laying hold of the fashionable clientele of the Quaker City?

An examination of the "hotel personals" which the *Daily Union* regularly printed in the 1890's is illuminating. While not captioned "social column," these lists clearly were the cream of the visiting crop in the newspaper's eyes. They were compiled from the registers of the principal (and most expensive) hotels that lined the Boardwalk, a selection device which simplified the editor's task, since these great structures embodied the town's most forceful claim to elegance and sophistication. An examination of twenty-six weekly lists—chiefly in 1890, 1893, and 1894, when they were prominently and extensively featured in the newspaper—yields 467 names of distinguished visitors. These were all from Philadelphia (if a visitor came from a different city, the *Daily Union* noted that fact). A comparison of these names with the appropriate *Social Registers* yields 10 definite listings and 5 possible listings. Lest it be thought that the resort press was too yokel an affair to recognize society when they saw it, similar data from the *Philadelphia Inquirer* may be added. Of 327 distinguished visitors to Atlantic City (1892, 1894, 1901), 14 are found in the *Social Register.* In addition, of 142 arrivals on a single day at a dozen hotels (including the prestigious Traymore, Windsor, and Chalfonte), 4 are listed.

But perhaps Philadelphia society, while not thronging the hotels, maintained a sizable cottage community at the seaside. The Social Register Association published a summer edition in 1900 which gave 763 addresses of individuals or families, listed in the winter register at Philadelphia residences, who had summer homes elsewhere. Only 31 of them gave a summer address for Atlantic City, and 7 of these are not private homes but hotels. Though this edition of the register gave the same information for society members from Baltimore, Washington, New York, Chicago, and Boston, only one individual from these cities had a summer residence at the resort. Taking the summer addresses of the first two hundred Philadelphians in the register, we find fully half of them choosing the fashionable Philadelphia suburbs (such as Chestnut Hill and the Main Line), with most of the rest scattered among various northeastern resorts and foreign countries. Seven preferred Atlantic City. In sum, if high society was not utterly absent at the City by the Sea, there was something less than a surfeit of tweed on the Boardwalk.

Who were these "distinguished visitors" then? The brief descriptions attached to some of the names in the *Daily Union* give an idea. They are offered as given, with no attempt to harmonize the syntax: "Pennsylvanic Cycle Co.," "the well known brick manufacturer," "a prominent official in the passenger department of the Pennsylvania Railroad," "candidate for District Attorney of Philadelphia," "a prominent businessman," "a prominent merchant," "a well known carpet manufacturer," "a prominent Philadelphia Civil Engineer," "a prominent member of the Quaker City bar," "manager . . . of the Philadelphia Press," "a well known Philadelphia letter carrier," "publisher and printer," "one of Philadelphia's most prominent physicians," "a well-known Philadelphia shoe manufacturer," "a well-known Philadelphia fruit dealer," "a prominent iron merchant," "Select Councilman of the Tenth Ward," "President of the Penn Mutual Life Insurance Co.," "President of the Fire Association of Philadelphia," "real estate agent," "publisher of The First Ward News," "of Common Councils," "the well known Philadelphia politician," "a prominent Philadelphia lumber merchant," "well known wholesale grocer of Philadelphia," "the 8th street shoe merchant," "Recorder of Deeds of Philadelphia." Also, twenty-one physicians.

These were the elite of business, manufacturing, government, publishing, and the professions. They were not high society. How a "well known Philadelphia letter carrier" made the list is anyone's guess; the inclusion seems ironic, but it was probably meant seriously. In six instances, ladies at the great hotels are specifically described as high society: "a pretty society lady of Germantown," "a popular acquisition to the large number of society representatives stopping at the Waverly," "a leader of society of Philadelphia," "a handsome blonde and prominent in Philadelphia social circles," and others. Yet none of these ladies is listed in the *Social Register*. It cannot be said that a blueblood never trod the strand, but society stayed away from the town with marked assiduity. Most of the rich who did come were the men who gave the Gilded Age its name, the nouveaux riches who were forging industrial America and growing fat on the proceeds. With them came the upper middle class, who could afford some of the same luxuries in more modest degree. The pseudo-snobbery of resort literature was partly aimed at both groups. If they couldn't be invited to Newport, they could buy their way into Atlantic City, but they would have to share the city with the classes they were escaping from. One article put it in just these terms:

> The ultra-swell and almost no one else go to Lenox, Bar Harbor, Newport. Swell and near-swell and folks "just comfortable" go to places like Asbury Park. Into Atlantic City every day in the season are dumped ultra-, almost-, and near-swell, folks comfortable and uncomfortable, and absolutely every other kind by the thousands; for that's Atlantic City.

There are numerous indications that those not having a vested interest in the promotion of the resort regarded it as lowbrow in atmosphere. The year 1894 was a black one for the national economy, but the *Philadelphia Inquirer* claimed that the resort had acquired new visitors from "influential society" and the "wealthy classes, ranging from the tens to the hundreds of thousands valuation." The author of the article, while seemingly sympathetic to the resort's interests, gave it a backhanded slap: "Some of these people came because they were tired of other resorts and wanted novelty, which they certainly get here, and others visited here because they could not afford to go to the more ultra and consequently much more expensive resorts." In 1909 a visiting journalist sardonically portrayed the nouveaux riches in the town. These are not the "Financiers" or the "Titans" whom Theodore Dreiser portrayed; these are bush-league robber barons:

These men are mainly railroad men and manufacturers—not the heads of railways, but assistants and deputies and lieutenants. They have money in abundance without being vastly rich, and they come to Atlantic City because it so exactly suits their barbarous ideal of what is fine.

They never think of anything outside the subject of iron or coal or pork or wheat or railway rates. They incarnate crass materialism in its most hopeless form.

The *Daily Union* complained in 1892 that the resort was failing to attract "the patronage of millionaires" because it lacked a really posh hotel of the "first class Ponce de Leon" variety. Indeed, by 1887 Atlantic City was already developing a suburb named Chelsea, to which its upper-middle-class natives were retreating. The locals had begun to sniff at their customers.

Although the resort's nouveaux riches might be crass materialists, they were not always humorless. The *Inquirer*, observing that powerful Philadelphia politicians are often seen at the shore, mentions an anecdote of "George W. Ledlie, the generous and big-hearted Port Warden of the Thirty-second ward, and the gentleman who has 4300 men working for him on his electrical traction work in Philadelphia and other cities." The tale is not without relevance to Atlantic City's moneyed customers and to Gilded Age ethics:

Mr. Ledlie tells a story, which is worth repeating, of an old firm of coal dealers who had as an employe an individual who was about as dumb and thick-headed as they come. This failing on the man's part became so apparent, finally, that the firm decided to discharge him. To bring this about, one of the members, with his visage full of foreboding portent, said: "Say, Bill, what do you know anyhow?"

The employe said: "Well, not much, boss. But I know that 1800 pounds makes a ton." That the man was kept on the firm's pay-roll, it is needless to say.

Quite apart from transient patrons, many of the resort's upper-middle-class users were resident throughout the summer in the city, renting the great number of cottages which the locals vacated for the season to pull in some extra money. Editor Hall estimated that there were over four thousand cottages on Absecon Island and that fully half of them were rented each summer. Such seasonal residents were often professionals and executives who commuted from Philadelphia, apparently each day, leaving their families by the seaside. A Camden and Atlantic Railroad brochure of 1883 encouraged this trade, while in 1893 the Reading Railroad sold twenty-trip commutation tickets for $17.50. This portion of the resort's clientele was reliable and dull, the least colorful part of the visiting population. It was certainly welcome, yet the garish, intense pleasure industries of the Boardwalk were aimed at the more transient customers. The cottagers spent their money peacefully and left comparatively little historical record.

At the other end of the social spectrum were the blacks, both resident and visiting. Evidence of their activities is hard to come by, for while the resort was highly dependent on black labor, it was anxious not to advertise the presence of blacks to potential white customers. Since most blacks were poor, they could hardly constitute a large tourist population. On the other hand, merely by working in Atlantic City they were able to avail themselves of some of the pleasures of the resort. The New Jersey state census of 1905 shows that, of 426 resident blacks, only 38 had been born in New Jersey. Of the vast majority not native to the state, 130 had been born in Virginia, 86 in Maryland, 43 in Washington, D.C., 34 in Pennsylvania, and 27 in North Carolina. A total of 47 were from fifteen other states, and individuals had come from Cuba, England, and Australia. A great many no doubt lived in Philadelphia before seeking work in the resort. Nevertheless, directly or indirectly they found themselves in a very special community, some of whose pleasures could not be denied them.

It was a situation not entirely agreeable to the local establishment. In 1893 the *Inquirer* complained:

> *What are we going to do with our colored people? That is the question. Atlantic City has never before seemed so overrun with the dark skinned race as this season, probably because the smaller proportion of visitors makes their number more prominent. At any rate, both the boardwalk and Atlantic avenue fairly swarm with them during bathing hours, like the fruit in a huckleberry pudding. This has gone so far that it is offending the sensitive feelings of many visitors, especially those from the South. . . . Of the hundreds of hotels and boarding houses which stud the island from one end to the other, it is probable that not a dozen could be found in which white help is employed. And when to the thousands of waiters and cooks and porters are added the nurse girls, the chambermaids, the barbers and bootblacks and hack drivers and other colored gentry in every walk and occupation of life, it will easily be realized what an evil it is that hangs over Atlantic City.*

Although this complaint is a good expression of the contradictory mentality of a white culture which employed blacks for every personal service and yet was distressed by the thought of mingling with them in the surf, it is nevertheless an admission that the city made no real attempt to exclude blacks from the beachfront. The article went on to say that in Asbury Park the problem had been solved by the founder and "original proprietor" of the resort, who restricted blacks to certain defined areas. But in Atlantic City, with ownership diffused in hundreds of hands, no such unified suppression was possible. The author conceded that only the collaboration of all the beachfront proprietors could keep the blacks in their place, a collaboration which (one suspects) was unlikely. Seven years later the *Washington Post* complained of the way local blacks by the hundreds were invading the bathing districts "heretofore patronized by the best visitors." Conditions were similarly lax off the beach: "After the colored waiter serves his master's supper he can go out and elbow him on the Boardwalk, crowd him in the cars, or drink at the very next table to him in almost any cafe." But it would be wrong to imagine that blacks at the resort were always coldly viewed. In July 1900 the *Inquirer* good-naturedly (if condescendingly) mentioned "a beautiful young colored lady becomingly garbed in broad, longitudinal stripes of black and orange alternating and carrying an indescribable, unmentionable parasol into the surf with her to shield her complexion from tan and freckles while in water up to her neck."

Of course, Atlantic City was not in fact completely integrated. Various kinds of informal segregation were practiced everywhere. The *Daily Union* records the criticism of a black Pennsylvania newspaper concerning the "color line" in the resort. Although black servants could sit in the pavilions along the Boardwalk, wealthy black tourists were denied admission. Such inverted discrimination in favor of poor over wealthy blacks was perfectly logical, given the racial convictions of the whites. After all, the servants had to be in Atlantic City: the black tourists did not.

The amount of black excursionism to Atlantic City is, as has been suggested, harder to determine than the use of facilities by local blacks. Nevertheless, it is clear that during the 1890's there was an annual outing to the resort for blacks from Philadelphia and the surrounding area. The *Daily Union* reported the visit of five thousand blacks to the Seaview Hotel and excursion district on September 3, 1891. They used public conveyances, swam, and enjoyed themselves at the Seaview's dance hall and carrousel. The date, September 3, is interesting. At that time Labor Day had not yet been made a national holiday and September 1 marked the end of summer at the shore, after which resort trade quickly dried up. It may be that the blacks who organized the excursion chose a date just after the close of the season to avoid offending the whites. Moreover, the money would be welcome as a post-season windfall.

The *Inquirer* observed in September 1896 that "one of the harbingers of fall is . . . the annual excursion of colored citizens from Pennsylvania, Delaware and New Jersey to the seashore." The visitors that year remained in the lower Boardwalk area, and "the beach below Texas avenue was devoted exclusively to the dusky bathers." The newspaper approvingly commented on their orderliness, for there were very few arrests and "the race weapon, the 'razor,' was conspicuously absent." In September 1897 the annual black excursion drew eleven carloads over the Pennsylvania Railroad and twenty-five over the Reading. Some travelers reportedly came from as far away as Maryland for the event. The 1898 convocation prompted the *Inquirer* to remark that there was "no more disorder than there would be were the gathering composed of an equal number of whites."

Whether Atlantic City's hospitality to blacks warmed as the decade advanced is not clear from the limited evidence, but in 1897 there was a holiday during the regular season in mid-August for "the belles and beaux of the colored quarter" of Philadelphia. They chartered two gaily decorated streetcars with musicians aboard for a round-trip party over the length of Absecon Island. Another August excursion took place the following year, and on August 22, 1899, the Baptist National Colored Congress met at Atlantic City, where "Miss G. H. Hoggers, of Philadelphia, caused a sensation when she said that God knew his business when he made the negro black, and that he should not seek to get white by using cosmetics." Black excursionism continued into the twentieth century, as evidenced by a postcard dated from Atlantic City in August 1909: "Never saw so many of the Colored race on any train. 11 cars of them. 27 whites *only*."

Thus it appears that while blacks suffered under the traditional exploitations and disadvantages of racial prejudice at the resort, they nevertheless enjoyed certain opportunities to outflank white society. Racial barriers more rigidly enforced elsewhere were hard to preserve at the seaside, and sometimes they were largely relaxed. Moreover, blacks were able to achieve some political power, as we shall see later.

At the very bottom of the heap of the resort's users was a group which contributed neither money nor labor, and therefore was not welcome. Atlantic City wanted a smiling face, for important reasons shortly to be discussed, and the presence of tramps disturbed the smile. There was a good deal of pathos in their situation: "Ten tramps, like a flock of sheep, being chased down the railroad track by officer Piner was an amusing sight witnessed by many this morning. As the summer season progresses these undesirable visitors make their appearance, stealing rides in freight cars." The city's policy was to hustle tramps as quickly as apprehended over the drawbridge back to the mainland. Bums who applied to the city jail, however, were given overnight lodging. Perhaps this service was granted on the condition of their leaving town, though this is only conjecture. At any rate, in 1897 a total of 471 persons were admitted as "Lodgers," "Tramps," and "Bums" to the city jail. The authorities had a habit of categorizing them: 229 were classified as "Americans," 129 as Irish, 38 as black, 36 as German, 4 as Jews, and 2 as English. The *Daily Union* complimented the Jews on their "excellent showing," "considering the large numbers in this city and the fact that many are constantly traveling . . . in their effort to earn their livelihood." The resort had particular trouble with tramps during the severe depression beginning in 1893 (the worst to hit America until the Great Depression of the 1930's); in that year a detachment of Coxey's Army passed through town, to the great amusement of the employed. This was a novel incident, but hoboes were a recurrent problem. In 1908 it was observed: "There are no beggars around to bother [the visitor]; they and the tramps are run out of town as soon as discovered." By 1912 the Salvation Army had an "industrial home" in the resort, and the Volunteers of America had a lodging house for transients of both sexes. Such was seaside life for those who tarnished the Gilded Age.

Between the extremes of the rich and the déclassé stood the lower middle and lower classes. Certainly these two groups were distinct from each other, but together they comprised the great mass of visitors to the resort. Evidence points to the numerical preponderance of the lower middle class, with the lower class coming in its wake and enjoying whatever its modest means would allow. In terms of numbers, the greater part of the accommodation industry was directed toward the lower middle class, while the values expressed in the resort's entertainment were those of citizens vigorously striving for the good life which they believed they could attain and which they imagined the upper middle class and rich to enjoy. It seems likely that upper-middle-class observers tended to lump the lower middle and lower classes together. A laborer in clean shirt with wife and family would be as acceptable and as "respectable" as a petty clerk and his family. So long as the lower-class visitor had money to spend, he might "pass" as lower middle class. From the visitor's viewpoint, the clerk in an insurance office certainly would not consider himself on a par with the hod carrier. Nevertheless, both belonged to the less-moneyed group of tourists, instead of the blue-ribbon trade which some promoters fancied Atlantic City should attract. The local upper middle class who ran the large businesses, edited the newspapers, and cranked out the publicity for the town viewed this great mass of visitors with mixed feelings.

Though the hosts wanted their money and recognized that the resort depended on their patronage, they often wished their guests were someone else.

It is necessary to consider how the hotel industry fit into the needs of the lower middle class. It is obvious that the great hotels were beyond their range. The Traymore charged $3.00 to $5.00 a day, as did the Brighton. The United States Hotel and the Dennis demanded $3.00 to $3.50, while Haddon Hall had accommodations from $3.00 to $4.00. No shopgirl from Wanamaker's or ticket agent for the Pennsylvania Railroad was going to pay that much unless he was on a mad spree. On the other hand, a study of 225 of the principal hotels in 1887 shows that most of them charged far less. The most common daily charge (73 hotels) was only $1.50 to $2.00 for room and board. On a weekly basis, the cost was lower. A total of 91 hotels offered weekly room and board for $8.00 to $12.00, this being the most common price range of the many schedules available. In 1890 clerical workers in steam railroads and manufacturing averaged $848 a year; thus $8.00 for a week's lodging and food would represent about half a week's salary. It seems reasonable to suppose that such hotels would be well within their range. Annual real wages for other kinds of workers included: $1,096 for government employees in the executive branch, $878 for postal employees, $794 for ministers, $687 for workers in gas and electricity, $439 for workers in manufacturing (nonclerical), and $256 for teachers. Here the economic blurring of the classes emerges, however different their aspirations and working conditions might be. Schoolteachers simply could not afford hotel rates; a trolley-car driver might. But in the main, the lower middle class could meet the prices of the majority of hotels in Atlantic City, assuming that their stay represented a holiday for which they had saved. Qualifications are in order. The larger the hotel, the more expensive it tended to be: with one exception, the eleven largest were above the $1.50–$2.50 range. They comprised 5 percent of the total number of hotels, yet had 23 percent of the total number of rooms. The 91 hotels which offered room and board for $8.00–$12.00 weekly comprised 40 percent of the total number of hotels, yet had only 25 percent of the total number of rooms. In other words, only about one fourth of the hotel space could be had at the cheapest rates. Yet these smaller houses were probably more consistently full. A newspaper clipping in a scrapbook compiled in 1885 indicates that at peak season only the big hotels had room available, whereas second-rate hotels and boardinghouses were crammed full. Moreover, when demand exceeded supply, hotel men practiced "doubling up" in the rooms, a maneuver which could hardly have been used in the most expensive and prestigious houses. Thus the smaller, cheaper hotels, though lacking in space, utilized their space more fully.

The principal bailiwick of the lower middle class was the boarding-house, not the hotel. Unfortunately, their rates are not recorded, though they must have ranged from the price of the cheapest hotels down to a good deal lower. In return for lower rates, the boarding-house offered relatively humdrum accommodations and food. One fastidious reporter for *The New York Times* was reduced to desperation in his search for a hotel room on a summer evening in 1883:

> *I passed a large boarding-house with a crowd on the front porch and somebody banging a piano in the parlor. I was almost far enough gone to seek for shelter in a boarding-house, but not quite. Even in my desolate condition I pitied the dwellers in an Atlantic City boarding-house and passed on.*

Still, boardinghouses, though lacking the glamour of even a small hotel, made available to the lower middle class a means of extended vacationing; without them they could have afforded only daily excursions. Estimating the number of boardinghouses is difficult, since there was no legal obligation for a proprietor to call his hostel by the name of "boardinghouse" or "hotel." In addition, the nebulous term "cottage" was often favored, no doubt for its implication of class as well as its lack of clarity. *Gopsill's Directory*, the standard Atlantic City guide in this period, lists the "hotels, cottages, and boardinghouses" for each year. A fair estimate would place boardinghouses, in name or in fact, at about three fifths the annual total:

1882–83	311	1896	610
1884	349	1897	582
1885	362	1898	590
1886	382	1899	621
1887	443	1900	649
1888	506	1901	715
1889	506	1902	739
1890	522	1903	665
1891	570	1904	689
1892	541	1905	696
1893	512	1906	683
1894	552	1907	682
1895	600	1908	716

The above figures show that, measured by the number of establishments, the accommodation industry developed steadily in the 1880's, wobbled but developed in the 1890's, and leveled off after 1902. Apparently the hard times of the 1890's did not drive many boardinghouses and hotels out of business. Nevertheless, prosperity was not identical with being open for business. The impact of depression on a mass resort is apparent in an *Inquirer* article of 1893:

> *Nearly every branch of business has felt the depression. The small hotel-keepers, who run their houses largely on speculation from season to season, have the most to fear, and several of them are tottering in the balance. A few weeks of good business would put them on their feet again, and this is what all are praying for. The big houses, like the Windsor, Brighton and Dennis, which draw their patronage almost exclusively from the fashionable and moneyed elements of society, are doing well, because these elements of society will always flock to seaside resorts as long as the resorts last.*

When the economic fortunes of average Americans faltered, those of Atlantic City faltered as well. Widespread hard times inevitably touched the majority of resort businessmen, and if the town's few most prestigious services had a clientele with a reserve to fall back on, it could only make the general drought more irksome.

Atlantic City could not have existed without the railroads, and the railroads could not have existed without the lower middle and lower classes. During summer weekdays, lower-middle-class families and young single people poured into town on their annual vacations, and their fares sustained the railroads, which waited for weekends to make the big killing. Just like the resort, the railroads needed successful weekends for a profitable season. On twelve or thirteen weekends hinged the prosperity of the entire year, and in fact Sundays were most critical of all. The six-day workweek was the general practice in the nineteenth century; thus employees not on vacation had one day a week into which to cram their summer pleasure. The excellent rail service between Atlantic City and Philadelphia made a round trip in one day feasible, and the railroads recognized that they must encourage this mass patronage with low rates. The narrow-gauge Philadelphia and Atlantic City Railway was built for this purpose in 1877, offering fares that Hall claims went as low as fifty cents for a round trip. Travel to the resort increased swiftly: "The crowds in the city were so large at times, especially over Sunday, as to nearly exhaust the supply of meat, milk, bread and provisions in stock." Generally, round-trip excursions cost $1.00 or $1.50, and in 1880 the fare was increased to $1.75. A protest meeting was organized in the resort, probably as a response to the threat the raise posed to the excursion trade. The West Jersey and Atlantic Railroad, controlled by the Pennsylvania, was organized in 1880 specifically to attract "the medium and poorer classes." The fare was "the astonishing sum of fifty cents each—less than hackfare from Market street, Philadelphia, to the Park." The expense of travel could be reduced still further from prevailing excursion rates by organizing charters, a popular practice. In 1880 Hillman and Mackey advertised themselves as sole agents soliciting group excursions on the Camden and Atlantic Railroad, and invited churches, fraternal organizations, and other interested assemblies to make early reservations for choice summer dates. On the mass patronage of the ordinary tourists the railroads were able to maintain service which provided for upper-middle-class and upper-class visitors as well.

There are many random indications of the essentially lower-middle-class appeal of the resort, in addition to the evidence of lodgings and transportation. Excursion houses had a long history at the seaside. Built at the terminals of railroads entering the city, they provided a reception point, an entertainment pavilion, a dining hall, and an amusement park for the weekend crowds. The Seaview Excursion House aimed at the popular market, with "its broad piazzas, its numberless facilities for amusement, and its enormous dining-hall, which can be changed on occasion into a Jardin Mabille, with flowers and fountains." The West Jersey Excursion House featured solid excursion-oriented food, like "fish, chicken, roast meats, vegetables, pies, pudding, ice cream, tea and coffee." It provided free music and dancing in the ballroom, a bar, a bowling alley, and a pool room, and bathing suits and lockers could be rented for twenty-five cents. The Seaview announced that "the large and spacious Ball Room will be used for Roller Skating every evening except Wednesday," while the Ocean House had a "Billiard Room Attached." Later, in 1911, the Hygeia Hotel promised the "Free use of shower bath," whence, apparently, its name. Its price range went as low as fifty cents, because it was on the "European plan," which meant that the visitor of modest means could bring his own food. Most amusements admitted customers at five cents or ten cents apiece, aiming at high-turnover, low-cost entertainment. Applegate's Pier let in baby carriages for free, with an eye to thrifty mothers. Heinz Pier, which charged nothing for admission, featured an "art exhibit" of fine rugs, ceramics, figurines, and paintings. But the company sought to develop a mass market for its "57 Varieties" through samples and demonstrations. A souvenir postcard introduced the housewife to the mysteries of canned goods. "Four Ways of Serving Heinz's Baked Beans With Tomato Sauce" included "The Usual Way" ("Place the can in boiling water for ten to fifteen minutes, then open and serve. *Especially desirable for luncheons*") and a fearsome recipe for "Bean Salad" ("Place portions of the contents of a can of Heinz's Baked Beans in individual salad dishes. Pour over each portion a tablespoonful of Heinz's Mustard Salad Dressing").

Endless details reveal the mass orientation of Atlantic City.

If Atlantic City was primarily a lower-middle-class resort, then the next question concerns the basic function it performed for its clientele. In simplest terms, the answer is: it was there to dispense pleasure. The thousands of different people who flocked to the city shared an extraordinary community of feeling which could not exist under normal urban conditions, because, unlike the conventional city, Atlantic City had a single purpose. The Boardwalk was a stage, upon which there was a temporary suspension of disbelief; behavior that was exaggerated, even ridiculous, in everyday life was expected at the resort. The rigidities of Victorian life relaxed, permitting contact between strangers and the pursuit of fantasies. The imprimatur of the absurd was upon Atlantic City. In later years it would be the scene of fantastic stunts which came to be expected in the merrily bizarre atmosphere of the place—aviation feats, a gigantic operating typewriter, a colossal marathon dance derby, the gaudy and grotesque Miss America Pageant. Examples from the 1890's include a balloon ascension and parachute drop, Pain Pyrotechnic Company's Battle of Manila at Inlet Park (together with the explosion of the *Maine* and a mammoth portrait of Admiral Dewey in fireworks), a female baseball club, and a challenge supper of "oysters and sugar, pure soap, watermelon and molasses" undertaken by three visitors who wagered that "the one who first became ill after eating certain dishes agreed upon by the trio should 'set up' a wine supper for the less distressed members of the party." The town was a gargantuan masquerade, as visitor deceived visitor, and entrepreneurs fooled them all. And people wanted to be deceived, to see life as other than it was, to pretend that they were more than they were. America was starved, as today, for festivals. The culture was groping toward common bonds in an industrial world, bonds that could humanize and integrate urban life without reimposing the restrictions of the old village form of society. Atlantic City provided a location of common understanding, together with a diminution of customary restrictions. The fluidity it offered was the countervailing force to a culture too rigid, with expectations in excess of possibility.

Pleasure at the resort meant not only fluidity but also the illusion of social mobility. Whether such an illusion is a good thing depends on the philosophical inclination of the observer, whose attitude will be affected by the degree to which the actual mobility of the society approximates the illusion. No attempt will be made here to improve upon Stephan Thernstrom's analysis in *Poverty and Progress*, which maintains that America did provide its citizens with real mobility, but not in the rags-to-riches manner of the Horatio Alger novel. For present purposes, let it be noted that the crowds at Atlantic City very much liked the fantasy world which surrounded them, and that it was skillfully and ingeniously presented by men who shared their hopes for the realization of the fantasy.

One form of fluidity found at Atlantic City was increased contact between the sexes. It is not possible here strictly to separate actuality from illusion, but only to make some observations. Common sense suggests that meetings between males and females of like class, socially and economically, were far easier in a resort than in the outside world. Young men with prospects, money to spend, and the desire to meet girls would take their annual vacations there. Single girls could visit the resort in the company of girl friends, or with relatives or parents who might well be understanding, or even alone. The excursions seem to have been gay parties from beginning to end. With the anonymity provided by a great transient city went a kind of prior legitimation of contact. No one went to Atlantic City for solitude, at least not in summer. So anyone who went there could expect to meet strangers, and could feel relatively assured in seeking introductions. This process was similar to today's computer dating, in which selection of mutually compatible couples is not the point. Rather, the computer, with its prestige in a science-worshipping society, provides a technological and therefore social ratification of the meeting of strangers with like motivation. Single people who went to Atlantic City could expect that other single people would have motives similar to theirs. This was a great breaker of barriers, and was of real benefit to the people involved.

Of course, not all mingling at the resort was of the approved sort, nor did the easygoing informality of seaside life always yield wholesome fruit. In July 1896, a local constable invaded a Kentucky Avenue hotel at one in the morning to arrest a couple who had registered as "Mr. and Mrs. C. R. Duff." "Sensational developments are expected at the hearing," the *Inquirer* duly informed its readers, for the adulterous pair were allegedly well known in Philadelphia. A detective, hired by an outraged husband, had shadowed them to discover who was plumbing "Mrs. Duff." Sometimes the temptation to exceed social proprieties proved compelling, as in the case of a young man who "implanted four osculatory bits upon the ruby lips of a woman whose acquaintance he did not enjoy." The judge before whom this scapegrace appeared rejected his defense that he was unable to restrain himself, and "decided that there was not sufficient provocation, though he admitted that the victim of the kisser was fair to gaze upon." He nailed the culprit for five dollars a kiss, and "would not consent to a discount on a lot of four, but insisted that the trespasser upon the dignity of woman should pay $20." "Dan and Mary," a couple from Chicago, found Atlantic City a bit too casual for the prosperity of their relationship:

> *She accused Dan of having boldly flirted with others of her sex, to which the lover mildly protested. With the cunning that is proverbial in the feminine world, Mary pretended that she believed Dan, and matters went along smoothly again. But the storm broke in all its fury yesterday, when Daniel, after having enjoyed a surf bath, during which he cast sheep's eyes at a fair female bather, returned to his bath house. Mary had seen his doings, and she was mad clear through, so she decided that in order to prevent a recurrence of such scenes she would treat her derelict lover to another bath. Straightway she procured a box of lye, which she poured into a bucket of water. Then, as Daniel hove in sight she prepared for the act of her life. When within a few feet . . . Mary took good aim and fired.*

Dan was obliged to seek a quick rinse before repairing to a magistrate to have his sweetheart arrested. But at length he gallantly declined to press charges, and was reunited with his fiery mistress. Incidents such as these doubtless were exceptions to the happier rule of pleasant boy-girl encounters.

As an aid to the mixing of the sexes, Applegate's Pier had a "Lover's Pavilion." The *Daily Union* snickered at a Baltimore ordinance forbidding public kissing, imagining what a riot such a law would cause if enacted at the seaside. Guvernator's Mammoth Pavilion had an inner sanctum, curtained off, which sold liquor to young people and was accordingly a popular place among them.

> *A noteworthy feature was that many of these young people who were entertaining each other did not seem to be very well acquainted. Their speech and actions did not indicate such, any how [sic]. As an example may be cited the determined efforts of a rosy-cheeked lad of not more than eighteen years, surely, to discover the "real name" of the maiden who accompanied him.*

Beyond this, increased sexual contact existed on the level of illusion. This in itself could have concrete results, because expectations encouraged fulfillment. It is undeniable that the public believed Atlantic City to be a great mingler of the sexes. A postcard from the turn of the century shows two ladies in a rolling chair who have just run down a well-dressed young man. Flat on his back, he gallantly salutes them. "Just ran across an old friend on the Boardwalk," says the caption, but behind the weak humor is substance, the fantasy of women assuming the role of sexual aggressors. A flowery bit of prose in John F. Hall's history extols the romantic milieu of the resort: "It must be borne in mind that the Goddess of Love is the divinity that presides at the seashore and the matches that are made within sight of the sea, while not as numerous as the sands on the beach, are of frequent occurrence." Such attitudes were congruent with the official sanction given the family, and in a city that prided itself on being the Family Resort, it is not surprising that faith in the availability of marriage is frequently proclaimed. This did not deny the element of chance, which made the game more exciting and poignant. Heston's handbook for 1888 shows a male hand clasping a female hand, and the legend: "The Autumn Break-Up—They May Never Meet Again." But at least they had met the first time, and getting contacts for the long winter was probably the strategic objective of many Philadelphians.

In spite of the make-believe atmosphere along the Boardwalk, however, it was necessary to bear in mind the prudent considerations of the real world which resumed after vacation's end. An 1873 article mentioned "whole rows of unmatched girls" who waited by the shore for partners "equal to them in social position." There was much latitude for deception here, the making of alliances that would end in bitter disillusionment. But when the Cinderella romance did come true, and in an honorable way, it was cause for celebration, a vindication of the capitalistic faith that the individual could transcend class. A story from the *Inquirer* in 1893 is straight out of Horatio Alger:

> A wedding will take place quietly at this resort tomorrow, which if all the details were known, would disclose one of the most romantic stories of the season. The bride is a young Philadelphia girl who is well-known among the employes of Wanamaker's, where she has held a position as saleswoman for several years past. She came down last week to spend her vacation at the shore, and during the gay round of pleasure she encountered a young Western man.
>
> The pair were strangely attracted to one another, and the upshot of the acquaintanceship will be tomorrow's ceremony. The bridegroom comes from Colorado, and is reputed to be the sion [sic] of one of the wealthiest families of the Centennial State.

But even without romance, the feeling of being part of a great crowd with a common purpose was intrinsically pleasurable. A promotional pamphlet exalted "the crowd itself," in which each participant figures as does another wave in the sea. A visitor mentioned how he liked to "bathe in people" at the resort. It was a huge party, with everyone putting on his best face as befitted the situation. The sores of industrial living and working were hidden from view, just as the resort took care to railroad its bums out of town.

Since there was a heightened awareness of forms of behavior appropriate to a pleasure city, fads arose which the masses seized upon.

They conferred a feeling of belonging, a "society" of those outside society. Fads also testified to the loneliness that was a part of city living, for a fad is an artificial attempt, inherently frantic, to create or to heighten identity where insufficient identity is felt. Fads in Atlantic City took such diverse forms as the use of certain words, the wearing of particular objects and items of clothing, interest in what is *au courant*, and even the adoption of certain roles.

> *Talking of love and pretty girls, we do not have any more flirtations, they are called "mashes"—"don't you forget it." This is the day of slang phrases; at cards you are told that "you can't sometimes most always generally tell how things will turn out"; as for the bathing "it is just too awfully nice for anything."*

The *Inquirer* warned its readers in July 1896 to avoid being judged "not in it" by laying in a supply of comic lapel buttons. Messages in use on the Boardwalk included: "If you love me, grin"; "I am somewhat of a liar myself, and there are others"; "I am mamma's darling, whose darling are you?"; and the succinct "Yes, darling." The young man could wear one proclaiming, "Give me your hand," to which the "summer girl" could respond with another which said, "I will be a sister to you."

In 1897, someone discovered that a burning incense taper carried in the coiffure would discourage Jersey's saber-toothed mosquitoes, and this practical innovation quickly became an item of fashion. As crowds of women strolled the Boardwalk by night, the effect was "quite startling, resembling somewhat the firefly." Vacationers also liked to have friends autograph their cigarettes as keepsakes, and white duck sailor hats were similarly used, the object being the hieroglyphic effect attained by great numbers of signatures. For a brief time, daring young men wore a single silk garter made of flashy ribbon with a silver buckle as they paraded the beach. Young women were fond of attracting attention by performing athletic exercises on the sand, such enthusiasts being generally of generous endowments and often of economical inclinations in the use of yard goods for bathing costumes.

At the century's end, "Hello, My Baby" was so popular that this "mongrel ballad" could scarcely be escaped along the waterfront, while the "latest dude dress" was reported to be a white jersey shirt worn "Chinaman style outside of the pantaloons." Men were advised to turn up the cuffs of their white flannel trousers if they wished to be in style. Palmistry was in favor, especially among the ladies, who queued up to consult various "professors," "gypsy queens," and other savants "just arrived from Paris." The palmists had "all sorts of queer-sounding cognomens, some of which are regular jaw-breakers," and were attired

in "some fantastic costume" to impress "the fair patron with the weight of their marvelous powers." Previously, phrenology had been the "summer girl's" pet interest, and her aspiring gallant might be cruelly diverted from "a conversation of particular personal interest" with "How's the development of your bump of amativeness?"

Ladies' bathing suits became more abbreviated and more colorful as the end of the century approached. Part of the reason was the increasing number of women learning to swim (who appreciated not having to drag pounds of spare cloth through the water) and part the growing hedonism of American society. "Time was," said the *Inquirer*, "when women went into the water with long, baggy trousers down to their heels, while over these hideous garments hung flannel skirts. But that was in the old days before the world began moving at the pace it seems to be going at now." Women were eager to keep up with bathing-suit fashions, and the typical costume of 1898 "would scarcely fill the much talked of collar box." The more daring abandoned stockings and began to abbreviate their skirts. Bicycle clothing influenced bathing-suit design toward trimness, much to the delight of male "kodak fiends." A new female type emerged, "the bicycle girl, mayhap astride a man's wheel, scorching up and down the strand, with her golden hair hanging down her back and robed in a natty bathing suit, the colors of which outrival the noise of the bell, with her jaws going at a rapid pace because of the wad of tutti-frutti she has hidden within." Novelty was possible in street wear, too. For the Fourth of July 1896, one enterprising young lady "combined patriotism and style" by wearing a shirtwaist fashioned from a silken American flag, with a body of blue studded with stars and sleeves of red and white stripes.

A more esoteric fad, the "widow craze," struck Atlantic City in 1893. The widow possessed a mystique of "experience" which the maiden never enjoyed, an earthly wisdom made respectable by the hand of God. The black clothing, drab in color but not necessarily in design, was an immediate attention getter, and widows were allegedly in demand. Their avowed bereavement recommended itself to the solicitations of gallant strangers. An attractive blond widow was to be seen every afternoon at a certain time on the merry-go-round, dressed in the "most exquisite style."

The "summer girl" has joined the great auk in extinction, but she was once a prevalent shorebird. She deserves to be considered more as a role than a fad, perhaps, for she reappeared with each *fin de siècle* summer to bewitch male vacationists. "At a distance you would take this creature for an angel and no mistake, for she seems the personifica-

TOILETTE
FOR THE SEASIDE

tion of modesty and grace. Nudge up a little closer—if you can—and alas, you will observe that she has that naughty little twinkle in her eye." With her "coquettish commingling of sea shore freedom, natural feminine vanity and womanly longing for admiration," she was a sentimental favorite of journalists. But the efforts of young ladies to act the summer girl could make for amusement, too.

> A sensation . . . was furnished on Tuesday by three very pretty, stylish and modest young ladies who went into the water wearing, for the first time, suits that had been made especially for them, cut from thin white flannel. They didn't know, poor things, the terrible shrinking power of salt water, or they would not have gone in. . . . They had not been in the water five minutes till a group of horrid men had assembled directly in front of where they were bathing. One of the girls, wonderingly, made a survey, and the result horrified her. The three of them were living pictures of "Venus Rising from the Sea." The white flannel was clinging with a tenacity worthy of a far better cause, and the black stockings showed through the material as though it was tissue paper, and indeed it was not much better. Being nice, modest girls they

made a break at once for the bath house, but on their way thither
ran a gauntlet far more awful than any ever encountered by
Fenimore Cooper's Indian fighters.

Fashionable yet unspoiled, alluring yet virginal, surrounded by im-
ploring suitors whom she coyly evaded, the summer girl was the
archetype of female desirability. She was altogether too delicate a
flower for the twentieth century.

New York City might have its Four Hundred, but Atlantic City had
its Forty Thousand. Anyone could join who had an aptitude for vogue
and a fancy to belong to an "elite." In the confined area of the resort—
and along its nerve track, the Boardwalk—fads could spread quickly.
They occupied the evanescent middle range of repetitive behavior,
halfway between the gesture too private to be stylish and the cliché
too well known to be distinctive. In a normal city, fads applied to
sections of the population, whereas Atlantic City was óne great show
on a city scale, and everyone was potentially in on the act.

Imitation of the upper class was a primary component of the symbolic mobility which the resort afforded its lower-middle-class users.
The many pseudo-sophisticated portraits of the city offered in promotional materials were designed to impart a patrician glamour to a plebeian spa, and far from substantiating the prestige of the place, they
prove just the opposite. Atlantic City was low-flung, but it palmed itself
off in high-toned terms. The promoters had a good ear for what
appealed to their audience, and they were not wanting in boldness. Dr.
Boardman Reed, a vigorous booster, composed a brochure for the
Pennsylvania Railroad which touted the advantages of his home town
as a health resort relative to Florida, the western states, and Europe,
but these places were noncompetitive with Atlantic City for 95 percent
of its customers. The object could only have been to gild the Jersey
coast with glamour rubbed off more remote utopias. Similarly, the im-
posingly titled "Academy of Music" presented lowbrow fare like comic
opera and "Professor Bartholomew's Trained Horses." Overstuffed
names like these were usual throughout the town. Many called the
fifth boardwalk, completed in 1896, the "Esplanade." But the events
of 1898 generated a rumor that this elegant title had a Spanish origin,
obliging the embarrassed Esplanadists to retreat hurriedly to the more
humble "Boardwalk" to·avoid "anything that savors of the Dons."

Probably the most baroque and certainly the most long-lived ersatz
phenomenon was the Boardwalk rolling chair. It began as an aid for
invalids, but one entrepreneur realized its wider potential. He started
renting a fleet of them with attendants, and they rapidly caught on.
They were floridly designed along the lines of Brown Decades' aesthet-

NOT MUCH DIFFERENCE
They—"Don't you think we are perfect pictures in our new
bathingsuits?"
He—"Yes, living pictures."

ics, with swan-necked prows and heart-shaped dips in the backrests.
Thickly padded with comfortable cushions and equipped with robes,
they offered to the most proletarian customer willing to spend some
change an American version of the sedan chair, the classic attribute
of effete aristocracy. The chair pusher was probably the only servant
most visitors ever had. Rolling chairs were popular subjects on postcards—just the thing to impress people back home. They were the
epitome of nouveau bourgeois.

*Afterward, well wrapped up, a ride in a rolling chair is within the
range of possibility, and when one has been wheeled for a stretch
along the Boardwalk, dined at the celebrated tables for which
our hotels are noted and afterward listened to a high-class concert, he or she is ready to smile a welcome to the sandman.*

One of the most important devices by which the lower-middle-class
visitor created the illusion of having a higher-class status was clothing,
for when nobody knew anybody else, clothes assumed an exaggerated
importance in attributing status. Victorian styles allowed rather more
yardage for creating effect than today's taste recommends.

*The Piers at Atlantic City are the happy hunting grounds for
those of the fair sex who love to see beautiful gowns or to display
stunning ones in their own wardrobe. Saturday and Sunday nights
the crowd is thickest. . . .*

*[One] simple but vastly pretty gown [recently seen] was white
organdy made over grape-colored silk. The yoke, which extended*

over the sleeve top, was of pleats and grape velvet ribbon . . .
alternately arranged in groups, edged with a quilling of organdy,
velvet bordered. The sleeves were mousquetaire, with a ruche at
the wrist, and the waist itself repeated the perpendicular lines of
the yoke, but at greater intervals.

The belt and stock were very deep violet satin ribbon and a
big bow nestled at the left corner of the yoke. The skirt had a
ruching laid in points, which was edged top and bottom with
velvet, and above it following the same outline were three rows
of the same ribbon. Ruche and ribbon rows were repeated at the
foot of the circular flounce. Stunning little gown it was even if
not specially original.

Dress standards were high at Atlantic City, both in contemporary
terms and even more so from the perspective of the melancholic informality of the present Age of Denim. Gowns, bonnets, and parasols
for the ladies and suits, cravats, and skimmer hats for the men were
in order for beach strolls. Victorian decorum prevailed right up to
mean high-water mark.

While fancy clothing was usual throughout the season, on one
particular occasion there was an immense resort-wide competition to
be the best-dressed. This was Atlantic City's Easter Parade, copied from
the older event on New York's Fifth Avenue. Like the Miss America
Pageant at a later date, the Easter Parade was a ploy of local businessmen to pull in shekels outside the normal holiday season. The mild
weather of springtime allowed promenading, even if the ocean was
too brisk for swimming, and the event was highly popular. One weekend near the turn of the century, for example, allegedly drew nearly
forty thousand passengers over the railroads. The Boardwalk each
year was jammed rail to rail by a crowd dressed in springtime finery.
An army of the nouveaux bourgeois, like the fevered vision of a megalo-
maniac haberdasher, marched in review past equally well-dressed
spectators. This was the white society which found cakewalks so
amusing. Yet in its turn it performed a ceremony that to the un-
anthropological eye was every bit as ridiculous. It was a mass imitation
of the upper class, an awkward assumption of the externals of elegance, and as such a parody of itself and its model.

Atlantic City was for sale. High society might be for sale too, in the
long run, but it erected barriers against the too easy assault of wealth
upon its ranks. A mellowing process was employed, to give time for
the aura of the stockyard or the dime store or the roundhouse to dim a
bit. New families seeking admission on the basis of wealth and power
passed through a generational apprenticeship which allowed sons or
grandsons into the ranks of the patriciate, but excluded the patriarch
who had done the dirty work. Edward D. Baltzell in *Philadelphia Gentle-*

men describes how this worked. But Atlantic City sold its wares cash-on-delivery, and the pocketbook was its only coat of arms. There was a limit to illusion, which the town never forgot: at the end of every fantasy was a hand poised over a cash register. An emphasis on buying and selling pervaded the resort and typified it throughout its history, producing an unabashedly vigorous commercial atmosphere. Every inch of the Boardwalk was engineered to tickle silver out of the jingling pockets of the throng. When the city of Chicago investigated the resort's water-recreation facilities in 1913 and compared them with its own, it was pleased to see that the difference was favorable to the boys in Cook County. It was noted that maximum profit, not convenience and service to the public, was the overriding purpose of the Jersey resort. Searching for upper-class trappings, Atlantic City inaugurated an annual horse show in 1899, prompting editor Hall to express equal enthusiasm for the horseflesh and the profits of the display. A visitor was disgusted when St. Nicholas' Church charged admission to its dedication, "in common with everything else" at the resort, and an *Inquirer* article remarked how the city's businessmen "pile it on" in their systematic extortions. That was a secret of Atlantic City. Though particular charges tended to be small, the methodical way in which everything had its fee led to cumulative effects unhappy for the visitor. The steady trickle of nickels and dimes was the making of fortunes and the undoing of personal budgets as well.

The principal shearing of sheep took place in the scores upon scores of small stores which abutted the Boardwalk on the land side. So long as the stroller was not looking at the ocean, he was looking at something for sale. These petty shops contrasted curiously with the pompous hotels, for they were lower in tone, a kind of lower-middle-class commercial foothills to the great structures behind them. They also moved huge quantities of goods to lower-middle-class customers who could not afford the swank hostelries. But, like the hotels, they encouraged a parallel impulse to consume, to revel in the first full flush of prosperity which urbanization and industrialization were bringing to the common people. The great hotels beyond the foothills would be conquered someday; today the masses could buy from the shops for a taste of high life. It was good stage setting. It encouraged the lower middle class to continue to struggle for utopia by way of materialism, in which it had unshakable faith. It peddled rhinestones by the curb, and held the diamonds a bit further off.

And the things that were sold! Racy postcards, "Genuine Japanese corylopsis talcum," tinsel brooches, agate ornaments, "lurid Naples landscapes on pearl shells," coral, Japanese fern seeds, "Indian" moccasins, Kewpie dolls, Swiss woodcarving, photographs bedizened with gold lacquer, and a heroic device to cut apples open in the shape of a water lily. The visitor could buy an improving tintype to grace his mantel back home ("A stalwart maiden . . . in a boat which stood on end, pulling through the surf with an oar, and dragging a drowning man . . . into the boat with her free hand. The legend was 'Saved' "). Or he could have a glass of "pure orange juice" from a big machine which consumed huge piles of ripe fruit before his eyes ("These machines in several instances are mere dummies, and the great stock of oranges that appear to be passing through the fake crusher is the same old pile that was doing business early in July"). Then there were deviled crabs, lemonade, soda pop, tutti-frutti, Gilt Edge Beer, Fralinger's Salt Water Taffy, Gage's Ice Cream, Zeno Chewing Gum, George Smith's Cream Java Coffee, and innumerable other syrups, jellies, doughs, liquids, and solids to lick, chew, munch, gulp, and swill.

Confronted with so much wonderful junk so relentlessly proffered, visitors engaged happily in recreational buying, as dozens of desires not previously known to exist suddenly sprang into being and demanded fulfillment. All of life seemed to be for sale. Buying itself as a sort of pleasure was institutionalized for good and all in American culture. So far from being simply a convenience for the crowds, selling became a chief entertainment, engaging the passions more deeply and consistently than the ocean ever could. Recreational buying was a new phenomenon at the time. Whereas today it is an obvious element in the success of the suburban shopping center, through which it has become a principal locus of community, in Victorian America it was a novelty that the beneficiaries—the merchants—discovered slowly. The Boardwalk stores at first sold souvenirs and refreshments, and only later extended their wares as they discovered what the crowds wanted. But the entrepreneurs of the resort rose to the occasion handsomely, learning to speak a materialistic language the masses understood. Washington & Arlington's New Unlimited Monster Shows shrewdly tacked on its bill of fare a note pointing out its "steam organ, costing [$]10,000." "Munkacsy's Christ Before Pilate" ("The young woman who recites a little piece and tells all about the picture, explains what is not on the bills, that the picture is 'after' Munkacsy") was touted as "the $100,000 painting." Roving Frank's Gypsies promised that the traditional service of palm reading would be done by "All New Gypsies," a message which belied the spirit of clairvoyance as completely as it fingered the pulse of the times.

The merchants, promoters, and hotelkeepers themselves could only be impressed by the success which had descended on the town. Like their customers, they were a bit overwhelmed by the place, and, as though rubbing their eyes to make sure it was all real, they liked to reassure themselves with endless recounting of the growth in profits and numbers of visitors. They had many anxieties, for their welfare depended on factors that were either partially or totally out of their control: the press of Philadelphia, the laws of New Jersey, public taste, weather, the character of the resort, competition among themselves, and so forth. They had always predicted success for Atlantic City, and yet, now that it was here, was not a certain alchemy involved? Hence they searched for unique factors that would explain their city's fortune, that would imply permanence and eliminate the alchemy of success. The world of things for sale which so appealed to their customers appealed also to themselves. One could sell the goodness of life, and one could buy it—or so it seemed. And if this was true, then the goodness of life had descended upon both merchant and customer along the Boardwalk. Since happiness could be approached by measurable units, the businessmen of Atlantic City were measurers by nature. The Victorians were no Puritans. It was not for them to hasten through this vale of sorrow; they had made it a valley of opportunity. It was necessary now only to remind oneself that opportunity had no sorrows.

Until he settled in Atlantic City, Joseph Fralinger was a loser. Born in 1848 and orphaned at the age of six, he terminated a sporadic education at an early age to work as a glass blower. When strikes drove him from his job, he tried his hand at the fish-and-produce business in Philadelphia. Next he managed the Quaker City Base Ball Club and organized his own team at Philadelphia's Jumbo Park, but the illness of his wife forced him to move to Atlantic City. Here he started the unsuccessful "August Flower" baseball club, then moved to Wilmington, Delaware, where he again failed to turn a profit on yet another team. Back he came to Atlantic City. "Foreseeing the possibilities in catering to the tastes of visitors who were beginning to flock to the local beaches," he dispensed cider, apples, and lemonade to the Boardwalk crowds, juggling lemons to attract attention. He also began to manufacture saltwater taffy, at that time sold in trifling quantities for five cents a bag, but he hit on the idea of putting up larger quantities in boxes to take home. One weekend he ventured a purchase of two hundred boxes, sold out before Sunday noon, and frantically turned to oyster boxes from a sea-food shop to satisfy the demand. Fralinger's fortune was made. He became so prosperous that he was able to buy an interest in amusement rides, acquire beachfront real estate, and build the Academy of Music on the Boardwalk. He rebuilt the Academy after fires in 1892, 1898, and 1902, and remodeled it in 1908 for lease.

It became the celebrated Nixon's Apollo Theatre. Before he died, Fralinger owned homes in Atlantic City, Miami Beach, and Schwenksville, Pennsylvania, and was a pillar of the resort community.

John Lake Young (1853–1938) was the kind of businessman who had the eye of the times. Born in the village of Absecon to an oysterman and his wife, he was left fatherless at the age of three. As the official story goes, he sacrificed education as a youth to labor for his living, and by the age of thirty was working as a carpenter doing patchwork on the Boardwalk and pavilions. One day he met Stewart McShea, a Pennsylvania baker who had come to the resort for his health. The baker had capital to invest, the carpenter had ideas. Together they bought a pavilion, converted it to a roller-skating rink, and "made loads of money." When the popularity of skating flagged, they turned to the carrousel. "If they made money before they made ten times as much in this new enterprise." In 1891 they bought Applegate's Pier opposite the carrousel, rented out its stores and booths for increasingly stiff fees, and "money just simply rolled their way." McShea retired to enjoy his wealth in 1897, but Young persevered, attracting hordes of customers to the pier's auditorium, theater, ballroom, aquarium, and net hauls of fish (Young could identify forty-eight species for the crowd). In 1906 he triumphantly opened the new Million Dollar Pier, "one of the big engineering achievements of the present day," on which he located his personal concrete "Italian-style villa," with three stories, twelve rooms, and a conservatory and garden. Eventually he owned ten miles of beachfront property ("a goodly part of which is marketable at the tidy price of $1500 a front foot"), more land in Florida, two steam yachts, a fleet of sailing craft, hotels and cottages, and the proud memory of having entertained President William Howard Taft in his home. For John Lake Young, "eminently noteworthy as an example of that product of American achievement known as the self-made man," the good life had been reached literally by way of nickels and dimes.

The popularity of vaudeville in Atlantic City is an excellent illustration of the kind of patronage the resort attracted and the aspirations these people had. Many vaudeville shows were performed at the lower end of the Boardwalk, the plebeian end, which contrasted with the relatively sedate section toward the inlet to Absecon Bay. An elemental atmosphere prevailed in the "pavilion theatre" district, packed with excursionists.

> *There we find the fakir who shouts over his counter of hot sausages, mustard and rolls, "Take a bit of courage and eat something, gents. You've got to eat, and here's the place to do it." We*

find the "Three baseballs for five. Everytime you knock a baby
down you get a good cigar" man, and hosts of others.

Here, too, were beer gardens, saloons, open drinking bars, "The
Haunted Forest" exhibition, shooting galleries, toboggan rides, "flying
horses," carrousels, dinner-ticket and rental-bathing-suit hawkers, a
champion weight guesser, "fake" shows, dancing pavilions, and a
number of cheap boardinghouses and hotels. Into this section flocked
a large fraction of the resort's trade, the less affluent part. These people
were the lower middle class which Albert F. McLean, in his book
American Vaudeville as Ritual, describes as the "New Folk," but which
in the present study are called the nouveaux bourgeois.

McLean believes that the bulk of vaudeville audiences consisted of
rising white-collar workers and their families, who were in transit
toward upper-middle-class status. This group increased eightfold between 1870 and 1910, to over five million members. They were only
one or two generations away from rural life in America or in European
peasant villages, but they were thoroughly acculturated and had left
their old ways behind. Vaudeville managers designed their shows to
appeal to the aspirations of the lower middle class while remaining
comprehensible to the lower class. Immigrants just off the boat would
need some familiarization with American life before they could appreciate vaudeville, a fact which is borne out by the kinds of shows
performed at Atlantic City. In 1903 Lew Dockstader and His Great
Minstrel Company staged a tableau entitled "The Sunny South," featuring a scene described as "The Colored Heaven": "Showing a Southern
colored man in one of his happiest moments. 'The Watermellon [sic]
Song' . . . sung by Manuel Romain." This same singer also offered
"Sadie, the Princess of Tenement Row." These were themes that the
immigrant could not really appreciate, while the slum dweller would
find it hard to share a romantic feeling about "Tenement Row." They
were lower-middle-class themes, suiting the taste of those familiar
with American life and above the dirt sill of urban existence.

Vaudeville managers came to emphasize the "moral" quality of their
shows, for two reasons: vaudeville was suspect to Protestant Christianity, and its basic appeal did not reside in sexual themes anyway. Rural,
evangelical Protestantism traditionally had been hostile to public
amusement, but in the late nineteenth century church leaders were
divided on the question. Progressive Protestant clergymen, eager to
relate their faith to the increasingly urban American population, began
to discriminate between the use and abuse of amusement, a concession
that vaudeville managers were quick to exploit. They were quite willing to keep their shows "respectable," since fundamentally their suc-

cess was due to the glorification of materialistic success in industrial society, a theme which the clergy did not construe as objectionable. Vaudeville began to separate into two paths, "high-class" vaudeville and variety. Variety, which was not aimed at a family audience, was more bawdy and vigorous. It eventually turned into straightforward burlesque. Its respectable relative advertised itself as "refined vaudeville," "polite vaudeville," or "family vaudeville" to make its purpose clear, while managers labored to eliminate any taint of vice from their theaters and to prevent obscenities from being uttered in stage speeches. As such, high-class vaudeville was widely regarded as safe fare for such vulnerable listeners as young children and pregnant mothers. But the emphasis on "refinement," while it pacified the churches, had a coincidental effect much more powerful with its New Folk customers. It had snob appeal, playing on their desire to share in the life of the upper middle class by surrounding vaudeville with the trappings of upper-middle-class taste. The managers' claim that they wanted the "carriage trade" was actually addressed not to the gentry but to the plebeians, just like the high-flown promotional literature of the resort.

There is a good deal of documentation to demonstrate that most of the vaudeville in Atlantic City chose to take the "high-class" route as the more profitable alternative to variety. Doyle's Pavilion on the Boardwalk presented "Highclass Vaudeville" in 1900, as did the highly important Young's Ocean Pier Theatre a year later. The Amphitheatre on the Boardwalk announced that "Ladies and Children Can Attend Unaccompanied," while the Iron Pier Music Pavilion at its grand opening in 1894 promised to be "Devoted Strictly to High-Class Vaudevilles." The Empire was most explicit of all. Besides presenting "Continuous Highclass Vaudeville," it was "Patronized By The Elite," who enjoyed its "Elegantly Appointed Buffet." In fact, it was "The Only Music Hall in the City Conducted on a Strictly European Plan." This meant that the Empire served food but one did not have to buy it. The nifty rhetoric made it seem a club for the patriciate, but it hastened to assure its customers that the gilt of glamour entailed no financial consequences that were not entirely voluntary. In such manner did morality and materialism, two themes constantly on the mind of the nouveaux bourgeois, go hand in hand in Atlantic City.

Nothing more vividly illustrates the lower-middle-class soul of Atlantic City than the class sensitivity in the promotional output of the town's boosters, within and without. These men were generally of the upper middle class or were in the pay of upper-middle-class interests. They included people like the reporters for the Philadelphia newspapers and pamphleteers for the railroads. Among them were John Hall, editor of the *Daily Union* and local historian, and A. L. English, founder of the *Atlantic City Review*, who sold out to Alfred Heston in 1884 to write a promotional history of the resort. Heston in turn issued his series of handbooks, the single most important publicity device besides the Philadelphia press. Such men found themselves in an awkward and contradictory position. Local promoters belonged to the city's upper middle class. They recognized the importance of lower-middle-class patronage to the resort, wished to encourage it, and at the same time felt superior to it. Ideally, Atlantic City should be an upper-class resort, even though they knew full well its real character. At the same time, they resented the upper class, because it enjoyed elegance and privilege they would never attain. A similar enmity was felt toward the upper middle class of Philadelphia, supposedly their equals, because they were estimable frogs in a much bigger puddle: the editor of the *Bulletin* was not in the same league as the editor of the *Daily Union*. In Philadelphia, writers for the great newspapers could hardly refrain from snickering at the lowbrows of the seaside resort and their plebeian trade. They knew they had great power to affect Atlantic City's prosperity in the articles they wrote, each one bound to impress thousands of readers with the desirability or undesirability of the resort. Moreover, journalists outside Philadelphia were not boosting the resort the way the locals were. They were attracted by an easy source for a colorful article, but they did not feel the necessity for strict loyalty which resort journalists did. They could afford to express some negative feelings about the people there. Still, their articles were a vital element in boosting Atlantic City, and hence may be considered a part of the promotional literature.

The concern with class in resort advertising and journalism is consonant with the history of the period. Turn-of-the-century America witnessed such disturbing upheavals as Haymarket and Pullman, and the depression of 1893, a plunge of unprecedented severity for the masses. Americans could see plenty of evidence of class structure about them and the poverty and hardship that were the lot of the unfortunate. Though it was widely believed that thrift, hard work, and exploitation of readily available opportunities would enable deserving citizens to transcend the barriers of class, and allow the society to assimilate the hordes of ragged aliens that swarmed into America in search of a livelihood, the specter of revolution could not be ignored. The promotional literature of Atlantic City contained many touching examples of class mixing by the seaside, reassuring declarations of harmony to quiet the fears of readers and visitors and to reaffirm their

belief that America successfully accommodated its different classes. Sometimes, however, these accounts were tinged with class antagonism which belied their benign intent.

Rand, McNally's *Handy Guide to Philadelphia and Environs* of 1895 identified Atlantic City as "a thoroughly democratic place" devoid of "caste prejudice." It was "no uncommon sight to see the children of millionaires and the little ones of laboring men riding happily on the merry-go-round at the same time, and perhaps to find the parents fraternizing on the Switchback Railway." Applegate's Pier fathered a jingle in the same mode:

> *Four spacious decks high in the air,*
> *The old, the young, the millionaire,*
> *The worthy poor as well,*
> *Seek health and rest, all find the same,*
> *Shielded from sun as well as rain,*
> *A paradise to dwell.*

Faith in the benevolence of American society is rather lugubriously embodied in a tableau presented at Young's Pier during the 1908 season:

> *When the curtain rises on the first scene the snow is falling on a busy street, where Christmas purchasers, moving rapidly past each other, present life in its different phases of wealth and poverty. A drunkard is about to be "run in" by a policeman, when the wife and child of the former make an eloquent pantomimic appeal and the good-natured officer releases his prisoner. A colored waif, with newspapers beside him, has fallen to sleep in the snow, and the man in blue, passing along, sees him and covers his face with a newspaper.*

An *Inquirer* vignette of democracy in the shallows depicted "the most haughty and conservative of Walnut street beauties in boldly neglige [*sic*] attire laughingly receiving the splashings of a denizen of 'de Fourt' ward." The "pretty shop girls from the big Market street stores" were taught to swim by "big, athletic clubmen who would scarcely deign to notice them in the scurrying throngs along Chestnut street after 6 o'clock." Another reporter claimed that "the four-dollars-a-week young man spending his year's savings in a vacation trip jostle[s] the pompous millionaire freely, and very likely flirts with the millionaire's daughter right before the old man's eyes."

The *Inquirer* covered the Hebrew Charity Ball of 1894, an affair of "Jewish society of the highest class," at which "we are elbowing men who hold in their hands the business of many communities" and who "can transfer millions by the stroke of their pens." These are "men who are respected more and more, admired, by their fellow men and their colleagues." The author of a Pennsylvania Railroad pamphlet of 1889 attempted to dazzle his readers with the high-class atmosphere of Atlantic City, but achieved a portrait both sardonic and curiously naïve: "When Lent comes and the fashionable world takes its well-earned rest, there is no more fitting refuge in which it can undergo its self-denial in pleasurable quiet, while it recuperates its wasted energies in penitential rest, than this haven by the sea." A somewhat different tone pervaded *The Casino Girl*, a two-act musical staged at the Academy of Music in 1901. Its characters included such gentry as "pilsener Pasha, a brewer, whose introduction of beer into Egypt won for him his title," and "Mrs. H. Malaprop Rocks, a leader of St. Louis Society, better half of 'Rocks and Company,' pork packers of the western town."

In contrast to these views of the wealthy at the shore, it was reported that "slumming" was among the amusements of the resort. "The smaller concert gardens further down the island, which put up a complete variety show in connection with their concerts, attract the lower elements of society, although it not infrequently happens that parties of fashionables who delight in breaking loose and doing unconventional things when away from home are seen in these places." A writer for *The New York Times* suggested a trip to Atlantic City to see "Tom, Dick, and Harry and their girls." "It is almost worth a visit to see how the average Philadelphian amuses himself at the seashore." There is "no ruffianism" and the resort is "well-policed." "On the whole" the place is "quite as attractive as Coney Island," surely a backhanded compliment.

Atlantic City's role in presenting the illusion of social mobility must be seen in light of the class sensitivity evident in resort literature. The attention to class among resort commentators emphasizes the fundamentally lower-middle-class character of the town, and not only expresses satisfaction at the harmonizing potential of American society but also displays class antagonisms at variance with the supposed harmony. The history of the great plebeian resort demonstrates why it is possible to see turn-of-the-century America as either the Gilded Age or the Brown Decades, depending on the surface from which the light is reflected.

3

Games for the Mauve Predicament

BY THE last decade of the nineteenth century, a large minority of the people of the United States—the urban portion—were living in a condition remote from Nature. The circumstances of their lives afforded them little comprehension of Nature or of how urban man should relate to it. They were surrounded by the world of the Machine, and of the City, which is the Machine's artifact. The Machine, too, was barely understood, and while it brought many delights, the ways in which it brought them were mysterious and sometimes threatening. Although urban Americans were not yet a majority of the population, they were on the way to becoming so. Their pressing psychological necessity was to arrive at some understanding of Nature and the Machine, if they were to adjust emotionally to the new society which was unfolding about them. Urban Americans occupied a mental middle ground that would prove increasingly dysfunctional for the culture. While they were passing irrevocably into an urbanized condition, they had not yet acquired the attitudes necessary to cope with the City, which they did not want to avoid and therefore were not able to avoid. Similarly, Nature was ceasing to be an unlimited resource and becoming a remnant in need of active protection; but the attitudes necessary to save it had not yet formed. This was the dilemma faced by the people of America in the Mauve Decade, and it found expression in certain important genres of amusements in Atlantic City.

Animal acts, and more extensive menageries of trained animals, were enduringly popular fare at Atlantic City. They took many forms, but in essence they were all the same. If an animal could be taught to imitate some kind of human behavior, at a level of performance necessarily lower than that of humans, man's newly won dominance of Nature would be expressed for the delight of the audience. Animal acts demonstrated that, in some areas at least, man could trifle with Nature. Though Americans of the next century would begin to wonder if such trifling was a good thing, it was nevertheless still possible in the 1890's to luxuriate in Nature's subjection. The resort audiences did just that.

In 1880 J. H. Martin, a Philadelphia lawyer, noted the "learned pigs" on display at Atlantic City. A later reference confirms their existence, since one of them caused a stir by escaping. In 1893 the Iron Pier featured "Daniel Boone and His Trained Lions," a curious incongruity apparently acceptable to the public because of an imagined spiritual identity between the African and American frontiers. The Amphitheatre, a Boardwalk amusement hall, offered "Bartholomew's Equine Paradox" in the summer of 1894: "24 Educated Horses." "Do everything but talk." "Refined, Instructive, Interesting, Amusing." "The only Entertainment patronized by all classes, and that never had an unfavorable criticism." Once again, the polite vaudeville emphasis on the social acceptability of the show is evident. "Instructive" was as magic a word to the Victorian middle classes as "scientific" to post-Sputnik Americans, or "creative" to progressive parents and sophisticated young adults in the 1970's. Admission prices of ten, twenty-five, and fifty cents encouraged wide patronage, while customers of means could find choice seats from which to contemplate the wise beasts.

During the same season of 1894, Inlet Amusement Park brought "Gleason, King of Horse Trainers" to Atlantic City, featuring "A Series of Exciting Contests With Wild and Vicious Animals." These wild and vicious horses could be seen for twenty-five cents, fifty cents, one dollar, and five dollars, indicating that this was a high-powered show able to command a substantial admission price. The *Daily Union* reviewed the performance:

> *Gleason the horse tamer, last evening first handled a thorough-bred race horse that was never harnessed to carriage. In a few minutes he had the animal thoroughly subdued and was soon driving it about in a wagon. Later he harnessed it double with another nervous, skittish horse and drove both over exploding firecrackers and arms-full of paper thrown at them. Both these horses were quickly subdued and made docile.*

This was followed by the parenthetical comment that "the horses are not hurt or injured. Kindness and firmness are the elements of control."

The same theme of human intelligence subduing the savage beast occurs again in the advertising for the Zoo, located on the Boardwalk at Missouri Avenue. In July 1900 the Zoo introduced "The Latest and Greatest Attraction of Atlantic City," the celebrated Frank C. Bostock. Just as Gleason was "King of Horse Trainers," so Bostock was the "Animal King." The vocabulary of power in Bostock's advertising ex-

presses the ideal of man as the manipulator of Nature: "Forest Kings
and Jungle Monarchs as Submissive as Domestic Pets. Ferocious Lions,
Fierce Tigers, Treacherous Panthers, Bloodthirsty Pumas Subservient
to the Human Master Mind."

The unnatural behavior required of animals in menageries involved
a certain amount of cruelty in their training. This did not leave the
public conscience altogether at ease, as the *Daily Union*'s hedging
remarks on Gleason indicate. Albert F. McLean, in his analysis of
menageries in vaudeville entertainment, shows how the unsentimental
and exploitative attitude of men like Bostock aroused a movement for
humane treatment. Bostock was one of the foremost trainers of the
period (a commentary on Atlantic City's importance as an entertainment center) and author of *Training of Wild Animals*, which appeared
three years after his performance at the resort. This book was a clear
exposition of the unsentimental school of thought, emphasizing the
savagery of wild beasts and the intelligence and heroism of the
trainer in mastering their viciousness. The humane movement, which
challenged the cruel effects of this attitude, advanced a sentimental
anthropomorphism which invested animals with human sensibilities.
By publicizing some of the more atrocious abuses in training and
handling, the reformers were able to force trainers to pay lip service
to their cause. Still, the popular Victorian attitude toward Nature was
actually confirmed, for the reformers protested not the ends of training, but the means. Reformers and trainers agreed: "Animals were
part of the natural environment to be manipulated for human
aggrandizement."

Consequently, menageries expressed the Victorian American's prevailing attitude toward Nature without suggesting alternative ways
he could relate to it. A different and highly popular kind of amusement,
nevertheless, did implicitly suggest the need for a more substantial
relationship than exploitation. Spectacles were a trademark of the
resort, from "Lucy," the grotesque building in the shape of a giant
elephant at the south end of Absecon Island, to the great electrically
lighted advertising signs on the Boardwalk. Anything that was lurid,
readily comprehensible, and preferably large was likely to find favor.
Atlantic City itself appealed to visitors for its spectacular qualities (the
vast crowds, the huge hotels, the seas of merchandise), but there
were also specific shows presented as spectacles.

In July 1894, Inlet Amusement Park staged the "Destruction of
Herculaneum," "The Crowning Mammoth Effort of Wise & Martin,
Pain's World-Famous Scenic Artists." This was promised to be "The

Most Magnificent, Spectacular and Pyrotechnic Production on Earth." While Herculaneum had the advantage of an exotic setting, and made possible some fire-and-brimstone work, an indigenous tragedy would be more of a gut clencher. Happily, just such a tragedy was available in the satisfyingly cataclysmic Johnstown Flood, which occurred in Johnstown, Pennsylvania, on May 31, 1889. In 1904 Herbert A. Bradwell presented his "Scenograph" of the Johnstown Flood on the Boardwalk opposite the Steel Pier. A little booklet describing the incident, a pocket companion to the display, promises that the Scenograph "will give a very full understanding of this greatest disaster of modern times." A third entertainment of this kind was a huge painting of Custer's Last Stand displayed in the Heinz Pier, opened by the famous pickle magnate in 1898. Here threatening nature takes the form of savage Indians, at whose treacherous hands the dashing champion of white civilization meets a barbarous end.

The Grand Opera House presented H. Rider Haggard's *She* in July 1890. The management promised the audience "the same People, Scenery and Wonderful Mechanical and Electrical Effects which made the play so popular in all the large cities":

> *The Company carry a complete carload of Scenery, consisting of THE ELECTRIC STORM and WRECK OF THE "SLAVE DHOW." Followed by the appearance' of HEAD OF THE ETHIOPIAN, Displaying all the beautiful colors of a tropical sunrise on the African coast. THE HOT POT SCENE, Showing the African in his cannibalistic state. "SHE'S" CAVERN PALACE, A marvel of Historical and Architectural Grandeur. A city of six thousand years ago, THE RUINS OF KOR, A wonderful stage picture. THE BOTTOMLESS CHASM, Showing "Holly's" Leap for Life. The most realistic scene ever attempted. THE FIRE OF LIFE. Words are inadequate to convey even a faint description of this weirdly mysterious and awe-inspiring scene. The Grand Production will undoubtedly be the Spectacular event of the season.*

Herculaneum, the Johnstown Flood, Custer, and *She* were all expressions of ersatz danger. An urban population that was largely removed from the grosser effects of Nature—famine, plague, storm —sought in them such thrills as could be obtained by encountering danger by proxy. The kinds of disasters depicted had never happened to these people and never would. No doubt this was a good thing, and yet the absence of encounters with Nature in urban life did leave an unfulfilled desire. These shows and menageries both had a "spectacular" quality to them, a lavishness in the display of danger, and both emphasized the perilousness of Nature. But unlike the menageries, the spectacles placed man in a passive relationship to Nature, and it may be that this very passivity indicates a desire to approach Nature rather than to dominate it. Phony danger was more satisfying than mere manipulation, and besides, Nature was not all bad ("the beautiful colors of a tropical sunrise"). On the other hand, the danger was in fact bogus. Notice how the advertisement for *She* emphasizes that the show will bring "a complete carload of Scenery" to its assistance, as if a quantity of deception made for less deception. The author apologizes for the inadequacy of words to capture the mystery and awesomeness of the spectacle, and indeed, a spectacle depended on the spectator's goodwill and desire to be convinced if it was to translate illusion into reality by means of grandiose effects. Spectacles fell short of relating urban Americans to Nature. Indians, cannibals, floods, and volcanoes were all unlikely to figure largely in the lives of nineteenth-century Philadelphians.

An occasional resort entertainment may have had some real educational value. The beach was too thoroughly scavenged by hundreds of thousands of visitors to offer many good specimens of marine life, but

CONSISTENT

Fond Mother—"Go to the bath house, Mabel, and put
something around your neck. I think it's
terrible for you to expose it in that manner."

in the summer of 1900, Wonderland, opposite the Heinz Pier, informed vacationists of its nature display. In the museum were "remarkably constructed birds' nests of the world. Fine collection of birds' eggs and rare fishes of America, etc. Strange Insects. Gorgeous Butterflies." At ten cents' admission practically anyone could enter. Far more typical

of the resort, however, was the nature spectacle. For the same dime the
visitor could (and probably would) see a perhaps less educational
show: "It Is the General Talk. Have You Seen the Petrified Woman?"
"Wonderful, Marvelous, Instructive."

Freak shows were an enduring, if minor, variety of spectacle at
Atlantic City. The *Daily Union* recorded them in a thoroughly bland,
routine manner:

> *A live double bull with six legs and two tails arrived on a
> freight train yesterday. It is a monster and will be on exhibition.*
>
> *A two-headed boy is a new attraction on the beach front.*
>
> *The wonderful two-headed boy, James and Jacob Tocci, is
> attracting crowds of people at Young & McShea's rink. It is the
> greatest living wonder.*
>
> *Among other interesting exhibits on the Boardwalk is that of
> Millie Christine, the remarkable woman with two heads.*

Such freak shows must have been crowd drawers, and at the same time
culturally approved entertainment, or else so important an amusement
pavilion as Young and McShea's would not have engaged them.

As a whole, Atlantic City's amusements had little to teach the
visitor about Nature. We shall see later how promotional prose uniformly sentimentalized Nature despite the urban realities of the town,
a contradiction also evident in the poetry, postcards, souvenirs, and
illustrations which emanated from the resort. Nature was essentially
a "reactionary" phenomenon in Atlantic City, for it usually appeared as
a harking back to vanished life styles largely irrelevant to the city
folk who loved the town for its urban features. This does not mean
that Nature had no important functions in the resort; on the contrary,
the use of pastoral rhetoric as ratification of city pleasures will be
discussed at length in a separate chapter. But if Nature was to be
something more for industrial, urban society than the object of
romance and exploitation, Atlantic City for its part was silent.

But Atlantic City was not lacking in fare more congruent with the
lives of its visitors. The Machine created Atlantic City: the indis-
pensable railroad and also the systematized volume of services (accommodation, refreshment, and entertainment), together with the
advertising that brought them to the attention of millions. Atlantic
City reciprocated with a cheerful symbol of the Machine, the mechanical amusements that dotted the Boardwalk and the oceanside blocks.

Mechanical amusements took three basic forms, still familiar to
everyone: the merry-go-round, the Ferris wheel, and the roller coaster.
All three were popular at the resort throughout the 1890's, though the
merry-go-round and Ferris wheel appeared there a good deal earlier.

In July 1890 the *Daily Union* remarked, in the profit-conscious diction of the town, that "the new carrousel of Young & McShea was in operation yesterday for the first time and gathered in the nickels with more than usual rapidity." Two weeks later it reported that "Young & McShea, of the merry-go-round fame are doing $300 a week more business at the popular South Carolina avenue carousel than last year." The same proprietors were at work in June 1893 building another merry-go-round in a pavilion at the foot of Massachusetts Avenue. The distinguished carrousel builder Gustav A. Dentzel erected a double-deck merry-go-round in 1890, but the difficulty of loading and unloading made it unprofitable, and it was dismantled. Gopsill's *Atlantic City Directory* for 1891 lists other carrousels: Caemmerer and Groff's, on Chelsea Avenue in the west end of town; Adolph Daut's, on Mississippi Avenue near the ocean; Flood and Company's, on the Boardwalk near Missouri Avenue; and LaMarcus Thompson's, on the Boardwalk near New York Avenue.

An undated picture in a scrapbook at the Atlantic County Historical Society shows what the compiler has captioned "the first ferris wheel" in Atlantic City. This is very possibly a valid claim, since the crudity of the construction suggests that this ride was built before 1872, when a far more sophisticated wheel appeared at the resort. In fact, this "first" Ferris wheel was not a wheel at all, for it had two sets of crossed wooden beams reinforced by wires and lacked a circular metal rim. If a machine powered this ride, the photograph does not reveal it.

Isaac N. Forrester built a much more complicated "Epicycloidal Wheel" about 1872 on the beach in front of the Seaview Excursion House, a strategic location. This ride consisted of four great wheels, much like wagon wheels in appearance, joined by axles into two pairs and crossed in an "X." A vertical drive shaft, attached to the axles at their junction, caused the wheels to roll around a circular track. Passenger carriages were suspended on the wheels. Bearing sixty-four customers, this amusement must have required metal construction and steam power. There can be no doubt that William Somers' "Observation Roundabout" was a powered ride. Local historians credit Somers with inventing the Ferris wheel in 1891, when he constructed one on the beach at Kentucky Avenue. Though of course the Observation Roundabout was not a first, it was similar to modern wheels and could claim to be a home-town product. Fire destroyed Somers' initial effort, and in its second incarnation the wheel was made double.

There were other wheels of various kinds at Atlantic City throughout the decade, including the Crystal Palace Carrousel at the Seaview Excursion House, the local Enterprise Manufacturing Company's

"Round-about wheel" at Young & McShea's pavilion, and the Smith wheel, mentioned in the *Daily Union*:

> The "Smith" wheel on the beach near Kentucky avenue started yesterday and run [sic] splendidly several hours till some of the machinery got hot. It is a great novelty picking up and unloading cars loaded with people without stopping. Dr. Rex Smith is the inventor.

The third principal ride, besides the merry-go-round and the Ferris wheel, was the roller coaster. Victorian Americans did not use this term, but called the ancestors of the modern roller coaster by such names as "toboggan slide," "switchback," "scenic railway," and "serpentine railway." The Seaview Excursion House offered the "Mt. Washington Toboggan Slide" in 1889, and next summer the Casino Toboggan Slide, "the most exhilirating [*sic*] and novel amusement in the country," was in operation on the beach at Ocean Avenue. In 1893 the *Daily Union* described an intriguing hybrid of the toboggan slide and Ferris wheel:

> One of the novelties that is expected to be a paying scheme the coming summer will be located near the foot of Kentucky avenue. It is a large round-about wheel and toboggan slide combined. The main wheel which will be 45 feet in diameter, will run continuously, and the coaches containing the passengers will shoot down a toboggan slide to a groove in the large wheel. Here it is caught up and whirled around five minutes. When time is up it shoots out of the groove again to the starting point.

An article written in 1895 shows a photograph of a switchback in Atlantic City, very likely the one belonging to the amusement inventor and proprietor LaMarcus Adna Thompson. This switchback consisted of two tracks laid side by side, but sloping in opposite directions (there were no curves to the ride). When the small train reached the bottom of the incline its momentum carried it partway up the hill at the end, where the passengers disembarked and walked to the top, while the attendant pushed the empty cars to the summit and transferred them to the other track. Thompson's "Scenic Railway" improved upon the switchback's limitations, though the older ride continued in use. A circular track eliminated the transfer of the train, while a power hoist dragged it up the hill to the starting point.

At the turn of the century a dramatic refinement took place in the switchback which is impressive even today. A photograph dating about 1901 in the Atlantic City Public Library depicts the "Flip Flap Railway" on Young's Pier. At the bottom of the inclined plane was a breathtaking vertical loop twenty-five feet in height. A small car carrying two passengers, one facing forward and one disconcertingly facing back-

ward, traveled bicycle-fashion along a single grooved rail. As it reached the loop, its momentum was sufficient to carry it through the circle, giving the passengers a thrilling somersault. The Flip Flap Railway was the pinnacle of evolutionary progress in the roller coaster by the end of the Victorian period.

There were other, less important mechanical amusements in operation in Atlantic City. Among these were the Horseshoe Curve, whose seventy-two wooden horses could be made to gallop or canter as they traveled about a horseshoe-shaped track. "The motion is exhilarating and not so dizzyfying as on a merry-go-round." Today the bicycle is not regarded as fraught with excitement, but during the Mauve Decade it had a brief time of glory when it appeared to be the transportation wave of the future. Amusements were developed using bicycles and bicycle-like apparatus to attract patronage. In 1891 Eaton, Eastwood and Fish had a ride styled the "Flying Bicycles" on the Boardwalk at Texas Avenue, and Henry Darnall opened his "Bicycle Railway" on the Boardwalk two years later. A newspaper article describes the bicycles as suspended from above, though it may mean simply that they traveled along an elevated track. At any rate, the bicycles were fixed to prevent upsetting, and patrons could ride them along a 1,400-foot track.

Finally, there were the Revolving Towers on the beach at Massachusetts and New York avenues. The inventor responsible for these ingenious curiosities was the remarkable Jesse S. Lake of Pleasantville (Atlantic City's homely sister just across Absecon Bay), one of those eccentric, vigorous minds who somehow survive the intellectual meanness of small-town life. Lake (1825–96) was an inventor from youth. From his fertile imagination issued a host of mechanical innovations and schemes. These included the forerunner of the caterpillar tractor (affectionately known as "Lake's Hell Wagon" because of its deafening operating noise—though, to be sure, he was a part-time Methodist preacher), a whistling buoy, an improved cable-car grip, a process to extract aluminum from the mud of tidal marshes, and a plan to put passengers on and off an express train passing at full speed! Lake obtained sixty-five patents, but was largely oblivious to the business possibilities of his work. In an age which has been called the Great Barbecue for its wealth gotten and misbegotten, his share was fried bananas; riches eluded him. Still, his Revolving Towers were monarchs of Atlantic City's skyline. Each was a steel tower 125 feet in height, carrying a circular elevator 60 feet in width slowly to the top. As the elevator rose, it revolved leisurely to give the passengers an impressive view of the city and miles of the flat Jersey coast. At ten cents it was a cut more expensive than most rides, but still within the reach of mass patronage.

The names applied to many of these amusements express the importance they had for Americans of the day: "epicycloidal wheel," "roundabout," "revolving tower," "switchback." The implication of mechanical action must have carried special force during the 1890's, when the effects of machine power were impinging on countless aspects of daily life. It is likely that "merry-go-round" meant something different to the Victorian than to the modern ear, signifying not "merrily we go around," but "merry go-round," with "merry" as an adjective modifying the noun "go-round." The mechanical nomenclature so often applied to amusements at the turn of the century emphasized the basic appeal, for they expressed one of the most dynamic and widely felt phenomena of the era: technological innovation in the form of large machinery. By providing an accessible symbol of the Machine, mechanical amusements humanized technology.

Technology is the means by which an end is reached. A machine is an artifact, the physical embodiment of technology. Totally pragmatic in spirit, it is designed to achieve an end without regard to the value of that end. In the United States the end of industrial design traditionally has been conceived to be maximum productivity, to the exclusion of other values. Certain kinds of large machinery, expressing the pragmatism of technology, became omnipresent during the Victorian age, notably the steam locomotive. Railroads were the greatest economic force of the time, reaching into every corner of the land and occupying the core of the national prosperity. The thundering, hissing, smoke-breathing locomotive was in turn the single object of the railroads which most struck the public imagination. Secondly, the stationary steam engine was also of great importance. The giant Corliss engine, the hit of the Centennial of 1876, represented in extreme form what was possible in the manufacture of power. In the cities of America great factories arose, using immense quantities of power from stationary engines. There were many other ways in which the mushrooming technology of Victorian America expressed itself, from typewriters to sewing machines. But the extreme forms like the locomotive were most visible, and hence most impressive and threatening at the same time.

And these artifacts of technological change were indeed threatening. Henry Adams' grim prophetic theories on power expressed an intellectual's reaction to what was happening, and while the masses of

ordinary Americans clearly were enthusiastic about cities, they too had mixed feelings about the contemporary technology. For example, Eugene Debs's mother persuaded him in 1874 to give up his brief career as a locomotive fireman, because she was justifiably terrified for his safety. Railroad tragedies were distressingly frequent, and Atlantic City had two sufficiently horrifying examples of its own. A speeding Philadelphia and Reading express barreled into a West Jersey train full of excursionists at a grade crossing just below the Thoroughfare (the channel separating Absecon Island from the mainland) on July 30, 1896. Splintered wreckage and the mangled corpses of forty-four people were strewn over a wide area. On October 28, 1906, a train approaching the resort plunged off a trestle into the Thoroughfare. Some eighty passengers drowned as the deep water of the incoming tide swallowed up the coaches, leaving but twenty survivors. A resident of the area sent a poem, written for singing to the hymn "Safe in the Arms of Jesus," to a Camden newspaper, which published it:

> Down where the murmuring ocean
> Breaks on the sandy shore,
> Swiftly a train is rushing
> Seventy souls or more,
> Eager with thoughts of pleasure,
> Light-hearted, gay and free,
> Speeding across the meadows
> On to Eternity.
>   Refrain
> Wildly the cries of anguish
> Fall on the Sabbath air,
> Hopes of a life-time lying
> Down in the Thoroughfare.

Besides these disasters, the Philadelphia press regularly reported ghastly squashings and mutilations inflicted on passengers, crew, and pedestrians on Atlantic City railroads and nearby lines.

Various observers criticized the effects of technology on the quality of life. For example, R. Heber Newton, rector of All Souls Episcopal Church in New York City and a leading advocate of social Christianity, testified to the Senate Committee on Education and Labor in 1883 that the laboring portion of society especially suffered:

> One after another the processes of every old-time handicraft are being transferred to vast and complicated machines, and production is no longer to be called a manufacture, but a machino-facture. The skill which of old lay in the deft fingers of the craftsman is becoming lodged in steely mechanisms. Men become the tenders upon the costly and cunning machine. . . . Thus . . . labor suffers severely from the modern mechanical improvements,

and from the monster forces which science has broken in to these engines.

The physician George M. Beard, in his book *American Nervousness: Its Causes and Consequences*, published in 1881, wrote that the whole of society was bound to suffer mentally from the principal technological innovations.

> *The modern differ from the ancient civilizations mainly in these five elements—steam power, the periodical press, the telegraph, the sciences, and the mental activity of women. When civilization, plus these five factors, invades any nation, it must carry nervousness and nervous diseases along with it.*

Thus a widespread enthusiasm for the new machines of modern society was tempered by an apprehension which produced a popular need for some way to make machinery "sympathetic" and unthreatening.

Mechanical amusements were machines in the service of pleasure. In effect, they went technology one better, and in so doing they turned it on its head. Whereas technology sought to maximize productivity, on the cultural assumption that maximum productivity would bring maximum pleasure, mechanical amusements sought to maximize pleasure directly. Although sufficient productivity in terms of the number of passengers per ride was vital to an amusement's success, it was even more important that the machine produce pleasure, or else it would not be competitive. An amusement designer who put capacity and speed of processing ahead of the pleasure-producing potential of his machine would merely be constructing an efficient white elephant. There was much more of an optional nature to the use of a mechanical amusement than, say, to the patronage of the only railroad that ran through one's town. The customer paid to ride because the ride was pleasurable, and while speed produced excitement, the last thing he wanted was for his ride to end quickly. The amusement customer wasn't going anywhere, and the longer he took to get there the better. In strictly technological terms, mechanical amusements were nonsense machines.

Enjoying these rides, Victorian Americans confronted machinery in terms of pleasure rather than efficiency. This in itself humanized technology, because the Machine was humbled to the point of serving the need for pleasure directly, rather than indirectly in the form of highest productivity. The serpentine railway was a train of delights, the kind the Machine never quite delivered in the sober economic world. It was small and comprehensible, and its dwarfish scale produced jerky movements which had a comic element in them. The switchback was erratic in principle, rising and dipping randomly,

whereas railroad builders moved mountains to avoid unprofitable grades. The Epicycloidal Wheel was full of motion without progress, as its four wheels chased each other about like a locomotive with epilepsy. A roundabout was a wheel that a human could get inside of, enjoying the motions as his carriage pendulated intriguingly to avoid upsets. Its structure was that of a great locomotive wheel or the gear of a huge machine, whose accommodating edge scooped up humans for an exhilarating ride.

The merry-go-round offered circular motion in a horizontal plane at a speed slow enough to be safe for children. Wooden horses presented a delightful incongruity, to which young people responded, and the mechanical wheezings of a power-driven organ set the rhythm. Still, it wasn't the horses the children came for, but the motion, as the *Daily Union* testified in 1890:

> *The new merry-go-round at the foot of South Carolina avenue has ceased running, pending contemplated improvements to raise the horses and hang them upon a mast so as to permit them to revolve faster. They were found to be too slow for Young America who wants more excitement for a nickel.*

As relatively tame as the merry-go-round was, even adults could respond to its appeal. The same newspaper observed in 1893: "Vice-President Charles Pugh, of the Pennsylvania Railroad, was recognized last evening as one of the patrons of the merry-go-round."

Today mechanical amusements strike us as quaint rather than daring. The Ferris wheel, merry-go-round, and roller coaster are objects of the past suggestive of a certain innocence, a naïve gaiety which is out of place in the anxiety-ridden city of the present. It must be remembered, however, that they had an altogether different effect on Victorians, to whom they symbolized the essence of the excitement of the age. The large machines born of Victorian technology possessed an eye appeal susceptible of mass popularity. Though parallels are not completely lacking today, nevertheless there is a difference. Passenger jets are large and dramatic, but they operate outside of urban centers and fly at remote altitudes; small boys don't wave to pilots. Rockets are something to be seen on television, accompanied perhaps by a canned sentiment from the President to relate the feat to national purpose. Computers, the epitome of modern impersonality, conceal their mysterious operations beneath the blandest of façades.

Each age has its own sources of technological excitement. The 1890's were flush times for large machinery, and the mechanical amusements of Atlantic City reflected the fact successfully for the popular culture. Not only did they symbolize the Machine, they also expressed Victorian Americans' love of using the Machine to triumph over Nature. The Casino Toboggan Slide, for example, embellished its track with scenery and advertised itself in 1890 as "Pikes Peak and Through the St. Gothard Tunnel." These allusions attracted contemporaries, since in 1891 a cog railway commenced service up Pikes Peak (and two years later allegedly inspired Katharine Lee Bates to write "America the Beautiful"). The great tunnel, over nine miles long, constructed beneath the St. Gothard Pass to provide train service between Italy and Central Europe, was finally completed in 1880. Next year, *Appleton's Annual Cyclopaedia* claimed: "The tunnel has been pronounced by engineers one of the greatest works, if not the greatest one, ever yet executed by man." Atlantic City rides challenged gravity and inertia. Most daring was the switchback, which bolted and twisted with motions that in the normal world were sure to lead to disaster. The Revolving Tower was a mechanical Olympus, from whose top godlike passengers viewed the prostrate flats of Jersey. The Observation Roundabout picked up the customer at ground level and swept him up into the clouds, in a delicious tension of excitement that came just below the threshold of fear. When the peak was reached, the rider plunged downward in what was almost a free fall, until the circular route quickly and smoothly decelerated him.

Mechanical amusements were fundamentally urban in appeal. Ever since the mid-nineteenth century, cities had been reaching out aggressively into the country, subduing Nature with the Machine. This is the process Leo Marx describes in *The Machine in the Garden*. The amusement machines of Atlantic City were also challenging Nature, for the sake of pleasure. Visitors to the resort, responding to the urban spirit of the time, were willing to pay to share the experience.

Evidence exists in the history of mechanical amusements to suggest why they were popular in Victorian America. First, while their appeal lay in their being a symbol of the Machine, it was not essential that they embody technology at a level of sophistication equal to the Machine of which they were the symbol. So long as they were Machine-like in appearance and operation, they could be quite primitive in construction and still be effective. If this is true, then the adaptation of more sophisticated technology to mechanical amusements would occur when they acquired a dramatically increased relevance to the condition of the culture. In other words, when industrialization and urbanization began to have a profound impact upon society, a previously existing symbol of the mechanical process would suddenly enjoy a great increase in popularity. At this point, patronage of mechanical amusements would increase to such a level that an updating of their

technology would be necessary if all the customers were to be accommodated (and all their fares garnered).

William F. Mangels' *The Outdoor Amusement Industry* (1952) offers an interesting chronicle on the subject. Mangels was involved in the amusement business himself, and he was able to draw on a lifetime's interest.

The origins of the merry-go-round go back at least a century before the rise of Atlantic City. Mangels reproduces a print dated 1770 of a device for training young royalty in ring spearing, a popular tournament contest. Rotated by hand, this affair had four wooden horses suspended from the ends of two crossed wooden beams. It became a favorite amusement, and took the name "carrousel" from the tournaments of horsemanship held in the Middle Ages. A carrousel factory appeared in Germany in the mid-nineteenth century, and commercial production brought such improvements as the use of animal power. Michael Dentzel came from Germany to Philadelphia in 1844, bringing knowledge of carrousel construction with him and operating his rides in various places in Pennsylvania. His son, Gustav A. Dentzel, started a factory in Germantown and placed a carrousel on Smith's Island, in the Delaware River adjacent to Market Street. Sometime before 1876 he moved it to Atlantic City, where it became the first merry-go-round at the resort. Significantly, it was powered by a horse harnessed to the center pole. Although S. G. Soames of Marsham, England, first applied steam power to a carrousel in 1865, Dentzel was the first to do so in America. This was probably at a site near one of Atlantic City's excursion houses, and must have occurred in 1876 or shortly thereafter. It might be supposed that machine-driven carrousels would displace other kinds quickly, and yet this did not occur. Fritz Landow, an immigrant carrousel maker from Austria, went on tour in 1880 with a crude portable ride operated by manpower; and as late as 1912 the Central Park carrousel in New York was powered by a mule. Nevertheless, the direction of development was toward powered rides, such as the widely used and superbly made "Steam Riding Galleries" which the Armitage-Herschell company began to manufacture in North Tonawanda, New York, in 1879.

Mangels finds the forerunner of the Ferris wheel in use since the eighteenth century in the Old World. The Russians were fond of rotary swings called *katcheli*, which incorporated a capstan-like device to allow a man to apply horizontal force in propelling them. An illustration of 1790 from Alexandria, Egypt, shows an X-shaped wooden pleasure "wheel" that is strikingly similar to the "first" Ferris wheel in Atlantic City, described earlier. Pleasure wheels were popular in early-nineteenth-century England under the name of "perpendicular round-abouts," but it was not until 1867 that Isaac N. Forrester of Bridgeport, Connecticut, obtained the first patent in the United States for such an amusement. It was Forrester who was responsible for the Epicycloidal Wheel in Atlantic City, suggesting that his patent was for this very device. In view of its size and complexity, it must have been powered by an engine. Other manufacturers appeared shortly afterward, and wheels were made in Brooklyn and Ohio. An Ohio company produced a ride in 1885 powered by a small gasoline engine. In the 1880's the Conderman Brothers of Clay City, Indiana, and Hornellsville, New York, designed a portable wheel also using a gasoline engine.

Finally, George Washington Gales Ferris, head of the Pittsburgh Bridge Company, designed a great wheel for the Columbian Exposition of 1893 in Chicago. According to William McMahon, in *So Young . . . So Gay*, his story is curiously involved with that of William Somers of Atlantic City. Mangels has it that Ferris was inspired to build his wheel at a banquet given for architects and engineers by the directors of the upcoming fair. One of the speakers pointed out that the Exposition would lack a spectacular attraction like the Eiffel Tower. According to McMahon, officials of the fair contacted Somers, who had already built wheels at Atlantic City, Asbury Park, and Coney Island. For some reason nothing came of this, and the Exposition sent Ferris to the resort to examine the Somers wheel. Ferris returned with a recommendation that was to make all the difference, a recommendation which he, as a bridge builder, was in a singularly good position to make. The Exposition's ride, he said, should be made of steel. He constructed a truly monstrous wheel 250 feet in diameter, carrying 2,160 passengers in 36 cars seating 60 in each. It was equipped with Westinghouse air brakes and two 1,000-horsepower steam engines. Obviously, only steel construction and skilled engineering could achieve such a gargantuan scale in a mechanical amusement. But Somers was wroth, so he traveled to Chicago to put up his own wheel outside the fairgrounds. A lawsuit followed, and the court actually found for Somers, though on what ground is not recorded. In the meantime, however, Ferris had died, and his name had become permanently attached to the pleasure wheel.

The late application of power to amusement rides is clearly illustrated in the development of the roller coaster. An early ride called "the Russian Mountains" operated in Paris in 1804. A modification of the popular Russian ice slide for the warmer French climate, it used rolling carriages instead of sleds to carry passengers down the inclined plane. In 1817 the spectacular Promenades Aériennes of the same city featured a ramp eighty feet high, with a circular track that brought the cars to a point next to and below where they had started. Then they were hauled up another slope for a new ride. Various patents were issued in France in the first decades of the nineteenth century for rides of this type. America, however, had an example of an industrial "roller coaster" on a spectacular scale to serve as a model. The gravity-operated inclined coal railway at Mauch Chunk, Pennsylvania, was converted to an amusement facility in 1870. A system of stationary engines and inclined planes carried passengers to and from the starting point, the reversal of direction giving the ride the name "switchback." In 1878 Richard Knudsen of Brooklyn, New York, patented an "inclined-plane railway" which was a modestly scaled switchback, but it was never built.

LaMarcus Adna Thompson's "Switchback Railway," built at Coney Island in 1884, was the first operating ride of its kind. It was similar if not identical to his ride in Atlantic City, examined earlier. This popular amusement depended upon manpower to drag the cars up the ramp at the end of one grade to the starting point of the other. Thompson's early lead in switchbacks stimulated competition, and Charles Alcoke built a circular roller coaster at Coney Island in 1885 with a power-driven chain to take the cars uphill. Thompson's answer was the similarly powered "Scenic Railway" (or "serpentine railway") that he set up on the Boardwalk between New York and Tennessee avenues. Tunnels containing natural and historical scenes illuminated by floodlights gave this roller coaster its name. Thompson Scenic Railways were the hit of amusement parks and fairs, and various elaborations followed in the wake of their success.

The predecessor of the Flip Flap Railway was a centrifugal railway operated in the Frascati Garden in Paris in 1848, which in turn was modeled after a smaller device in England. Forty years later, Lina Beecher of Batavia, New York, installed a centrifugal railway in a park in Toledo, Ohio. In 1889 he built a second device for Sea Lion Park, a Coney Island amusement center established by a former Atlantic City lifeguard. Beecher organized the American Railway Company and built other Flip Flaps in Atlantic City and St. Louis, but the ride was unpopular because the violent motions of the loop gave passengers sore necks. An elliptical loop, which eliminated discomfort to the customers, appeared at Coney Island in 1901, yet the ride was never profitable.

The history of mechanical amusements makes it clear that the basic forms popular at Atlantic City existed well before their appearance at the resort. Moreover, we know that the first merry-go-round and the

first roller coaster in the city were powered without the benefit of machine. It is very likely that the first Ferris wheel was driven by man or animal, and in basic structure it is the twin of a ride of the eighteenth century. Inventors and proprietors were slow to apply the technology of the day to mechanical amusements, because the appeal of these rides depended upon symbol, not actuality. As the need for the symbol increased, the patronage increased, and appropriate technology was used to accommodate the demand. This technology had existed for decades. Steam engines drove the nation's railway system long before their use in rides, and the magnificent steel engineering of the Brooklyn Bridge preceded by ten years the steel engineering of the Ferris wheel. It is not correct to assume that available technology was used in industry before amusement because tools are more important than toys. The operators of amusement rides were looking for profits, not good times, and, like manufacturers, they would apply the technology necessary to make the profits. The application of technology to mechanical amusements came only when they were so heavily patronized that their backward design could not keep up with the possibilities of profit.

When inventors finally responded to the market for more sophisticated amusement technology, they pressed forward to achieve monopolies by patenting the rides themselves. They were disappointed. An article in the *Daily Union* in August 1891 advised the entrepreneurs of the resort who were considering building mechanical novelties to hire a patent lawyer for advice on how to avoid paying royalties for necessary equipment. Switchbacks, figure eights, gravity roads, toboggan slides, merry-go-rounds, all depend upon simple mechanical principles which cannot be patented. Gravity roads have been used in Europe for centuries, and merry-go-rounds "are as old as Methuselah." In 1904 a court decision held that the basic concept of the rotary swing was ancient in origin and unpatentable. Men like William Somers, who placed a sign in front of his Observation Roundabout declaring himself the patentee, and who tried in 1893 to sue two competitors in the roundabout business, were to find that they had built the greater part of their castle on sand.

Curiously enough, though individual entrepreneurs might exaggerate their pioneer role in developing rides, Atlantic City itself did not seem to be anxious to advertise its leadership as a mechanical amusement park. Indeed, sometimes it appeared that it was not even aware of this aspect of its character. In 1893 the *Daily Union*, in its article on the unveiling of the Ferris wheel at the Columbian Exposition, referred to Ferris as the inventor and made no mention of the home-town boy, Somers. The brakes on the Scenic Railway failed to work one day in August 1891, and the passengers were hurled to the ground. Among the seven people injured was Bessie Wanamaker, niece of John Wanamaker of Philadelphia, a man of imposing reputation. The *Daily Union*, obviously reflecting anxiety in the resort over the costly consequences of bad publicity in Philadelphia, questioned the value of the ride. It could not understand why 800,000 people had ridden the nickel amusement in its two years of operation, since it was noisy and dangerous. "This scenic railway has been no advantage to this city or its locality since it was built. Many people wonder why so many people patronize it or why it is permitted to exist." It is possible that Atlantic City's tendency to ignore its mechanical amusements can be explained by its desire to avoid identifying with Coney Island, a still greater amusement park which nevertheless, in Atlantic City's opinion, was altogether lowbrow in its appeal. The illusion of swank was critically important to the Jersey resort, and the protection of that illusion took precedence over all else.

No matter if Atlantic City was unaware: its mechanical amusements were a smashing success. Through these rides, the resort helped Americans understand the age they were living in, the age of the Machine and the City. As for Nature, Atlantic City had little to teach.

If, however, the best the city can do for the country is to make itself work, then the resort succeeded more than it failed. By suggesting that the Machine could serve man, Atlantic City pointed to the possibility of avoiding a middle "Garden" world of a landscape raped by the Machine, and a City devitalized and decentralized by an ersatz landscape. It is a possibility our culture is still struggling to discover.

The Perspectives of Janus

4

ONE OF THE most troubling problems the citizens of Atlantic City had to face was the character their town should have. Specifically, what balance of discipline and pleasure would be most profitable and at the same time lie within the bounds of the community's sense of propriety? Atlantic City was to be the great Family Resort, yet it was also to be the great Pleasure Resort. These two demands placed upon the seaside city, by its builders and also by the public, were hardly compatible. The extent to which they were antagonistic constituted the agonies of a Victorian American resort.

In the last decade of the nineteenth century, although the urban world of industry and commerce was giving the city masses increasing leisure and relative affluence, it was also imposing new burdens and frustrations. Work conditions in an economy progressively influenced by technology led to insecurity, hostile rivalries, and lack of satisfaction in the job. Consequently, the traditional cultural emphasis on discipline gradually yielded to an emphasis on pleasure, a hedonistic compensation for the shortcomings of the new life. The Pleasure Resort was a response to this emerging hedonism in American society.

In apparent opposition was the ideal of the Family Resort, in which good order, wholesome entertainment, piety, and temperance would shelter families from destructive temptations, particularly those aimed at fathers and children. Still, the Family Resort versus the Pleasure Resort was not a simple case of discipline versus pleasure. Though restraint was a necessary adjunct to the welfare of the family, the family was not a negative phenomenon. The emotional warmth, loyalty, and cooperative effort which could be found within the family salved the injuries sustained in the outer world, where efficiency, competitive struggle, and impersonal obligation reigned. Pleasure in a family setting, though not perhaps the most luxuriant form of hedon-

ism, was an appealing goal, for it further enhanced the desirability of the family as an institution.

Atlantic City prided itself on its ability to deliver pleasure. Advertising literature emphasized the deluge of joys offered the visitor, and the hot time that was possible. Unofficially, an even hotter time could be had, and the information must have circulated widely, through barroom gossip, reports of returned friends, inferences from newspaper accounts, and other sources. Officially, Atlantic City sought to cram the visitor with all the entertainment, food, liquor, souvenirs, and assorted oceania that it could. It might be supposed abstractly that this atmosphere of license could still result in entirely legal and morally acceptable behavior. Naturally, a spree was the very thing to compensate for the boredom of a repetitive, dull, routinized job in industry or business. Yet, though the resort definitely cultivated the institution of the spree, there were no effective boundaries to decide at what point the spree was to end. That was a loose thread.

The resort offered a middle ground. It should not be a sink of iniquity, but neither should it be a Sunday school. After all, a Sunday-school resort existed in the form of Ocean Grove, a notoriously dull and straitlaced Methodist retreat appealing to those who believed the main pleasures were deferred to paradise. Atlantic City, being a much more heterogeneous section of American society, wanted nothing to do with that notion. The town should somehow be freewheeling yet virtuous, scintillating yet sober, fashionable yet Christian. There were two fundamental classes of visitors to Atlantic City, the minority of riffraff who might be expected to want pleasures the culture did not sanction, and the overwhelming mass of respectable tourists who wanted a good (but clean) time. This was one way of structuring the resort's patronage. But there seems to have been a second way, which was held simultaneously. Most of the visitors were relatively urbane people who wanted to enjoy themselves at the resort, and who would be annoyed and perhaps driven away by pestering restrictions on their behavior. This group was theoretically the constituency of the Golden Mean, and included none of the riffraff but a majority of the respectable group. These people would respond to and help maintain the compromise between the Family Resort and the Pleasure Resort.

Consequently, Atlantic City was trying to respond to a whole range of demands by sustaining an elusive compromise between familial duty and pleasure. Of course, it all depends on whose viewpoint we consider. A local minister, a hotelkeeper, and the owner of an unlicensed saloon would have different views on what Atlantic City

should be like, and so would a father in the company of his family, a young salesman on a one-week holiday, and a shopgirl on her annual vacation. But there was a net effect proceeding from the different viewpoints, which was a compromise indeed, but a compromise tending toward paralysis. The decorous features of a strict Family Resort— church, soda parlor, ladies' sitting room—were available. The culturally acceptable concomitants of a Pleasure Resort fairly shrieked at the visitor as he made his way along the Boardwalk. And the nitty-gritty fundamentals of a full-blown Pleasure Resort were but a step down a side street or alley, a flight upstairs, or a sidelong glance away on the Boardwalk.

Atlantic City represented a culture often in danger of lying to itself, clutching with its left hand what it pushed away with its right. The culture, not the city, was to blame, yet the city was frequently criticized for results that it could not control, but only modify. Atlantic City was an expression of the desires of Philadelphia, and as such its defects were but the defects in the general culture. This does not exempt local individuals from blame, but it does mean that outside pressures determined the general form Atlantic City took. Thus one must sympathize with the resort in the face of recurrent hostile scrutiny. It appears that no one bothered to point the accusing finger elsewhere. It was more reassuring to regard Atlantic City as a sinful magnet luring respectable Americans to misbehavior than as an excrescence of the culturally unsanctioned desires of America.

The ideal of the Family Resort permeates the literature of Atlantic City, in statements both declarative and defensive. Promoters for the city were forever proclaiming it to be such a resort, and apologists were forever saying it had been once and would be again. When business was going smoothly, it was possible to tout Atlantic City as a model of propriety, but once the municipal slip showed, it was time to refurbish the ideal. In the summer of 1890 the *Philadelphia Bulletin* assailed the resort's iniquity in an impressive series of front-page articles which appeared daily throughout August and into September, having as their target liquor violations, gambling, prostitution, and official complicity. As part of its journalistic technique, the *Bulletin* dug up a local figure representative of the respectable citizens of the town, whom it identified as "Squire" John Gobley. Gobley was a retired citizen who had held several public offices; the title "Squire" seems to have been conferred by the newspaper to conjure up an image of rural integrity. The *Bulletin* drew on Gobley for commentary on the city, picturing him as a bluff and honest old nestor, grown gray in the service of his community. The Squire was steadfast for the Family

Resort: "I would like Atlantic City to be known as a place where mothers could send their daughters; and husbands send their wives without fear."

Alfred Heston, in his handbooks, repeatedly championed this viewpoint. In 1887 he said of the resort: "The solid character of its patrons from the better elements of society, the quiet, homelike aspect of the place, the natural scenery and charms peculiar to itself, conspire to make Atlantic City the very ideal of a summer resort." The advertising material in Heston's handbooks expands upon this scheme of recreational respectability with particulars. Of the Winter Ocean Parlor and the Seaside Parlor, he says: "The regulations are such as to make these places at all times desirable for ladies and families." The same tone is evident in his description of the Park Baths and Annex ("Protection to ladies and families on the beach front"), but here he makes a curious recommendation over which he dwells suspiciously long. This quotation suggests the peek-a-boo eroticism which often appears in the literature of Atlantic City.

> *The regulations are such as will ensure perfect propriety in every department and the convenience of guests. Robes are provided at both places of plain or stylish designs for gentlemen, ladies, and children. Special care has been taken in the selection of material and in the making to secure comfort and freedom from annoyance by faulty seams or fastenings. Everything of an immodest character is strictly avoided.*

By reassuring the reader of the management's concern for structural failure in its bathing suits, Heston goes a bit beyond the necessities of Family Resort rhetoric.

A promotional brochure of 1904 presents a peculiarly antiseptic picture of the Family Resort, expressing a fear of contamination by contact between humans and morbidly estimating the resort on the basis of its ability to keep its visitors from encroaching on each other.

> *Visitors, ladies or gentlemen, singly or together, may pass and loiter at all times of the day and evening in perfect safety, free from intoxication annoyance and without danger of being spoken to by other than their friends. This feature is considered by travellers of world wide experience to be the most wonderful thing in the world. Upwards of a quarter million of people, bent upon pleasure and recreation, congregate here by the ocean side and enjoy thoroughly, each in his or her own way, the pleasure of a holiday in a thoroughly respectable manner and without giving offense to anyone else.*

This disciplinary extreme belies a basic purpose of the city: the mixing of people and the maximization of experience. It is the vision of a man fearful of human nature, who sees perfection in isolated individualism and who is fastidious about physical contact.

An observer's comment in 1908 reveals the ignorance of the author through a naïve comparison between Atlantic City and that traditional city of gratified desires, Paris. It is the classic native assumption of America's moral superiority to decadent Europe. "There is this difference between Atlantic City's cafes and those of Paris—you can safely take your wife and daughter into any of those of the former,

AN ATLANTIC AVENUE
SWELL BAR

whereas one would think twice before taking them into all the cafes of the French capital." Such assurance befitted only the willfully blind in Atlantic City, since there were a good many places whose thresholds were never graced by the step of wife and daughter. Even Heston belies the universal respectability of the resort's business by claiming in 1887 that "none but the better class" of hotels and businesses were invited to advertise in his handbook, their appearance guaranteeing their character. If there was a better class, obviously there was a class that was somewhat worse, and though the author may not have meant this, it was a simple fact nevertheless. On the other hand, assurances of a moral atmosphere suitable for family entertainment and accommodation were appropriate at a time when working males wished to seek in the company of their families what was missing in their jobs.

In August 1890 the City Council of Atlantic City passed an ordinance

prohibiting the operation of public amusements on Sunday, including rides, games, exhibitions, and sports, a legislative act that ostensibly spurred the *Bulletin* to begin its crusade. The Philadelphia newspaper believed that this law struck at respectable families out for a holiday, not at real malefactors, by banning innocuous amusements in favor of real evil.

> *What bosh [is] all this!*
> *Innocent children are denied the pleasure of riding on the "merry-go-round," but excursion loafers can revel in free-flowing beer and whisky! . . .*
> *The switchback railroad, with its entertainment for women and children is closed by the law; but the doors of low drinking dives are open to the touch of the debased and the degraded. . . .*
> *Atlantic City is an inviting summer resort—it is just the spot for the family, the tired worker, the seeker after health and the lover of recreation!*
> *But a halt must be cried to the gambler, crook, dive-keeper, prostitute and black-leg; they have nothing in common with the family, the tired worker, the seeker after health and the lover of recreation!*

The *Bulletin* imagined a family outing on Sunday. When they arrived at the beach, the children found that they couldn't play with the sand, for sand throwing was illegal, nor could they throw a ball. When Mom and Dad took the kids to the merry-go-round and the toboggan slide, they found them closed. "And so it goes on. At last the father, in desperation, leaves wife and children to the puritanical monotony of the beach front, while he seeks a beer saloon. *It is open to him!*" At the end of the day, the idyllic Victorian family scene has become a dismal tableau:

> *Father returns—drunk! A sad-eyed, heavy-hearted woman, cross, surly children, and an intoxicated man take the cars for home. This is the end of a day that perhaps has been looked forward to for weeks! This is the awakening after a woman's dream of a pleasant holiday for the children! The picture is not overdrawn; it is a faithful reproduction of that which occurs here every Sunday.*

Here the *Bulletin* clearly sees the family as the proper customer of the resort. Interestingly enough, it holds that too much emphasis on discipline is conducive to a flight to hedonism. Excessive restriction of pleasure ruins the time of women and children, and drives despairing men into the clutches of the dive keepers. The *Bulletin*'s rejection of the "puritanical monotony of the beach front" implies that the Family Resort and the Pleasure Resort have a certain interest in common. Pleasure in moderation is the goal. Still, the unbridled

Pleasure Resort is intolerable. The *Bulletin* chides "Dutchy" Muhlrod, a local dive owner, reminding him of the low opinion in which the family holds him: "You have no friends, except those you have to buy; mothers and wives hate you, 'Dutchy' Muhlrod; even children despise you!"

The propriety of Atlantic City allegedly encompassed its entertainments as well as its lodgings, businesses, and social customs. Schaufler's Garden is mentioned in the *Daily Union* in 1891: "The proprietors strive their utmost to make the garden a resort of innocent amusement. . . . How they have succeeded is well attested by the ever increasing number of gentlemen who visit the pavilion with their wives and families and sweethearts." In 1893 the same paper reports that Fred Albrecht, manager of Albrecht's Concert Garden, "has determined to engage only first class performers and give his patrons a clean and pleasing show." In English's history of Atlantic City, written in 1884, there is a suspicious apology for the resort's concert gardens, which it will prove worthwhile remembering in Chapter 5:

> A feature of Atlantic [sic] is the open air concert gardens. One at first thought would perhaps not class these institutions as special attractions, but the standard at which they are held elsewhere, must not be judged by what they may be regarded here. They are conducted with order and decorum. Many people who never venture into them at home visit them in the cool of the evening here, and enjoy the excellent music which is provided. Solid businessmen of irreproachable reputation, distinguished people from all parts of the country, and church-going people are frequently seen in these places. Mr. Alois Schaufler of Schaufler's Hotel, opened the first and largest place of this kind, followed by Mr. Wm. Albrecht, of Albrecht's first-class hotel. Each furnish proper and interesting entertainments, and are managed with a strict regard for decency and proper enjoyment.

"Order," as was seen earlier, is an important theme in Victorian society, but when writers use this word, they sometimes mean not just political order but moral order as well. Many visitors wanted to be assured that masses of people bent on pleasure would not produce libertinism on an urban scale. Consequently, Guvernator's Mammoth Constitution Pavilions and Concert Gardens advised readers of its "strict order," and editor Hall claimed that, on the Boardwalk, "every civilized nation on earth is represented in the cosmopolitan process." "Civilized" is a weighty qualifier. Were Italians from a civilized nation? Were Irish? Were blacks? Hall is conveniently vague, allowing scope for the favorite prejudices of his middle-class readers. His newspaper assured tourists in 1897 that for nineteen years the Fortescue Pavilion "has maintained an unblemished reputation, not the slightest complaint

ever having been entered against it." These claims for orderly pleasure were designed to fetch the family trade, which officially desired excitement always bounded by decency and security.

There are many explicit examples of the city's desire to be a Family Resort. In 1891 a committee of prominent local citizens, including the chief of police, six doctors, and two ministers, visited the showing of Miss Millie Christine, the two-headed woman, to determine the authenticity and wholesomeness of the exhibit. They declared themselves satisfied: "She is not repulsive, but on the contrary, pleasant and interesting to talk to." Other entertainments stressed their elevated nature, such as the "high class Vocalist Miss Minnie Lee" or the "high-class vaudeville" previously discussed. In 1897 the Fortescue Pavilion introduced "the Zartinis, a family of German artists. The exhibition is chaste, artistic, beautiful and worth seeing." One finds many other claims of this kind throughout the turn-of-the-century era.

Sunday in a resort was a problem, for the weekday amusements tended to obscure the Sabbath. Since the American family presumably was pious in the tradition of its forefathers and required religious facilities, a Mrs. Williams, proprietress of the Victoria Hotel, built an open-air church on the Boardwalk to provide a convenient place of worship for Sunday strollers. Applegate's Pier staged "select Sunday-night sacred concerts" in 1887, and Young & McShea's Ocean Pier advertised a program of sacred music for the Sundays of 1893: "Manager Willard promises that nothing but a sacred concert will be rendered." In 1891, in fact, Young and McShea opposed a Sunday-opening movement, declaring that "there will be church services as usual at the merry-go-round on Sunday afternoons." The efforts of churches and citizens to make Sunday in the resort holy persisted for many years, despite the long odds against righteousness presented by the critical Sunday excursion trade. As late as 1927, the local Minister-ial Union protested the performance of a circus on the Sabbath.

Appeals of a fundamentally disciplinary nature were balanced, indeed overbalanced, by attractions of a pleasurable sort at Atlantic City. The lure of the seaside involved letting down your hair and acting a little wild, a fact fully realized at the time.

Much of the public did not want censorship of its activities at the resort. As far back as 1856, a letter to a Philadelphia newspaper stated:

> There are many delightful flirtations on the beach, a favorite spot for lovers. The blind god also seems to have sought the sea shore and brought with him the bows and arrows for matrimonial purposes. . . .
> I would advise a man before getting married, to see his sweetheart in her bathing dress. There is no deception there. He can

see exactly the size of the human nature he is in love with. . . .
And no harm . . . the salt water washes away all impropriety.

Atlantic City was indeed celebrated as a center of lovemaking and all
the activities that go with it. In a society which had erected too
formidable barriers against contact between the sexes, the resort
was a godsend. The atmosphere of the beach—thronged with strangers
all out for a good time, the greater part in a state of relative undress—
was a perfect antidote to the stifling restrictions of everyday life. The
holiday atmosphere offered a further suspension of the normal rules
of sexual propriety. A few people were irked, such as one prudish
commentator, who complained: "Shock-headed youths lie with their
heads in the laps of frowsy-looking women who comb their hair; and
those who are interested in the subject may classify at least a hundred
new varieties of public love-making." But the *Daily Union* more
accurately expressed the general feeling in 1893:

> *The Baltimore police have been instructed to arrest all young*
> *persons kissing or "spooning" in the public parks of that city, and*
> *a fine of twenty dollars is imposed for each offense. A similar*
> *edict in this city would greatly swell the public revenues, but it*
> *would not be submitted to; it would raise a riot.*

There were innumerable places of rendezvous throughout the city,
and all kinds of entertainments and facilities to accommodate couples
according to their familiarity with each other. Applegate's Pier, a
double-decker, had a Lover's Pavilion in the middle of its second level,
which provided privacy from the crowd on the beach for those couples
whom even strangers made nervous. This was fine for established
pairs, but those looking for a partner also benefited from the informal
atmosphere of the resort. The fastidious informant cited earlier out-
lined the process:

> *Thus it is that women who in their home towns are wholly*
> *decorous and will never go to anything more exciting than an ice-*
> *cream sociable or the strawberry festival of the First Presbyterian*
> *Church will, in Atlantic City, be absolutely careless about the*
> *minor mores. One of these women, staying alone at a hotel,*
> *will, after the third meal, become acquainted with some man who*
> *sits at the same table with her. On the next day she will be rolling*
> *about with him in a "chair," while in less than a week she will*
> *be visiting "grottoes" with him in the evening, and drinking*
> *highballs.*

The young lady in question had good reason for covering the basics
"in less than a week": she probably had to leave the resort and get
back to her job in little more than that. If she was fortunate, she had
a marriage prospect, or at least an escort for the fall.

The seal of Atlantic City was designed before 1900 by a city doctor, James North, who fancied himself the local bard and wrote a poem to his creation as the personification of the resort. It reveals perhaps more than intended about the contemporary mentality. The symbol of the city itself, as depicted in an illustration accompanying his poem, represents the town goddess riding tiptoe on a wheel, surrounded by the hokum of popular heraldry, including symbolic devices, a motto, and so forth. Absecon Lighthouse springs from the goddess's head like a unicorn's appendage, and through her thick and heavily draped robe, a nipple improbably and coyly peeks. And the poem:

> *Here crowned with light she stands*
> *Holding in outstretched hands*
> > *Pleasure and health,*
> *With her emblazoned shield*
> *Poised on fair Fortune's wheel,*
> *Hinting joys unrevealed,*
> > *Greater than wealth.*

This "hinting of joys unrevealed" characterized Victorian sexuality; thus the peek-a-boo eroticism of the seaside was one of the promised delights of Atlantic City.

Viewing beach scenes was a principal attraction. Heston advised the tourist: "Bevies of girls dressed in dainty costumes are scattered about on the sand." Bathing suits of light-brown linen which appeared in 1897 met with one journalist's approval: "This latter will become popular with women of exceptionally fine figure for it clings to the body as tightly when wet as would a sticking plaster and the graceful contour of a Venus-like form is made conspicuous, though by no means obtrusive." The same year, in an after-dinner speech predicting Atlantic City's future, a friend of the city foresaw that the wooden Boardwalk would be replaced by a permanent structure of cement and stone, "where the 'Peeping Tom's' of the future cannot lie upon their backs under its shelter and gaze into the celestial firmament in broad daylight." Commercial entertainments could be erotic, too. In 1900 the pretentiously named Academy of Music, an important entertainment hall of the Boardwalk, presented the "Black Patti Troubadours, Greatest Colored Show in Earth." The show consisted of "Black Patti and thirty Ebony Estasies [sic]. A Darktown Frolic . . . on the Rialto."

J. H. Martin's scrapbook of the resort, completed in 1885, contains several trade cards of the "naughty" genre (which persists in postcard form today). Trade cards had a picture on one side and a merchant's name, address, and advertisement on the other. One such item, advertising the *Republic*, an excursion steamship on the Philadelphia–Cape May run, has on the front a colored engraving of a sedate man and woman strolling past a bathhouse on which are hung two ladies' hats. On the back, the area behind the man and woman is devoted to advertising the excursion, but the space between corresponds to the reverse side of the bathhouse. The door says, "Ladies Bath House. No Admittance," and the head of an occupant is visible over the door. A second card advertises Henry C. Blair's Philadelphia Apothecary Shop and its branch store in Atlantic City. An artist on bended knee implores a demure lady (a model?), who modestly hitches her skirt. There is a warning: "Don't Look on the Other Side." Unfortunately, the card is firmly pasted to the page of the scrapbook! A third card again shows our sedate man and lady, symbolic of the polite façade of society, walking past a bathhouse, hiding the joys of sex. This time the reverse of the card shows the interior of the house, where two shapely girls in chemises are seen. One combs her hair and the other, particularly well built, adjusts her stocking. Not much by today's standards of

commercial nudity, but spicy stuff in an age of concealment.

A number of actual postcards survive from a later period. A colored print from 1911 shows a busty bathing beauty clad in a low-cut scarlet suit and black stockings. A 1906 black-and-white card has a bathing-suited girl bending down to pull up a stocking which is slipping down her thigh. This card is captioned: "I miss the Rubbers down here." A more obscure double-entendre, "Have you ever been ripped up the back?" accompanies another card in which a girl is attended by a kneeling friend who hooks up the back of her suit. A card titled "Going Crabbing—Catching a Crab" has three girls and a man in a boat. Two of the girls have fallen backward, with their legs upraised, revealing their black stockings, petticoats, and underwear. A 1907 card is similar, with three girls and one man in a boat; the girls lift their skirts over their knees to keep from being splashed.

In addition to these double meanings, playful activity between the sexes is a common subject of these "racy" postcards. In "Sport on the Beach," four girls in bathing suits prepare to leapfrog their kneeling boy friends. An uncaptioned colored print shows a girl giving an impossibly high kick, which exposes her stockinged leg, to knock her boy friend's skimmer hat off. But the most frequent topic of all is a promised surplus of unaccompanied girls or boys at the seaside. The assurance of a 1960's rock song that in "Surf City" there are "two girls for every boy!" has a predecessor at least as far back as 1910, and judging from the conservatism of postcards in abandoning old themes, probably earlier. A card dated that year depicts three men and one woman sitting arm in arm on the sand, and is titled "Girls Wanted, Atlantic City, N.J." A 1918 card of six girls, arm in arm, puts the message into prose: "There are plenty of nice girls here but not enough boys. Why don't you come out and have a good time in Atlantic City, N.J.?" The same photo, tinted and retouched, is used again, with a more terse caption: "Waiting for company at the beach, Atlantic City, N.J." The publishers of these cards catered to the universal hope of men and women of finding someone at the seaside, and were quite willing to present the surplus as male or female. Whichever side had the balance, the fact that there were many unattached persons anxious to make the acquaintance of the opposite sex gave substance to the postcards.

And what were these postcards used for? One didn't send a card reading "Girls Wanted" to his aunt. They must have been sent by relatives and friends to single men and women, to emphasize that the sender had struck it rich and the receiver could do the same. In-

terestingly, a card located recently at a Philadelphia flea market supports this interpretation. The picture of two women lying on the sand is labeled "Girls you meet in Atlantic City, N.J.," and the reverse bears a message: "Dear Brother: Emmie said they give these girls away down here . . . , Sister Anna." The use of cards like these suggests that their buyers believed the resort to offer an unusual opportunity for sexual encounters. Such meetings could be the spicy kind ("Atlantic City Is No Place For a Minister's Son") or the eminently respectable kind that led to marriage.

While many of the natives of Atlantic City were worried about preserving the sanctity of the Sabbath, most of the visitors were indifferent. They came to the resort just so they could escape the boredom of a Sunday in Philadelphia; or worse, in Lancaster, Trenton, or Reading; or worse, in Troutville, Trexlertown, or Pine Grove Mills. The rich could evade the religious responsibilities of an entire season, namely, the somber Christian celebration of Lent. J. H. Martin sardonically described this maneuver in 1882:

> The quietude of Lent in the large cities offers inducement for going to some secluded resort, where select coteries of nice people from different cities—all presumably invalids, more or less—can meet and have a good time without any censorious neighbors across the street to criticize them. Nearly every young lady who has been at numerous entertainments through the winter and worn herself out becomes "an invalid" and can always go away with great consistency for her health from Ash Wednesday until Easter.

As said previously, passages like these were not really addressed to the rich, but were written by and for the middle class to encourage travel to the resort through snob appeal. Martin repeated this stock theme (he did not originate it), and one is struck by the frequent borrowings his contemporaries made from a meager pool of descriptive clichés about Atlantic City. When someone felt called upon to describe the City by the Sea, he turned automatically to the familiar pap written decades before by a nameless booster. What is noteworthy here is the middle-class ambiguity toward the decline of religious feeling in the culture. Neglect of religious observance in favor of pleasure was projected upon the rich, allowing middle-class guilt to be externalized in hostility toward the higher class. At the same time, there was envy for the imagined liberation from religious restraints which the rich were supposed to enjoy. The middle class, upper and lower, was abandoning its religious ideals, substituting secular happiness for deferred bliss, and the conflict between traditional conscience and the lure of pleasure

was manifested in such prose as the above. Hall was at his wit's end, in his history of the resort, in making Easter by the Sea digestible for his readers. In the same passage, he juxtaposed two incongruous sentiments. First there was piety: "The sublime majesty of the deep teaches a silent lesson of the omnipotence of the Creator and the dependence of frail humanity." Then came policy: "Easter week, as a rule, is devoted to card parties and dances which are toned down to meet the requirements of the season." In one paragraph he exclaimed: "When the sun shines forth on the glad Sabbath morning, sackcloth and ashes are cast aside and Queen Fashion, arrayed in all the bewitching beauty of her gracious loveliness, is revealed to the crowd that promenades the Boardwalk." And in the next paragraph he added: "The churches are usually largely attended."

But for all that there is a middle-class crisis of conscience taking place here, the impending resolution of that crisis is clear in retrospect. Pleasure and materialism were triumphing over piety at the resort, and apologies for transgression of the Sabbath would become fewer and fewer. Heston's 1887 *Handbook* shows how the odds were stacked against religion:

> *Aside from the attractions of land and sea—the drives, the beach, and boardwalk, the fishing, the yachting, and the bathing, the bracing air, and other attributes of the grand old ocean—aside from these, Atlantic City affords diversions of a secular or religious character above and beyond those of any other seacoast resort. One can go a-shopping here, find books, papers, small wares, material for embroidery, painting, and drawing; can visit a circulating library, or take an interest in the church, get acquainted with the minister, and help along the good work.*

Heston presents religion as an item of consumption; yet it is obviously an article of inferior appeal compared to what else is available. Its inclusion in the paragraph is utterly parenthetic, and rather pathetic. Atlantic City's Easter Parade attracted tens of thousands of people to an orgy of display, as crowds of strangers undertook to impress one another with conspicuous consumption on a mass scale. The religious would be hoping to fill the churches, but the stylish would be filling the Boardwalk—literally, rail to rail, for hundreds of yards.

Summer Sundays were particularly busy days because of the huge excursion trade that could afford to come down to the shore for only that day. An 1893 article in the *Inquirer* pointed out what a novelty it was for a visitor from staid Philadelphia to be able to buy all the beer he wanted on the Sabbath without having to search for some surreptitious dive. In fact, the author claimed, the beer gardens of

Atlantic City did most of their business on Sunday. A newspaper clipping in Martin's scrapbook expressed one observer's wonderment over conditions on the day of rest:

> One queer thing about Atlantic City is its Sabbath—or rather the place where its Sabbath ought to be. Atlantic City can give Paris and Chicago points on the second commandment. You can always tell when Sunday comes in Atlantic City—if you have a trustworthy calendar.

Methodists tried to have religious services in the skating rink on Sunday evening, but the few hundreds they attracted compared pitifully with the thousands drifting by on the Boardwalk. A minister who preached at Young and McShea's Pier on Sunday in 1891 was aghast to discover that the resort was going full-tilt, with shops and stands doing as lively a business as if the city were a pagan metropolis.

We see, therefore, the elements of discipline and pleasure in the faces of Atlantic City as the Family Resort and Pleasure Resort. Some kind of popular resolution of the conflicting strains was necessary, if the people who lived in Atlantic City and who purveyed its amusements, the people who visited it, and the people who observed it from afar were to make sense of what was going on and to preserve their vision of themselves as moral beings.

During the 1890's, the idea of the Golden Mean of pleasure, to which the majority of the society supposedly subscribed, provided the necessary resolution. The Golden Mean for behavior allowed pleasure that was genuinely exciting but not truly sinful. Off at one extreme of the mean were the degraded, outside the pale of civilization and worthy of punishment. Off at the other were the bluenoses, who held worthy ideals but pursued them too vigorously for the comfort of the easygoing generality. Unfortunately, the Golden Mean was difficult to define precisely, differing as it did with the one describing it. It was dangerously similar to hypocrisy, and was therefore vulnerable as a debating device. And it was legally useless, since either an act was not a crime or it was, and the job of the law was to catch and to punish criminals. Finally, for all these drawbacks, the Golden Mean was nevertheless unavoidable as the only viable guide to behavior for the city and the culture.

The idea of the Golden Mean is simply stated in the *Bulletin*'s 1890 crusade: "This paper concedes that a certain liberality—necessary to seashore life—should prevail at Atlantic City. But it emphatically protests against the abuse of that liberality." Squire John Gobley also spoke for the compromise approach to resort conduct, and the view-

point of this seaside Cincinnatus was intended by the newspaper to represent the conviction of the honest majority of the town's citizens.

> *The Squire is a good deal of a philosopher. He knows that the world will be worldly and that no sect can dominate. "There are two classes," he says, "that can never rule this city—the extreme temperance people and the extreme rum people. There must be a happy medium. It would be as damaging to the city's prosperity to allow one to control as the other."*

When Gobley says "prosperity," he is referring both to morals and to finances. The people of the resort saw the two as connected, and they realized moreover that the highest moral prosperity was not automatically synonymous with the highest financial prosperity, as the following chapter will show. Of immediate interest is the Squire's candor in recommending public sanction of compromise between pleasure and discipline in Atlantic City.

> *Now I advise our policemen here, when they see a young man of good address who has succumbed to the influence of liquor to find out where he lives and send him there. . . .*
> *We must be considerate and we must know how to discriminate. No good can come from throwing a young fellow into a cell because he has committed some light offense. It disgraces him by exposing him to public criticism.*

What is a young man "of good address"? Could a man without money be such a person? Could a black? There is no way to know definitely what he means, but one must suspect that he is describing the white upper- or lower-middle-class youth, who is well dressed and probably, therefore, has money to spend in the town. Gobley is standing forthrightly for the unequal application of the law, for the sake of a resort flexible enough to mediate between discipline and pleasure. He can be even more unabashedly frank:

> *We can't stop the sale of liquor here on Sunday altogether, but we can make the liquor sellers show some respect for the day. That is why I advise those in authority to make these people at least pull down their blinds on Sunday, so as to be less offensive to the many who object.*

The median between pleasure and discipline—even the coat of arms of Atlantic City (in distinction to James North's city seal) expresses this desired conciliation. It is described in 1900 as consisting of a shell, showing a view of the ocean, a stretch of the Boardwalk, and yachts. This mélange is supported by dolphins and two Greek maidens, one holding a caduceus supposedly meaning power, wisdom, and activity, and the other flowers, meaning pleasure. The message of "pleasure but wisdom" is reinforced by the motto, "Consilio et Prudentia," recommending counsel and prudence.

While many were agreed on public compromise between pleasure and restraint, just whom or what to restrain was a sticky question. The *Bulletin* thought that "the puritanical monotony of the beach front," the result of the 1890 city law against Sunday amusements, drove fathers into the saloons, which were allowed to remain open. The Philadelphia newspaper is relatively egalitarian in observing that this act penalized chiefly little people willing to obey the law or unable to defy it. "The industrious glass blower and the harmless card writer are denied the possible profits of the heaviest day in the week." The *Daily Union*, on the other hand, subject to the wrath of local powers, had to consider that its bread was buttered on a different side from the *Bulletin*'s. It agreed with the Golden Mean: "All appreciate that the radical enforcement of stringent and obsolete laws would provoke a widespread spirit of hostility and very greatly injure business interests and the popularity of this resort." Still, most people would modify their behavior for "the betterment of general appearances." It was perfectly reasonable to meet the needs of Sunday tourists for lodging and "innocent diversions," and "average Christian people" would insist only that the Sabbath be kept somewhat more decorous than weekdays. The real culprits, then, were not the substantial businesses which provided the room and board and refreshments to the Sunday crowds. No, the *Daily Union* identified the true scoundrels: "Peanut vendors and others of like character who are catching nickels all day and all night, Sundays and weekdays alike, can have good notice in advance what to expect here and if they do not like Atlantic City, its local government and the public sentiment of the place, they can go to Cape May or elsewhere."

In working out the compromise between discipline and pleasure for the resort, public officials as well as the press would return again and again to this device of tokenism to satisfy the forces of discipline that they were doing their job, while leaving the large purveyors of pleasure unmolested. An occasional raid, an occasional crusade, some little people made to toe the line for a while—these were the economical gestures used to put a smiling face on the dubious condition. The distance between the Family Resort and the Pleasure Resort was significant and troubling. During the Mauve Decade, the culture wanted to be fooled somewhat; it wanted its respectability, as it defined it, and its pleasure, as it felt it needed it, at the same time. Atlantic City was the place where both the fooling and the pleasuring were to be done. The City by the Sea did a dazzling job of both.

5

Babylonian Days

BESIDES the conflicting needs of late-nineteenth-century Americans for pleasure and discipline, the highly specialized role of Atlantic City as an urban amusement center for transients predisposed it to tension, vice, and scandal. The accelerating impact of technology, particularly transportation and communications technology, resulted during this period in the growth of urban regions. The resort, though politically part of New Jersey, was economically bound to Philadelphia. A small machine within the greater metropolitan machine of Philadelphia, its function was to dispense pleasure to the masses regularly disgorged by the patron city through the agency of the railroad. As a specialized pleasure machine, Atlantic City admirably discharged its task for the greater metropolis. Nevertheless, the service role of the resort imposed particular stresses on the values of the year-round inhabitants.

The population of the resort was 13,000 in 1890, increasing to 18,000 in 1895, 28,000 in 1900, and 46,000 in 1910. This rate of growth in itself was an obvious strain for the informal enforcement of moral standards on which even great cities depend, because there were just too many strangers in each neighborhood to enable older residents to keep track of what was going on. Still more important, however, was the vast transient population which descended upon the resort each summer. Weekends were particularly heavy, as hordes of excursionists roared into town on train after train, all of them trying to extract the maximum pleasure out of means too modest to allow an overnight stay. Trains from Philadelphia were fast, frequent, and cheap; the resort was altogether more accessible in 1895 than in the 1970's. Consequently, so long as the weather held, large crowds could be expected each day throughout the summer. On the weekend of June 10, 1893, well before the prime of the season, the Reading carried 6,000 passengers to the shore and the Pennsylvania 4,000. Even on an early-summer weekend, therefore, transients numbered more than half the permanent population. But on July 1 and 2 of the same year, the two railroads brought down 20,000 passengers. On July 3, 4, and 5, the total was 46,680. The *Philadelphia Inquirer* estimated 75,000 people at the resort on August 5, 1894, and 100,000 on August 27, 1893. Even though these figures might be exaggerated, there is no doubt that the crowds were huge. The vast transient invasions, several times the local population, produced curious social statistics for the resort. New York had 27 beer gardens; Atlantic City had 12. Philadelphia had 1,203 saloons, or 1.15 per 1,000 population; New York City had 7,579, or 5.00 per 1,000; Atlantic City had 190, or 14.55 per 1,000.

It is not surprising that summer was an annual crisis for the resort. While the city had to have large crowds to make enough money to last a year, it also had to accommodate an influx of strangers, some of them up to no good. Into the uneasy town poured a throng of sharpers, thugs, and swell deceivers in that rich variety of which Victorian society was so wonderfully prolific. One visitor complained: "We have had an inroad of bunko players and other confidence men during the week and the crowds which have arrived today have included many operators whom Philadelphia has undoubtedly been rejoiced to be relieved of if only for a couple of days."

The criminal repertoire at the resort included the "flimflam game," in which the perpetrator paid for a trifling purchase with a large bill, received a portion of the correct change from the hapless merchant, and then "discovered" a smaller bill in his possession. The flimflam artist obligingly offered to pay with the smaller bill, deftly shuffled coins and notes, and in the process managed to nick his victim for a tidy sum in excess change. "Shovers of the queer" passed counterfeit money to unwary businessmen, while practitioners of "hotel sneaking" went thieving among the city's hostelries. Other thieves took jobs hawking tickets for dinners and rental bathing suits in the excursion district to provide themselves with plausible cover for their true profession, and sometimes supplemented their income with the earnings of prostitutes who infested the Boardwalk in that vicinity. Confidence routines were popular. One crook befriended a young man he met in the surf, filched his bathhouse ticket when they came back to the beach, and excused himself for a rendezvous with his companion's gold watch. Lewis Jerome, an executive of the National Cash Register Company of Dayton, Ohio, was enticed by an acquaintance he had made to a gambling establishment on Arctic Avenue. Befuddled with drink, he was fleeced out of five hundred dollars at the faro table. Jerome challenged his defrauders, but they boldly claimed to have protection from influential quarters. Nevertheless, they fled town to avoid prosecution.

There were humdrum pickpockets aplenty in the town, some of whom made the post office their base of operations, but certain unscrupulous females perfected a more creative routine. An attractive young lady would select a southern gentleman in his dotage, lure him into a dark alley, and charm his senile fancy with a display of affection. In the course of a few embraces, the old fellow's wallet and valuables would transfer ownership. The lady would then add a professional touch by treating her friend to dinner at a nearby restaurant to impress him with her generosity, inflame his hopes with promises of a return engagement, and disappear for good. Those victimized in such manner were usually too embarrassed to seek revenge.

Less gracious than this ruse was the shakedown of a luckless young man from Philadelphia working as a waiter on the Boardwalk, who fell prey to "a blooming widow of forty or more summers." "According to his story she invited him to call on her at the Arctic avenue cottage and have a good time. He called and when he asked to see her privately she took it as an insult, but offered to overlook the offense for $15." The "badger game" added muscle to indignation. A woman would entice a sucker into a compromising position, an irate "husband" or "brother" would appear from the wings, and the sucker would pay handsomely to extricate himself. Nastier than the badger game was the "knockout game," whose essence was a few drops of chloral surreptitiously added to a target's drink. One detective reported that the knockout game prospered in certain dives near Mississippi Avenue in the excursion district.

While indigenous knaves may have executed some of these typical shakedowns, there is direct evidence to demonstrate the Philadelphia origins of many of the resort's vice personnel. "Dutchy" Muhlrod, the prominent dive entrepreneur mentioned in the previous chapter, had been driven out of the Quaker City in 1888 for operating a gambling den on Eleventh Street. In 1890 the *Philadelphia Bulletin* identified the resort madams Maria Weed, Mary French, Hattie Brown, Lottie Wilson, Lavinia Thomas, and Kate Davis as expelled brothel proprietors of the larger city. "One of the best known liquor firms in Philadelphia" operated a low saloon on Atlantic Avenue, which "reminded one of the old spots of pollution around Eighth and Vine." A number of resort saloonkeepers had been denied liquor licenses in the metropolis but had found Atlantic City more receptive. "They brought with them the scum of Race and Vine Streets, from the nest of the Swamp Robins on the Delaware, to the 'Gut' on the Schuylkill."

The natives of Atlantic City looked about them as summer descended, and took note of these sinister strangers. A city-wide feeling of mild paranoia blossomed with the onset of warm weather, generating precautionary actions: "Officer Retzbach arrested a man named Frees this morning as a suspicious character. The man's conversation and some property he carried warranted the officer in holding him, particularly at this time of year." Paranoia helped produce the numerous assurances that the crowds were well behaved, that the children of millionaires frolicked with the children of the poor, that never had so many strangers mixed so peacefully. The authors were trying to reassure themselves as well as their audience.

Atlantic City's participation in the Philadelphia metropolitan region produced a rather confused situation when interests and jurisdiction came into conflict. Though the resort made its living from Philadelphia, it had to abide by the laws of New Jersey, and this made for trouble. In August 1908, the local Citizen's League, responding to the campaign initiated by the governor of New Jersey, John Franklin Fort, sought to suppress violators of the Sunday-closing law among the saloon trade. But most of the residents of Atlantic City were unmoved by the crusade. Their sympathies lay with the demands of their Philadelphia customers, not the government of New Jersey.

A STRIKING
CONTRAST

"Of course, no one made any complaint," said one of the officers of the Citizen's League, "the visitors are satisfied. Ninety-nine per cent of the inhabitants never have kicked against the present conditions and never will, while we reformers have learned the futility of such a proceeding. Our only hope of breaking the rum power lies in the Grand Jury, and, judging by the surface attitude, I have no expectations whatever of securing indictments against the liquor law breakers. But we mean to keep up the fight,

and sooner or later the State will be able to show the defiant
interests that the whole is greater than any of its component
parts."

If morally outraged reformers hoped to use the coercive powers of
state government to override Atlantic City's social sympathies with
Philadelphia, there were those who suspected the other communities
of New Jersey of provincial envy. The *Bulletin* reported: "The consensus of opinion seems to be that the other counties of the State
are jealous of Atlantic City's prosperity and would like to make the
town as dead as many other resorts are now." John J. White, proprietor
of the renowned Marlborough-Blenheim Hotel and therefore a leading
resort citizen, appealed to the practical interests of the state at large.
Suggesting a liberalized Sunday liquor law, he observed that Atlantic
City annually harvested $180,000,000 from its visitors, "90 per cent
of them from outside of the boundaries of the State." Since the state
as a whole benefited from the resort's participation in a regional
economy, there was a strong incentive to overlook the resort's involve-
ment in the morality of that region.

Appeal could thus be made to Atlantic City's regionalism when it
suited the appellant. On the other hand, there were times when
certain resort interests found an isolationist stance more to their liking.
In 1890 the *Daily Union* commended the *Bulletin* for its exposé of
vice and corruption in the seaside town. But the *Atlantic City Review*,
Republican in politics and therefore sympathetic to the Republican
machine which habitually governed the city, was incensed by outside
meddling: "Not a word of commendation is heard of the *Bulletin*'s
efforts, and the articles are read and discounted." The *Bulletin* reported that two Atlantic City policemen had tried to interfere with
the selling of the newspaper in the city streets. Moreover, Isaac F.
Shaner, a street-paving contractor and an informant of the *Bulletin*,
had been threatened with the loss of city contracts if he did not
discontinue his cooperation with the paper. Even the *Daily Union*,
reformist in outlook and sometimes quite bold for a home-town newspaper, could not refrain from mentioning the more pragmatic incentive to local rather than outside reform. In 1900 it urged "respectable
hotel and business men" to cleanse the resort of vice: "It is time a
halt was called *before investigation lays bare the ugliness of all* [these]
transactions." Opportunism naturally colored the way various groups
in the resort, reputable and disreputable alike, dealt with their town's
regional posture.

For the purposes of studying value and conflict as evidenced in vice
at the resort, the balance of this chapter will draw heavily on the two

principal scandals and accompanying crusades during the turn-of-the-century decades, those occurring in 1890 and 1908. Supporting data will be included from 1895. No attempt is made to catalogue all the details of vice, the goal being to explain the critical problems of conscience it presented to the permanent resort population, and the larger implication of these problems for the culture in general. Nevertheless, the question whether there was a constant level of vice activity during these years, with an ebb and flow of crusade, or whether vice itself was subject to growth and decline, merits brief consideration. An unequivocal answer would require mountains of data, most of which have probably long since vanished. Nevertheless, there are some useful indications, which complement later parts of this chapter, to offer a partial answer.

Drinking and gambling very likely prospered in all seasons, except for very exceptional and brief occasions. Mayor Franklin P. Stoy, when questioned by an investigator of the New Jersey Excise Commission in 1908 as to the city's failure to observe Sunday-closing laws, "demurred, but was forced to confess that only twice in ten years had there been any general effort to close up all places on Sunday." Dutchy Muhlrod, keeper of the Hotel Lochiel, figured prominently in 1890 as a selected target of the *Bulletin*. Despite the stink the newspaper raised over lax law enforcement in Atlantic City, Dutchy managed to hang on, and appeared in the news again in 1908 as proprietor of the same "popular resort for the big contractors and politicians of Philadelphia." "Roulette, faro and poker are played on the second floor of his place and he has never been raided or closed up in seventeen years. His pull is iron-clad and has never failed." The tides of reform never ran high enough to reach this principal figure.

But there are clues to suggest that although such milder illegalities as Sunday liquor sales and gambling were resistant to all reform, and benefited from a favorable or at least not a virulently hostile attitude among the local public, the most serious vice—prostitution—did have its ups and downs. Prostitution was a major issue of 1890, and there is evidence that the city's failure to contain whores and brothels within a well-defined district sharply aggravated the threat to community respectability posed by an increasing number of prostitutes. Three years later, regardless of what the *Bulletin* may have accomplished, the *Daily Union* declared:

> Would that the Review *were not so funny in its claim that Atlantic City is so "free from the vices which flourish openly at other pretentious watering places." Where along the coast from*

*Maine to Florida, is there a "pretentious watering place" where
the law is winked at as it is here? . . .*

*Here disorderly people are allowed to do a lawless business all
the year without a license and it is useless for respectable people
to protest and remonstrate against the establishment of gin mills
and bed houses [brothels] in respectable neighborhoods.*

In 1900, when prostitution seems to have experienced another up-
swing, an apparent districting of vice emerges in newspaper reports.
The *Review* fretted:

*There are just about half as many more houses of ill-fame in this
town this year as there have been any summer for the last ten
years. This is stated on the authority of a police officer who ought
to know and who says the patrolmen have no orders to interfere
with the "joints." The denizens of the Whitechapel district were
never so shameless in their operations.*

Whitechapel, of course, was the notorious red-light section of London.
The *Daily Union*, in turn, mentioned "the 'tenderloin' or 'beefsteak'
section" of the city, and the *Bulletin* asserted that following a private
reformers' raid on August 27, "for the first time in years the tenderloin
district was closed all night." The local group responsible for this
purge, the Citizens' Committee, found that its good work was not
unequivocally appreciated.

*As a result of the raid on the "White Chapel" district last night,
all the disreputable houses are closed, and the inmates, Chief of
Police Eldridge states, are scattered all over town and liable to
cause the authorities much trouble. The Citizens' Committee de-
fends its raid on the ground that the houses sell liquor illegally
and should be obliged to contribute to the city treasury.*

The feeble justification that the Committee felt compelled to advance
for what at first blush seems a virtuous act could only have been due
to its recognition that it had upset an equilibrium in vice containment
which the general public and city government regarded as a blessing.
In 1890 prostitution was decentralized and therefore especially ob-
noxious; basically centralized by 1900, it was a sleeping dog most
people were content to leave at rest.

The best answer available to the question of vice continuity in the
resort is that milder forms endured with little difficulty in bad times
as well as good. Vice that was truly vicious in the eyes of the culture
could proliferate or contract a great deal over periods of several years,
depending perhaps upon public willingness to act against it. There
are signs of particular public discontent in 1893 and 1900. In 1890
and 1908 the lid blew off. At other times, Atlantic City was a mod-
erately freewheeling resort, whose mostly respectable citizens did not

trouble themselves with needless questions or with inquisitive looks down the wrong alleys.

Let us look more closely at 1890 and 1908. As we have seen in the previous chapter, the immediate cause of the 1890 uproar was a city ordinance against the Sunday operation of amusements, which struck the *Bulletin* as hypocritical and prompted its investigation of the resort. It discovered and disclosed to its readers much evidence of vice and corruption. Liquor licensing in the city was both dishonest and ineffectual in restraining excess. City law required that application for liquor licenses be accompanied by supporting signatures of reputable propertied citizens testifying to the honesty and sobriety of the applicant. But licenses were granted upon the signatures of brothelkeepers and operators of illegal saloons and gambling dives. Applicants used names without initials to impart a salutary vagueness as to who was signing, and the signatures of esteemed local citizens were forged. All this the city let pass, because the effect was a great increase in the number of licenses granted, bringing in more license revenue to the city coffers. How much graft officials obtained for overlooking glaring irregularities is a matter for speculation, but the harvest must have been bountiful. However, graft was not the end of the problem. The *Bulletin* claimed that not only did saloons proliferate but much of the increase came in the form of "disorderly houses" which conducted gambling, opened on Sunday or after hours, sold to minors, and acted as pickup joints for prostitutes.

It was easy for the visitor to find a gambling den in Atlantic City, regardless of his means. "They are run from away down below Mississippi avenue, where they play a five-cent limit, up to 'Dutchy's' on Delaware avenue, where some of the best known politicians and down-grade business men of Philadelphia stake their five to ten dollars on the deal." Levy's "aristocratic gambling house" was located near the prestigious United States Hotel to accommodate the wealthy, but the little man could find a game in progress in the back of cigar stores in the town.

The *Bulletin*'s strongest feelings were against prostitution:

> *What community would hail, as a blessing, or as an evidence of prosperity, the establishment of a vile brothel in its midst? There are more than one hundred of these dens of infamy in Atlantic City. Just think of it—one hundred such places in a city of this size!*

On August 9 it listed the names and addresses of twenty-four of them, including May Woodston's "pestilential hole," and the "Sea Breeze," owned by Minnie Wiegle, "the high kicker in Fox's Theatre fifteen

THE SUMMER'S CROP OF CONQUESTS

years ago." Besides the brothels, there were sixty-six saloons and restaurants with "ladies' entrance" signs which provided meeting places for prostitutes and their customers. These were mostly located on the four major avenues of the city, with almost half on Atlantic Avenue, the main street. And, of course, brothels and bars were supplemented by an unknown number of transient prostitutes.

The presence of brothels, not in a clearly defined district, but throughout the city, embarrassed respectable citizens who discovered

themselves living adjacent to them. Bella Thomas' place, for example, was cheek by jowl with the parsonage of the Methodist Church. She had a habit of leaving her windows open and a light on, making the activities of her patrons visible across the way, and sometimes the action spilled onto the front porch. Local inhabitants were also bothered by strangers knocking on their door under the impression that it was the desired brothel, actually located next door or around the corner.

> *There is a notorious disorderly house at No. 20 North, in one of the leading cross avenues of this town; at No. 20 South, on the same avenue, resides a lady highly esteemed in this city.*
> *The despicable creature who is tolerated by the authorities at No. 20 North circulates throughout the town cards bearing her "business" address. These cards are skillfully and openly distributed by brazen females who solicit customers on the avenues and in the gardens.*
> *Now these cards fall into the hands of gay young men and disreputable old men who are not familiar with the system of street and house numbering that prevails in this city.*
> *They confuse No. 20 North with No. 20 South, and the consequence is that life has been made a burden to the highly esteemed lady who lives at No. 20 South. Her house is invaded at all hours by drunken loafers; her door bell is rung late in the night, and scandalous inquiries are put to her!*

The vice industry was not confined strictly to whites in Atlantic City. Charles Coleman kept a gambling house for blacks on Arkansas Avenue, whose crap games were particularly frequented by hotel waiters. A disorderly saloon serving blacks and whites seven days a week was located on Baltic Avenue, while Harry Smith operated a saloon and gambling den for an integrated clientele on Arctic Avenue. There was an interracial house of prostitution on Arctic Avenue, run by a black madam with a white husband, and the *Daily Union* claimed that W. H. Furney was allowed to conduct his "low negro resort" at the corner of Baltic and North Carolina avenues because he was a political power, controlling the black vote in his neighborhood.

By impressing its readers with the foregoing facts, along with much other lurid material, the *Bulletin* did its best to keep the skillet sizzling for the balance of the summer. In the end, very little practical reform was accomplished, save that the city fathers and the overseers of illicit pleasure no doubt acquired a taste for the *Public Ledger* or the *Inquirer*. As for the *Bulletin* itself, it had the constraints of popular journalism to contend with, for it would hardly do to have run all those front-page exposés in vain. The public wanted some appropriate result. It would have been still less satisfactory to have continued the crusade

throughout the year: who cared about Atlantic City in November?
So the newspaper ennobled its labors with self-proclaimed success.
It promised:

> *Next summer will be garnered the harvest of purification sown
> by the* Evening Bulletin. . . . *Atlantic City of next year will not
> be the Atlantic City of this year! Municipal authority, once lax,
> will now be firm.*

September was the end of summer, and September was also the end
of Philadelphia's interest in Atlantic City. The *Bulletin* subscribers
were coming home, and the paper happily titled its article of September 2: "Things Can Now Be Said to Be on the Mend."

While disorderly saloons, gambling, and prostitution all figured
prominently in the 1890 exposé, the problem of vice in 1908 was more
narrowly defined, though it did not begin that way. For two decades,
the state of New Jersey had made no legislative attack upon liquor
selling within its boundaries, but in 1905 a group of four bishops
from the Catholic and Episcopal churches pressured through the
legislature a bill designed to suppress Sunday operation of saloons.
The new law forbade the sale of drinks in back rooms and required
the interior of bars to be open to public view on Sundays. Since there
was already a state law prohibiting Sunday opening, it was hoped that
local authorities of communities reluctant to impair the saloon trade
would be coerced into applying the law once no tactful evasion could
be made. The larger cities of New Jersey were not amused.

In the summer of 1908, the newly elected Governor Fort decided
to honor his campaign promises to promote civic righteousness by
enforcing the Bishops' Law. His Excise Probing Commission had reported unfavorably upon the behavior of Atlantic City, and on August
12, Atlantic County Prosecutor Clarence Goldenberg made public a
list of sixteen known gambling houses, eight for white customers and
eight for black. Fort decided to make the resort the battleground of
executive will, demanding of Goldenberg that "gambling houses, opium
joints and dens of a similar character be wiped out" promptly. Shortly
afterward, following the failure of the grand jury to indict saloonkeepers obviously guilty of Sunday opening, he went considerably
further. On August 27, the governor threatened to call out the militia
to rule by martial law unless Sunday closing laws were strictly observed. But his public proclamation was not confined to the abuse of
potables in the resort.

> *To the People of the State of New Jersey:*
> *The State Excise Commission in session at Atlantic City on
> the third day of August, last, took testimony and heard state-*

ments which it can safely be said astonished all good citizens of the State. . . .

No one in office or before that Commission questioned the fact that street walking, gambling, houses of ill-fame, people of ill-repute, and obscene pictures and open violation of the excise laws existed in Atlantic City. A leading citizen said before that Commission: "The citizens are alarmed that it is as it is now, and conditions are something terrible right here at the present time in this city. Never in the history of the city has it been worse. Never have the notorious street walkers been worse than they have been recently. Never has gambling been more open and more of it in the city than it is right now."

Continuing, he said: "The police department and officials of the city all know it; they are all aware of it, or could find out if they wanted to. . . ."

Next to a twelve-weekend rain, this was the kind of event resort businessmen feared most. The chief executive of the state had declared, for the benefit of whichever newspapers cared to run the prepared statement, that the nation's Family Resort had truck with nefarious saloons, gambling, prostitution, and pornography. It was enough to curl the pages of Heston's *Handbook*. The Philadelphia press attended carefully to unfolding events, and there was much excitement at the prospect of the nation's leading popular resort under military occupation. But instead of a broadening of the crisis, the reverse took place. A *Bulletin* editorial castigated Fort for extreme measures, suggesting considerable sympathy with Atlantic City's position in Philadelphia. The municipal government and the leading hotel and saloon proprietors took conciliatory steps. Gamblers were obliged to shut down, at least temporarily, and the organization of saloon men announced that there would be no Sunday opening. The season was near an end anyway. The cup was nine tenths drained: the governor could have the last swig. Atlantic City knew the virtue of patience, for in the long run its thirst was always slaked.

It is especially important to remember that the great majority of the citizens of the resort, including most of the businessmen who retailed pleasure to visitors and even most government officials, were honorable men by their own lights and by the judgment of their fellow residents. Atlantic City might vibrate in the pages of the Philadelphia press and in the minds of local reformers as Sodom and Gomorrah, but to the majority of local people it was mostly a town bent on making a living by exploiting its only valuable resource, which the Creator in his unknowable way had designated as the Atlantic Ocean instead of a lead mine or unending fields of onions. The inhabitants of the resort had the same measures of virtue and iniquity as Americans generally,

but the extraordinary pressures inherent in the confrontation of morality and pleasure in Victorian society had baleful results for which the locals could not ultimately be responsible. Nevertheless, there were men of ill repute who flourished amid just such pressures, and it would not be a true portrait of Atlantic City to neglect corruption altogether.

Evidence of skulduggery in 1908 is fairly modest. The political boss of the city at this time was "Commodore" Louis Kuehnle, who happened to be treasurer of the Atlantic City Brewery. Needless to say, he took a personal role in the issuance of liquor licenses. In four years, he would be jailed for contract frauds. Councilman John Donnelly, an agent of the Philadelphia Brewery, and Councilman John Westcott, counsel for the Weisbrod and Hess Brewery, voted on licenses. The grand jury which refused to indict saloonkeepers had, according to Governor Fort's investigators, three members who were themselves violators of the Sabbath. Harry H. Graff was proprietor of the Hole in the Wall tavern near the beach on South Carolina Avenue. W. B. Stafford had a saloon on the corner of Arctic and Michigan avenues. And finally, Anthony M. Ruffu, Jr., who as mayor in 1930 was to die in an automobile accident while facing ten indictments for personal interest in municipal insurance contracts, had yet another saloon on North Mississippi Avenue. The collaboration between local government and favored interests no doubt went much further. And of course, there was always Dutchy Muhlrod, who had evaded the law for seventeen years and whose establishment coincidentally catered to "the big contractors and politicians of Philadelphia."

The situation in 1890 had been decidedly more unsavory. A member of the City Council and Chief of Police H. C. Eldredge were both seen conferring with Dutchy Muhlrod, and Levy's "aristocratic gambling house" received a mysterious tip after a newspaper reporter urged Eldredge to make a raid upon it. An observer passing Harry Smith's "notorious negro dive" saw officer No. 66, a black man, unselfconsciously taking his ease with a cigar on the porch. Another officer, who was celebrated for his brutal skill with a blackjack, then a novelty, was seen to pick up a girl at Mabel Haines's brothel. City authorities, who demanded scrupulous formal complaints from the general public before they would take action against a dive, nevertheless forced a madam to leave town without trial after Mrs. Haines complained that she had opened a rival facility next door. The *Bulletin*, disgusted with Samuel Hoffman's friendly relations with Dutchy Muhlrod, then just beginning his career, wanted to know why the mayor had collected $470 in fines during 1890, but only $55 in 1889. Most of the money

came from violations of the liquor laws and related "disorderly house" offenses.

A particularly revealing incident among the events of 1890 occurred when one James O'Neill came before the Council to show cause why his liquor license should not be revoked. He had a $175 license which allowed him to sell anywhere except within twenty-five feet of the Boardwalk, a stipulation he had violated. O'Neill disconcerted the assembly by blurting out that many hotels and saloons in the resort sold liquor without a license, whereupon Mayor Hoffman jumped to his feet and replied that O'Neill should know because he had leased his saloon to another (unlicensed) party. Things were getting out of hand, and some members of Council began to have conciliatory feelings. They offered to let O'Neill keep his license if he would obey the twenty-five-foot ordinance. But O'Neill stood his ground, and with "a malignant look" retorted "that some of the very people who had complained of him were daily violating the law, and then in a sort of heroic manner declared that he was a true-born Irishman, *and did not come before any one to make complaint of others.*" The Council unanimously supported a motion that further action be suspended against Mr. O'Neill.

Although there were residents who by society's standards—even as modified by the easygoing local construction—could hardly be regarded as innocent, most citizens fancied themselves decent folk. They had built Atlantic City as the Family Resort, and pridefully identified themselves with it as such. But the exposés illuminated the compromise morality they had evolved for their community. Indeed, the compromises were so extensive that when they were clearly revealed it was difficult to stretch the citizen's rather inarticulate notions of community decency to encompass them.

The 1908 episode is particularly useful for its revelations of moral compromise. The governor's dark accusations of opium dens came to naught, apparently because they were a trifling, if colorful, problem. The city acted to suppress gambling, and prostitution was not an issue save for isolated cases. The contest, then, came to be focused on the Sunday sale of alcohol, and here community opinion clearly held that the state had no business tampering with the thirst of man. Indeed, in August 1900 local reformers had tried to obtain ordinances prohibiting Sunday amusements and regulating saloons more strictly on the Sabbath. Becoming ambitious, they sought next to prevent the opening of saloons entirely on Sunday, to restrict business generally on that day, to reduce the number of liquor licenses, and to supervise the honesty of the police. But they overextended themselves. "There

is no doubt but that the program will not have the full support that the first plan had of more efficient control of saloons and the closing of amusement places on Sunday," said the *Inquirer*, which also claimed that the zealousness of the Reform League irritated hotel men.

At the hearing of the State Excise Commission in August 1908, the unwillingness of the community to act against saloons was manifest. "[County Prosecutor] Goldenberg frankly admitted that the Bishops' Law . . . was ignored in Atlantic City. 'Nine out of every ten property holders in Atlantic City,' he said, 'are opposed to Sunday closing, so it has proved impossible to obtain a Grand Jury that will find indictments against saloons and hotels for remaining open on Sunday.'" Isaac Bacharach, a city councilman and chairman of the License and Police Committee, "frankly, even cheerfully, confessed to knowing that Sunday selling laws were fractured every seven days," while Judge Enoch Higbee of the county court informed the Commission that although indictments could be obtained against "disorderly houses," no action against the orderly sale of liquor on Sunday would succeed. Questioning Mayor Stoy, a member of the Commission declared: " 'In effect, you close up notorious places, but let the others alone?' The Mayor demurred, but was forced to confess that only twice in ten years had there been any general effort to close up all places on Sunday."

Efforts to structure illegal activities rather than to eliminate them had of course existed all along, even while Atlantic City touted its uniform wholesomeness. Prosecutor Goldenberg said of the gambling houses identified in his public statement of August 13 that "the majority of the white gambling joints were run exclusively for visitors, and no resident was admitted." This would spare the feelings of local people and, at the cost of a certain amount of the revenue derived from local residents, protect the establishment's transient harvest. Similarly, Dutchy Muhlrod, of the Hotel Lochiel, had no desire to make enemies by fleecing working people, and "only men who are wealthy and well able to stand their losses are allowed inside his doors." Parallel illegal services for blacks and whites respected the racial prejudices of the white community and its visitors, lest aroused hostilities incite reform.

Particularly illuminating was the testimony before the State Excise Commission of the head of the resort's organized saloonkeepers:

> President of the Royal Arch Association, the secret league of the license holders, Charles M. Speidel, revealed some of the inner workings of that association. It has 120 members, who are sworn to obey the majority of the society[,] and the [Excise Commission] showed that they had deliberately banded together to prevent the enforcement of the liquor laws of the State.

They showed that the liquor men had pledged themselves to stop selling beer and liquors to be taken from the premises on Sunday, that front doors were to be barred, and back doors open; that places must be closed at 2 A.M. or the society would recommend a revocation of license; that back rooms must be closed and that no liquor was to be sold to minors or girls, and that the organization use its influence to prevent any license to be granted south of Pacific avenue, in the beach front section, to any building with less than one hundred rooms, and was absolutely opposed to any additional saloon licenses in that district.

Speidel admitted that it was in violation of the law, and then he startled the commission with the declaration that these regulations had been indorsed by the Business Men's League, Hotel Men's Association, Board of Trade and other organizations.

If Speidel spoke truthfully of his organization and its supporters (and we shall see further evidence to suggest that the business community approved of the Royal Arch's work), then saloon operation in the resort followed an articulated code having the favor of a substantial part of the respectable community. The code sought to limit the visibility of Sabbath violation, to prevent offenses to family life through juvenile drinking, and to contain the proliferation of saloons in the symbolic heartland of the resort, its beachfront. While from the state's point of view this code represented criminal conspiracy against the law, from the saloonkeepers' side it was an attempt to enforce a responsible conduct of business and included major concessions to hostile opinion.

Initially, there was a certain insouciance in the resort's reaction to Fort's threat. The grand jury failed to indict, and prominent witnesses candidly admitted that the city was not in the habit of harrying Sabbath breakers from the town. The Reverend Sydney Goodman shocked the orthodox resort ministry by opposing Sunday restrictions and maintaining that gambling was an ageless vice which did not reflect upon the character of the resort. Nevertheless, Goodman was pastor of the "Men's Church," and aimed what the *Bulletin* styled his "entertaining church services" at single males, whom he invited to smoke at the Sunday-evening service. Most resort businessmen shared his conviction that "the laws should be adjusted to meet the views of the communities to which they apply," but infinitely preferred peaceful subversion of the law to martyrdom for legal change at the expense of the Family Resort image. A councilman's proposal for a "continental Sunday" ordinance devoting the forenoon to God and the afternoon to the Devil never emerged from committee.

Instead, upon sober reflection, businessmen contemplated the governor's threat of military seizure with anxiety, agreeing with Sheriff

Enoch L. ("Nucky") Johnson that "thousands of people would never come here again if the soldiers were in possession of the resort for even so much as one Sunday." Large hotel proprietors and leading businessmen, at most marginally interested in Sunday liquor revenue, forced the Royal Arch to accede to Fort's demands. Speidel, president of the Arch, was able to pressure the 110 saloons outside his organization (a number doubtless including the less responsible portion of the saloon establishment) into falling in line.

Atlantic City showed its willingness to retrench in other ways. The grand jury, though adamantly uncooperative in prosecuting liquor dealers, nevertheless acted in cases it considered offensive, and indicted the proprietor of a club of "New York sports" and a vendor of "immodest postal cards." The police raided two illegal speakeasies. Gamblers took warning that they had lost immunity, and by August 17 the *Bulletin* could find no games in progress.

> And maybe the gambling fraternity did not weep, wail and beat its collective breast as it "stood around" and watched the shekels pour into the cash registers of the thirst parlors and thought of the harvest it might have reaped if public opinion only included games of chance among the necessities of the place.

By early September it had dawned on the gambling interest that it was expendable in the judgment of the respectable resort community and that during hard times its only course was retreat. Unlike saloon-keeping, gambling did not enjoy a sound base of community support and could not expect respectable intercession against hostile forces outside the resort. Though there were "liquor men by the score" at the September 5 grand jury hearing at Cape May, no gamblers attended, leading the *Bulletin* to conclude that "the gamblers believe they are to be made the 'goats' of the present inquiry and are keeping under cover."

Such concessions having been made to the governor's demands, it remained to dissect what had happened. A lively debate rattled the clapboard walls of the city, as various analysts blamed the mess on the municipal government, the glum peasantry of rural New Jersey, the independent booze lords, and others. Reverend Goodman delivered a defiant sermon, "Fear Not, Atlantic City," and declared that the public did not expect the resort to be "a paragon of virtue and pose as an example for the entire State and Nation." Atlantic City was "not a village"; its customers were "cosmopolitan," and gambling was an inevitable feature of city life.

The *Bulletin*, the exterminating angel of 1890, was now distinctly sympathetic to this viewpoint. In an editorial on August 28, it judged the moral complexion of the resort to be satisfactory. It defended

Atlantic City for the large portion of decent people who frequented
it. Vice did exist in the town, but there was no "grossly obtrusive
viciousness." Instead, "orderly enjoyment" and "rational recreation"
were the characteristic offerings of Atlantic City. "Multitudes of intelligent and respectable residents of Philadelphia" and "an army of
visitors from other States" agreed, with "practical unanimity," that
discipline was properly maintained. The governor should enforce the
law, yet he should not regard Atlantic City as uniquely needful of
law enforcement. The resort was a credit to "the good sense and
decent instincts of the holiday masses of American citizenship."

Thus the *Bulletin* upheld Atlantic City's functional image as the
national resort and its moral image as the Family Resort. But then,
having identified its clientele with a cross section of respectable
America, the newspaper referred to the "exceptional character of its
summer population" which visited "frankly for pleasure." This population was "drawn from many portions of the Union," suggesting either
that the morals of some parts of America were not as satisfactory as
those of other parts, or that the mingling of Americans from different
places made for moral problems. The net effect of this contradictory
line, expressed in skeletal form, may thus be summarized: Atlantic
City was a national resort creditable to the decency of average Americans; Atlantic City had exceptional problems which excused it from
being "a sinner above other municipalities." The *Bulletin*'s indulgent
attitude must have cheered many in the beleaguered resort.

The most important commentary on the crisis took the form of a
letter from the Atlantic City Board of Trade, the Hotel Men's Association, and the Business Men's League, which was sent to Governor Fort
on September 8 and printed in the *Bulletin*. A kind of "Atlantic City
Manifesto," it argued that the resort had been wrongfully treated by
the state and in defense of its conduct advanced customary social
practice, traditional governmental policy, Atlantic City's economic
importance to the state economy, and the peculiar needs of a resort.
These were the arguments of shrewd, upright businessmen, especially
the observation that the contribution of "$110,000,000 annually—
drawn from without the State—to the commonwealth" was "certainly
an interest or industry to be conserved and fostered." But the balance
of the letter demonstrates that the tensions of a pleasure resort in
Victorian America forced its respectable residents into a position of
complicity with, or at least toleration of, phenomena incompatible with
their conception of themselves.

The *Bulletin* had offered Atlantic City a way to step down from the
chilly pedestal of the Family Resort, asserting that it was "unfair to

hold up" the town "as a sinner above other municipalities" and that "the exceptional character of its population" excused its failings. But the authors of the letter were quite unwilling that their city should forswear the role of Family Resort. No, "women by the thousand" were free from "molestation" there. And lo! in this self-styled City by the Sea, which had ever regarded its great hotels as the chiefest of urban jewels, these same hotels were pronounced to be "so carefully conducted that they seem rather like select family boarding houses than great metropolitan hotels." Wondrous are the ways of booster prose: many was the time a resort boardinghouse had palmed itself off as a hotel, but this was the first time that a hotel had shriveled to a boardinghouse.

A sense of guilt is evident in the phrasing of the city's refusal to shut down offending services in response to Fort's initial demand, a demand which "was not complied with." The authors took care to pad "intoxicating liquors" with "newspapers, ice cream, cigars, soda water and various other commodities" when they enumerated the items the resort had habitually been allowed to sell on Sunday. Whereas some communities had evaded Sunday closing laws "surreptitiously," Atlantic City had "frankly, openly" tendered liquors on the Sabbath. Though "music was prohibited in the cafes, and other regulations were observed," this was not a surreptitious evasion of the law, but was done to avoid "intruding" upon those who found the sale of liquor "distasteful." The resort had a "great necessity" for Sunday liquor. Not, to be sure, the 120 saloonkeepers in the Royal Arch or the 110 independents, but the hotels, which needed to serve their patrons "wines and liquors [not beer, the workingman's drink] with their meals in the hotel dining rooms." Atlantic City, ever dissatisfied with its status, was high-toning it again.

The letter pouted that the State Excise Commission had struck the resort "in the midst of the summer season," as if the city would have preferred action at the *beginning* of the season. Furthermore, how would the Commission have gathered evidence of Sunday violation in December, when there were but a few doddering invalids sucking brandy for their health? The authors were indignant at Fort's behavior, for Sunday drinking was a "right which all consider it without harm to any one."

The balance of the letter included some political jabs at Fort, attempting to embarrass him by resurrecting an endorsement he had routinely given to a publicity agent from Atlantic City. The manifesto also asserted that "gambling is virtually unknown" in the town, and that the city fathers had stoutly resisted attempts to import it. The

authors presented a homely tale of the shrewd prosecution of some
"leading gambling men of New York," who were forced to sell their
den at a ten-thousand-dollar loss shortly after it opened. No mention
was made of Prosecutor Goldenberg's action a month earlier, when he
had identified sixteen gambling dives in a public release.

This letter was quite a bag of tricks, principled and practical, reasonable and coercive, sincere and deceptive by turns. It had the endorsement of the foremost businessmen of the town, yet it contained plain
lies and less distinct distortions of fact. Just as the Golden Mean provided the rationale for the behavior of visitors to the resort, so it also
governed the behavior of natives who catered to the visitors' needs.
They believed they had achieved a successful compromise between
what the law allowed and what the opportunities of resort life made
possible. This compromise, be it noted, was somewhat to the "left"
(in the direction of pleasure and away from morality) of their own
highest notions of propriety. Anxious to believe that the compromise
was satisfactory, they hotly resented outside attempts to unsettle it,

and to defend that compromise they were willing to employ means that at times were extremely dubious.

This attitude of moral compromise must have affected the resort profoundly, by allowing less-principled men to settle on a compromise morality far more divergent from what the culture conceived to be acceptable. In later decades Atlantic City was to suffer heavily from men of easy conscience who found the atmosphere congenial and who boldly struck a chord that was sympathetic to the fainter community note which they discerned.

The Golden Mean of community morality was closely related to a second important phenomenon. There were three kinds of Babylonians in Atlantic City—buyers, sellers, and supervisors. The culture tended to be aware of them in differing degrees, a hierarchy of awareness which is revealing. The sellers were constantly in the public eye and were a standard item of newspaper reports. If vice became too rampant, the activities of supervisors would be called into question. But as for the buyers, the public preferred not to scrutinize them, but to imagine them as some other group, some other class, some other type of humans than the garden variety to which we all belong.

In the chronicles of resort misconduct, there was much evidence which might have led to disturbing reflection about the relation of crime to respectable society. Men of power and substance—leaders of society—frequented Levy's gambling den near the celebrated United States Hotel. The executive of the National Cash Register Company of Dayton, Ohio, who was swindled at the faro table must have been part of the blue-chip trade that the resort preferred to attract. The Boardwalk was the most respectable avenue of Atlantic City, but illegal "blind horse" bars did a lively business along its length, using bath-houses, soda fountains, and drugstores as a front. Drugstore bars were common, selling liquor in rooms marked: "No Admission to the Laboratory."

The Boardwalk was particularly gamy in 1895, with numerous "living picture shows," "The Pink Venus" attraction, nude portrait exhibitions, a bawdy phonograph parlor, and "Turkish dances" by "dark-eyed lassies of the Orient." A variety show in the lower Board-walk excursion district "is made up of negro minstrels, whose old jokes are varied by indecencies, a female singer whose success not in-frequently depends on the amount of double meaning in her songs, and the suggestiveness of her gestures, and last but not least, there must be a couple of dancers who can be depended to bring down the house by a liberal display of lingerie." The celebrated "Streets of Cairo" (a natural child, begotten of a certain "Little Egypt" at the

World's Columbian Exposition, Chicago, 1893) was much in vogue that year. An *Inquirer* reporter attended a performance of this renowned "danse du ventre": "Several women in the audience, who probably expected something of the kind, showed delicacy enough to blush, and four young girls from a prominent Pacific avenue hotel who held seats in the background gazed in astonishment, giggled, and finally, unable to stand the stares of the men in the place, walked out." After the conclusion of this diverting entertainment, a dancer in the "Cairo" troupe appeared outside: " 'You buy me lemonade?' she asked, with an arch smile, a summer youth who cast his eyes on her. The youth didn't refuse. . . ."

In 1890 the *Bulletin* vainly ranted against "those despicable scoundrels who sell intoxicating poisons to boys and girls," for there were a number of places in the resort which sold liquor to minors. This situation provoked sharp adult criticism, such as that of "a leading citizen of Reading," who abandoned his vacation in disgust because his son returned drunk to the boardinghouse where the family was staying, "a thing he could not do in Philadelphia or this city." The man from Reading claimed to know five other families who were deserting Atlantic City because of its moral laxity. Guvernator's Pavilion Theatre, "so-called," was a chief violator. It had a "sample room" which was a popular tippling place for young people, sherry cobbler being the preferred drink of the girls who frequented the spot. The *Bulletin* found that the ages of twelve youths, male and female, who drank there ranged from fourteen to eighteen years. The "sample room" was separated from a lesser hall to which admission was free and in which "the only lady mandoline orchestra in America" performed. To escape this rather pale entertainment, a young customer had to pay an admission fee to the inner sanctum, where "a grand company of twenty-five European and American vaudeville artists" presented a lively show. Guvernator's obviously was aiming at a young clientele:

> Beardless boys by themselves emptied glass after glass, boys whose appearance indicated that the correcting hand of the parent would do them good. The waiters supplied their wants and the special officers attached to the place looked on and never said a word.

And the action could be a good deal less innocent than underage drinking. Young men of seventeen to twenty-two years of age attended Mrs. Thompson's brothel on Mississippi Avenue. Minnie Mason, arrested for streetwalking in 1897, was only fifteen, and "a respectable

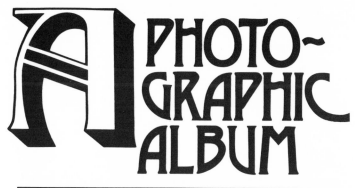

A PHOTO-GRAPHIC ALBUM

*Lounging about on the sand, generally in company with many
other holiday-makers, was a favorite way to spend
a hot day. Costumes made sunburn unlikely, but didn't
inhibit showing off* (below).

Sheer numbers, on the beach or in the water, was the usual state of affairs in August. A gradually sloping ocean bottom made swimming relatively safe except during stormy weather.

*In a 1905 view the Boardwalk was crowded with prom-
enaders and rolling chairs, but in
1888 there was privacy available on the beach.*

The 1880's version of cheesecake involved wringing out one's bathing costume (opposite, below). In a 1900 stereograph (opposite, top), the pail and spade brigade displayed their enjoyment of the beach, while a mixed group mugged for the camera in the 1890's (below).

viii

An 1897 stereograph picture bears the title "A Jolly Crowd" (bottom).
The inscription on the postcard below ("What are the wild
waves saying?") implies an interest in nature, but the young man
who sent it noted "Lots of arms going to waist here. . . ."

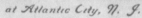

What are the Wild Waves Saying? Sister!   *at Atlantic City, N. J.*

By 1902, bathers were liberated to the point of rolled-down stockings, but the typical visitor found such displays dubious. On the card at bottom, postmarked 1908, the sender wrote "Am not doing such stunts as the above lady. Do you know her?"

6 1261a. "A Seaside Belle", Atlantic City, N. J.

READY FOR A BATH

4"

*"Ready for a bath," says the card opposite, dated 1905, but as can be
seen from the large beach view, strolling and
sitting in pavilions were more to the taste of most visitors.*

xii

"Dear Bertha: I recieved your letter and was glad to know that everything is O.K. I wish you could see the children in bathing it is certainly sport . . . This is us coming home. . . ."
Thus observed Mrs. M. Sager in 1906 (top). A very early group is at left below. "Happy and Beautiful" is the label on the charmer at the bottom.

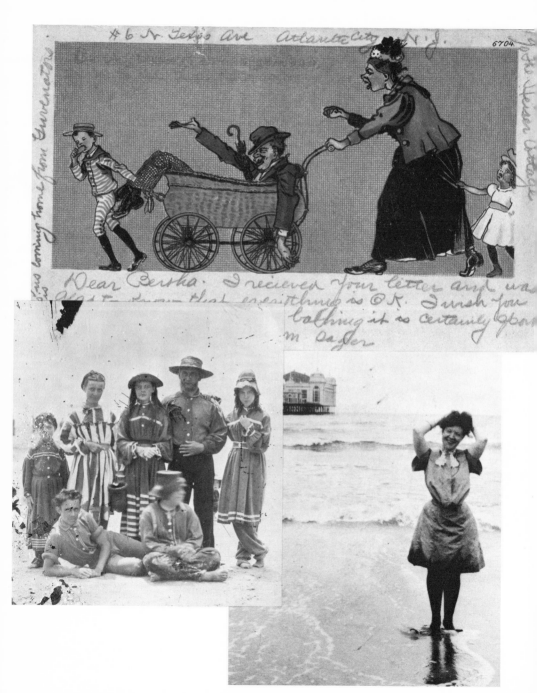

*Good clean fun on the beach (top) was a draw, but there were others.
Norman's Cottage and Dining Rooms promised easy
congeniality (the address was on the other side),
and on the card at bottom "Your Friend Ed" wrote: "Phila
is all right, but Atlantic goes it one better."*

xiv

*Then there were the donkeys. No matter what the date, from the 1880's
on, in posed pictures or group portraits or candid
scenes, the amiable and patient little creatures played a part.*

279—The Whole Family at the Beach, Atlantic City, N. J.

Atlantic City was a place where many blacks found employment, but it was
also a place for vacationing. At top, a group of Philadelphia
Negroes wait in front of an excursion house. Blacks were welcome
to paddle in the surf (at left). The Steel Pier
(bottom) served as a promenade and a place to sit.

xvii

"The Sandman" made sculptures out of sand, complete with uplifting epigraphs ("A Few Grains of Sand" was the exhibition title), collected donations, and prayed against rain. At bottom, an impromptu band concert—with a note by the sender of the card—"I could stay here forever."

S/S1

*Young's Million Dollar Pier (large picture), photographed in 1906, contained
theaters, exhibition halls, and a great amount of marble, some
of it real. Inside was a fine ballroom (opposite, below). If you preferred
disaster, there was an authentic re-creation of the
Johnstown Flood (below). A card (opposite, top) said
"Postcard" in 15 languages on the back.*

"JOHNSTOWN FLOOD" THE ORIGINAL
PAN AMERICAN PRODUCTION

ATLANTIC CITY
BOARD WALK

XX

*The trip out from Philadelphia was normally uneventful, but things
did go wrong. The Meadow Wreck occurred
in 1896. In the same year, the Lady Orchestra (including
a few ringers on bass, trumpet, and oboe) held
forth at Columbia Gardens.*

xxi

The various piers were major attractions. At Young's Ocean Pier (top) you could take "a trolley ride across the ocean" for a nickel or see a seven-foot shark in a tank. To the Heinz Pier, an advertising triumph, admission was free.

xxii

The Atlantic City–Moorish façade of the Academy of Music building, squarely on the Boardwalk, also housed Fralinger's famous pharmacy, home of saltwater taffy. The turn-of-the-century postcard at bottom shows visitors eagerly stocking up before they return home.

"Ice cold milk and buttermilk" were the only beverages that required advertising in the 1880's saloon below. At bottom, one of the resort's finer establishments—the Windsor Hotel, photographed in 1904.

xxiv
Two more places for those who could afford to sneer at boarding houses:
the Hotel Rudolph (at left) and the Traymore
(bottom). The 1898 stereograph at right bears the label
"Seeking health from Mother Earth."

XXV

*At top, John Lake Young's residence on his Million Dollar Pier. The address
was No. 1 Atlantic Ocean. The lavish interior of the
Old Vienna restaurant impressed "Cliff," the sender of the postcard
at bottom. "A great place," he remarked.*

The Marlborough-Blenheim Hotel (top) was a great stone pile containing
hundreds of rooms. In front of it were
sand artists at work and, of course, the beach.

s/s

*The Steeplechase Pier featured dozens of flagpoles, huge windows
and something known as "the Niagara Slide."*

xxviii

In 1902, from a platform high on the Revolving Observation Tower
(the whole platform rose like an elevator from ground-
level to the top of the tower), you could get a splendid aerial
view of Young's Ocean Pier (at left).

xxix

*In 1894, lesser versions of the Observation Tower were the Ferris
wheels. The ride at bottom, not for the
lazy, appears to have involved pedaling oneself along a rail.*

xxxi

*The Epicycloidal Diversion (opposite, top), a sort of multiple Ferris wheel,
photographed in front of the Seaview House in 1875.
Later, for bolder souls, there was the Loop-the-loop (below),
a centrifugal stomach displacer.*

Bluenoses might complain about some of Atlantic City's enter-
tainments, but the best were free and utterly
wholesome—the sun, the sand, and the smell of the sea
when wind made the flags whip.

married woman" living on Arctic Avenue near the notorious Burnett Cottages told the *Bulletin* in 1890 that "it makes her heart sore to see so many young girls go into these houses." Mrs. Burnett was not the only madam who believed that youthful prostitutes were desirable employees.

Despite unsettling evidence of this kind, observers who wished to blame someone for the unsavory side of Atlantic City often turned to scapegoats. The "Atlantic City Manifesto" ignored local gamblers and assailed the "leading gambling men of New York." Many resort citizens attributed Fort's intervention in 1908 to the envy of other counties in New Jersey, whose residents "are jealous of Atlantic City's prosperity and would like to make the town as dead as many other resorts are now." City officials often quite cynically attempted to displace local attention from genuine reform to the adjustment of trivial annoyances, as in 1900, when Mayor Stoy brazenly responded to criticism of his inaction by denouncing "abbreviated bathing suits and the frisky bathers, saying some of these scenes were revolting."

The black portion of the community provided a convenient scape-goat for local frustration with criminal activity. Blacks were allied with the Republican political machine, which in turn had comfortable rela-tions with vice operations. When a Democrat managed to win the mayoralty election by twelve votes in 1892 (a rare event in the resort), the *Daily Union* rejoiced that "the coons and gamblers did not run Atlantic City." The Republicans found their alliance with blacks use-ful when the city government was embarrassed with the necessity of a token cleanup, but the transparent motives of the city authorities on such occasions drew contempt from some independent observers. When the police sought in 1900 to spread oil upon reformist waters by squelching a petty crap game, the *Daily Union* sneered: "The Police Crusade. Swooped on a Penny Game of Crap. Got Eight Colored Culprits. Beginning Easy." In 1908, Prosecutor Goldenberg, claiming that the large white gambling clubs were too discreet to allow them-selves to be caught, raided the three leading black clubs. A prominent local citizen criticized the persecution of the smaller black gambling dens while the "big protected white places" went unmolested.

The inclination to seek scapegoats is mainly important as part of the general tendency of observers, within and without the resort, to allot blame according to a pattern. To reiterate, the culture clearly preferred to blame the seller of vice first, and next to blame the politician who supervised or at least tolerated the existence of the vice trade, but it hesitated to blame the customer of vice. The best answer

that can be given for this behavior is the fervent (but usually covert) desire of the culture to protect the family, particularly when it might have been implicated as the patron of illicit pleasure. A typical exclamation from the *Bulletin* in 1890 illustrates how responsibility for misbehavior was imposed:

> *The flaunting, brazen women* [sic] *of the town* [*does not come under this ban*]. *She can induce the boy of sixteen to come to her disorderly house when he should be with his parents. She can sell him liquor, though she has no license. She can send him away reeling drunk, caring little or nothing if he be picked up and cast into a filthy cell and fined for drunkenness.*

Though the *Bulletin* and *Daily Union* might mention an individual who had been victimized by a vice seller, their customary usage was to regard vice customers as a class, a vague dustbin of ne'er-do-wells, a group of riffraff outside respectable society. The line between the criminal and the family was distinct: "A halt must be cried to the gambler, crook, dive-keeper, prostitute and black-leg; they have nothing in common with the family, the tired worker, the seeker of health and lover of recreation." Or again: "Hotel men—and they have the larger interests at stake—say that their profits come largely from the steady trade of families. The low saloons are patronized by a class of patrons who will drive the family trade from the town." The governor of New Jersey made the same distinction:

> *Surely the women and children, and a vast majority of the men, go to that resort for health and pleasure, and go for no such purpose as those interested in these illegal practices would have us believe. A quiet Sunday in Atlantic City would induce people to go there rather than detract from their going.*

Excursion visitors could be included among the "undesirables." Though they were the city's bread-and-butter trade, they were too humble to be able to retaliate through the press or in other practical ways, and they were too poor to go to other resorts if offended. Newspaper commentators felt themselves to be of a superior class, sharpening their critical opinion: "Innocent children are denied the pleasure of riding on the 'merry-go-round,' but excursion loafers can revel in free-flowing beer and whisky!"

The culture's refusal to connect the family with vice was in no way contradicted by journalistic rhetoric of "the family endangered," since the family was seen not as an apple having a worm within, but as a castle having dragons without. The *Bulletin* flayed Mayor Hoffman:

> *The near-sighted and weak-kneed Mayor—who has allowed disorderly houses to flourish in the finest watering place in America, where thousands upon thousands of respectable gentlemen bring*

A beach flirtation—"May" and "December"

*their wives and children; the cowardly official who has stifled
the force of his own city ordinances against gambling; this miser-
able apology for a chief executive. . . .*

This same newspaper exploited the culture's defensiveness about the
family to lend its exposés impact, selecting incidents contributing to
a moral tableau of the family sorely besieged by the forces of evil.

The *Inquirer* seconded the *Bulletin.* In 1895 it portrayed the
notorious Peter's Beach at Brigantine (Atlantic City's mundane neigh-
bor), a swell dive and brothel which could be reached only by boat
from the Inlet. Run by a certain Charley Smith, Peter's "Beach" was
really a two-storied house on piles completely surrounded by water.
It customarily drew big spenders to its superb bar, "hotel" accommodations, and amiable damsels. The *Inquirer* became concerned through
information it obtained from an Atlantic City boatman who had been
employed by "Mr. ———'s family" during their summer stay at the
resort. The family's two young ladies, with their respective fiancé
and boy friend, had asked to be taken to Peter's Beach on a lark,
despite the boatman's warning. "They got in the parlor and the piano
started playing. They were in there only a few minutes when I heard
the girls shriek, and the door of the room opened and they rushed
down the pier, their faces scarlet with blushes." If Mr. ———'s
daughters bit off more than they could chew, so did respectable minors
who stumbled on the Oceanic Dancing Pavilion, where the dancers
were "tough young lads who wear their hair banged and hats over
their eyes, and young girls of the 'chippie' order." Well-bred girls of
fifteen and sixteen, visiting Atlantic City with their families, were
attracted to the Pavilion by the music and free admission. "Two
pretty young girls who came in while the Inquirer correspondent and
artist were in the room, took one turn round the floor, sized up the

company, appeared quite sorry for their venturesomeness and quickly left the room."

The temptation to ignore the Sabbath, well-nigh irresistible in Atlantic City, was an important snare in the family's way. The *Bulletin* reported a resort policeman who rudely rebuffed a prominent Philadelphia lawyer anxious to locate a particular church, but who smilingly directed a young man to a disorderly house, with his personal recommendation. Moreover, the Atlantic City police scotched the "Galatea" panorama and "sacred phonographic concert" of W. R. Lynn and A. Vivian for Sunday operation. This was the kind of story the *Bulletin* liked: a harmless and instructive entertainment suppressed by venal authority, while saloons sluiced out hooch to debauched fathers and painted ladies introduced tender youths to the path of destruction. The newspaper was pleased to report in 1890 that its exposé had the support of eight resort ministers, who called on "the better and best portion of this community," "the fathers and mothers, the young men and maidens," to make a moral cleansing of the city. Tales of dragons without diverted attention from a possible worm within, and conversely, anxiety for a worm within created a ready audience for tales of dragons without.

It is a striking fact that during the 1890 scandal Atlantic City never seized upon its most cogent defense, arguing that its vice customers came from Philadelphia, and that hence the bigger city should more correctly point the accusing finger at itself. Of course, those who made their living directly or indirectly from the conditions described in the *Bulletin* were naturally not eager to admit their complicity in crime by defending their role in terms of the social demands made upon them. Reflection, however, suggests a far more potent reason for Atlantic City's restraint. Its citizens shared the basic needs of the general culture, and even more important than their need to exculpate themselves was their need to preserve their image of the sanctity of the family. Atlantic City rallied to a sacred cultural shrine, even when it could have deserted its post to its own advantage, for to point the finger at Philadelphia might have been to point the finger at the family. Though it would argue its guilt, the resort passively accepted its right to be impeached, and the *Bulletin* was happy to take advantage of this passivity. How much more flattering it was to Philadelphia to see Atlantic City as an example of peculiar depravity rather than as a product of its users!

6

Not Too Far from the Madding Crowd

ATLANTIC CITY was a self-contained incongruity. It contradicted itself. It liked to style itself "the City by the Sea," a title about as unimaginative as the worst that American urban boosters have come up with. And yet there are important implications to this title. Atlantic City made its living as the City confronting Nature. The extreme juxtaposition of urbanity and wilderness was the trademark of the resort. Certainly many lesser resorts profited from the same phenomenon, but the sheer magnitude of the City-Nature confrontation in Atlantic City insists on its being studied in this place. The real problem is to determine the function of Nature and nature rhetoric in the resort; that is, the way they relate to the urban reality and urban preferences of the town. What emerges is an interesting commentary on the old theme of the frontier in American history, of the Machine which has sought to subdue it, and of the City which has resulted.

There is, after all, an ocean at Atlantic City. If Philadelphians came to the resort only for its urban pleasures, they might well have stayed in Philadelphia and built whatever man-made amusements they liked in their own city. Swimming (for most, wading would be the more precise term), lounging in the sun, breathing salt air, and looking out over the water were basic activities of undeniable importance to the resort's success. On the other hand, it is impressive to find that in temporarily "abandoning" the City for Nature, masses of Americans repaired to something very far from Edenic wilderness. They did not really leave the City: they added Nature to the City.

To begin with, Atlantic City was undeniably a city. It had a permanent population in 1895 of 18,000, a number which was rapidly increasing, and a transient population several times that figure. It was heavily serviced during the 1890's by the rival rail systems of the Pennsylvania and Reading companies, which provided it with unexceptionable communications with Philadelphia, New York, Balti-

119

more, and the other large cities of the East. *Gopsill's Directory* for 1891 lists 570 hotels and boardinghouses in the resort.

An article of 1908, which records the fictional experiences of "Bertha on the Board-Walk," comments on the subject:

> *The minute Bertha and her friends get their suit cases and stuff out into Atlantic Avenue in front of the railway station, they find it's frightfully towny, like Main Street. . . . The very trolley-cars are run by electric power, whereas new arrivals have a vague notion that they are at least sloop-rigged and started by motormen garbed like a sailorman.*

Main Street didn't stop at the Boardwalk, either. The *Philadelphia Inquirer* estimated ten thousand people in the surf on a July Sunday in 1893 and the Boardwalk was so crowded that visitors could hardly move. With such crowds, pollution was unavoidable. The sand just couldn't take the traffic load and keep a Tahitian purity. "Between the Boardwalk and the sea there is at low tide a great strip of sand which is probably white at the beginning of summer, but which assumes the colour of pepper and salt after a few millions of human animals have wallowed in it during the heated season." It was customary to take carriage rides along the beach, particularly near the water, where the sand was hard-packed. Horse manure ensued. In 1892 the mayor prohibited driving on the beach during bathing hours, meaning the few hours about noontime, alleviating the problem. But in the crowded shallows where the thousands waded, the sparkling waters were fortified by candy wrappers, bits of fruit peel, and the urine of little boys. Robinson Crusoe was astounded to find a human footprint on his unblemished beach; a visitor to Atlantic City would have been thunderstruck to find ten inches that hadn't been stepped on.

The first boardwalk was a crude, portable affair that could be dragged out of the ocean's reach each winter, but the popularity of beachfront strolls encouraged successive improvements. By 1884 the walk was a permanent structure twenty feet wide, five feet above the sand, and lit by electricity. The fourth walk of 1890 was twenty-four feet wide and ten feet above the sand, giving a cavernous effect from a beach perspective. Finally, in 1896 the Phoenix Bridge Company erected a structure forty feet wide and about four miles in length. As befitted the institutional status it had achieved, the boardwalk was officially uppercased to "Boardwalk" and acknowledged as the spinal cord of Atlantic City. But there was a continuing dispute about whether the Boardwalk constituted a boundary between the City and the Sea. Those who made their money on the City side thought it should, whereas those who sniffed lucre on the Sea side disagreed. By 1885 complaints could be heard: "A big roller skating rink . . . stands on the water side of the walk, and in some places the booths have crept over to the same side for lack of room on the other."

Then there were the piers. The West Jersey and Atlantic Railroad built a pier from its excursion house at the foot of Georgia Avenue in 1881, but it survived only a couple of months before an Atlantic storm claimed it as a souvenir. Colonel George W. Howard constructed a 650-foot offering to the sea adjacent to Kentucky Avenue in 1882, and saw his investment float away on a storm tide two months later. His second effort, 856 feet in length, came to grief after a single season when a gale-driven schooner smashed into its pavilions. Although Howard rebuilt again, he sold his pier to the city in 1889 for demolition to make way for the fourth Boardwalk. John R. Applegate, a Boardwalk photographer, opened a 625-foot pier off Tennessee Avenue in 1884. With an alleged capacity of ten thousand people, it had free checking for baby carriages, a large public ice-water fountain using a ton and a half of ice daily, and poetic advertising:

> Balmy breezes of the ocean
> Bigger crowds than waves in motion,
>   Babies and their coaches free
>   Parents save a doctor's fee,
> A well known fact without presumption,
> Physicians say it cures consumption.

The Iron Pier, which commenced business at the foot of Massachusetts Avenue near the Inlet in 1886, was located too far in the resort's wings for mass patronage. In 1898 it became Heinz Pier, the toe in the surf of the famous pickle manufacturer. Much more successful was the Steel Pier, at Virginia Avenue and the Boardwalk, which with the Spanish-American War completed the major new public entertainments of 1898. John Lake Young and Stewart McShea bought Applegate's Pier in 1891 and lengthened it to a whopping two thousand feet, but the last pier of the nineteenth century was Auditorium Pier, opposite Pennsylvania Avenue. Thus, by 1900 Atlantic City's beachfront was greatly changed from the long sweep of sand and sea that a half century before had seemed so promising of eventual profit to a certain group of capitalists. Now the harvest was home, and it was plum pie for all hands.

But where was the beach? It was becoming apparent that while a pier or two might be a desirable public attraction, too many thumbs in the pie would leave no room for the plum. Some citizens were alarmed when merchants who had developed both sides of the Boardwalk began in 1884 to roof over sections with tin. Another bad portent

was the accretion of sand along the length of Applegate's Pier, so that by 1890 bathers had to walk a hundred yards beyond its end to find water deep enough for wading at low tide. There were rumblings in favor of removing the structure. The city government, pressured by businessmen who stood to lose from seaside blight, beseeched the New Jersey legislature, and by 1894 won eminent domain over the beachfront through a Beach Park Act. Easement agreements which gave private developers the right to build piers only if they were at least 1,000 feet in length had mixed success, and the Auditorium Pier Company blandly added its 500-foot entertainment wharf in 1889. Major hotel owners complained: they hadn't invested their hundreds of thousands of dollars to offer guests backside views of amusement docks. The *Inquirer* bewailed "the utter destruction of the bathing section" by the proliferation of piers, for various schemes were afoot. It was bad enough that currents about the piers caused sand bars and menacing gullies which spoiled bathing, but the last straw was the announcement of plans to build an actual hotel on the beach projecting right out over the ocean. There were outraged howls from businessmen, who realized that the panoramic view from the Boardwalk would be completely ruined. And there was another pungent objection: "The slops and filth would undoubtedly wash toward the beach, and at times make bathing very undesirable." The only real solution to the resort's dilemma was to cut off all further development, which the Park Deeds did. With certain exceptions stemming from prior legal rights, no more structures could be built on the ocean side of the Boardwalk, though landholders could connect buildings with the walk on the land side.

Given contemporary values, the partial conservation of the beachfront was a major accomplishment of the businessmen and politicians of Atlantic City. The struggle for protection of the resort's shoreline would make an interesting chapter in a history of environmental concern in the United States, and would show that even under extreme duress of profit seeking, one community was able to reach a consensus sufficient to salvage something of its chief natural asset. Nevertheless, restriction of development on the beach did not limit a free-for-all on the other side of the Boardwalk. There were the great hotels, such as the Dennis, Windsor, Brighton, Traymore, Chalfonte, and Haddon Hall. There were many other less-distinguished hostelries. Besides these, in 1891 fifty-seven commercial bathhouses, ten mechanical amusement centers, six dealers in "fancy goods" (novelties), thirteen sellers of shells and curiosities, nine mineral-water sluicers, a merchant of "Turkish" goods, four "Japanese" goods dealers, and eighteen confectioners breathed the hot breath of profit seeking on the Boardwalk. The effect was extraordinary. On one hand, the ocean stretching serenely to the horizon. On the other, a jumbled wooden battlement of gingerbread balconies and jagged towers, gaudy storefronts and dowdy piers, stretching for miles. The City itched, jittered, and trembled to advance further against the Sea. It could not. At the boundary between the two, a vast human stew amassed to savor itself.

The reason for this titanic assault on what had once been an empty, windswept stretch of flat Jersey coast lay in the hearts of Americans. They weren't satisfied with the virgin strand. People loved to look at other people. Jane Jacobs emphasizes this point in her *Death and Life of Great American Cities*; she notes that city planners and architects have imagined that city people seek emptiness, order, and simplicity, when the reverse is true. A picture of the Steel Pier from about 1903 shows a double-decked arrangement between the admission gate and the central pavilion. The pier was double-decked on the land side so that the patrons could sit and view the crowded beach. A view of the wild ocean might seem aesthetically more appealing to a minority, but the operators of the Steel Pier knew where the majority preference— and the greater profit—lay. A collection of 536 postcards in the Atlantic City Public Library indicates a marked preference for scenes of crowded beaches over tossing waves; only a dozen or so of these cards show the ocean exclusively. Some of the beach scenes have revealing captions: "$5.00 Reward if you can find me in this crowd of bathers"; "Crowded Beach"; "Bathing House, Find me in the Bunch"; "A Jolly Crowd." These were the scenes visitors liked and wanted to convey to their friends back home. Serenity had limited appeal. The guests came to join the mob, and the city came to depend on the mob's regular appearance. " 'Fairly good attendance' is not what Atlantic City counts upon when she makes her ante-summer preparations. She must have a rush, a mob, a regular overflowing jam in order to make things pay." Because masses of people were such a prime attraction, the Boardwalk was the real focal point of the resort. The City Commissioner said in 1914: "As far as the lure and prosperity of Atlantic City is concerned it might as well lose the sea as its Boardwalk."

On the Boardwalk, the true city-ness of the resort was evident.

Atlantic City was a city not only in terms of statistics of population and structural development, but even more importantly in the density of experience peculiarly characteristic of true city life. Few events occur in cities which cannot occur in villages, yet it is the concentration of events in cities which produces their lushness of experience and their iridescent fascination. Atlantic City was an urban tableau. The visitor to the Boardwalk could see oddities, like an excursion of Chinese: "Last Monday was wash-day sure enough for Philadelphia's Chinatown. . . . This odd procession was . . . the Christian Mongolians of the Race Street Mission." He could see tragedies, like the one recorded in an old postcard of Steeplechase Pier:

> *Dear Bessie: Was glad to hear from you. I would of wrote sooner but was not able. A boy pushed me down the Niagara slide in this Pier one night. I fell to the bottom senseless. The Dr. was afraid of concussion of the brain. . . . They brought me home in a rolling chair, every body excited.*

And he could see comedies:

> *An amusing and at the same time most ridiculous spectacle on the beach during the bathing hours today was a young fellow who was dressed in a woman's bath suit. It was of white, with black braid trimmings, black stockings with white slippers, and white braid wound about the limbs, a la Roman style. The Kodak fiends were kept busy taking snap shots.*

People came to Atlantic City very much in order to join this human potpourri, presenting at every hand the pungent variety of life.

Atlantic City evidences the predominance in American culture of the active over the contemplative impulse. In business, transportation, foreign policy, urbanization, and many other areas, the Victorian period during which the resort rose to greatness was a time of explosive activity in American life. Both the men who laid violent hands on the raw Jersey coast to shape it in myriad ways and the tourists they attracted were animated by the active impulse. The visitor liked to bathe and to stroll, to see the sun over the water and to breathe clean air, but these attractions did not satiate him. At length, the vast natural panorama could be unengaging, if not actually burdensome in its impassivity. The visitor had only to turn his back to find the city, bristling with things to do and sights to see. Consequently, the benches on the Boardwalk faced the city and not the ocean. The resort's businessmen, sharing a preference for the active impulse, and having the added incentive of profit, were eager to contrive hundreds of ways of engaging tourists' attention, dooming Absecon Island to the obliteration of its primitive natural attributes.

Leo Marx, in *The Machine in the Garden*, identifies three possible conditions for the landscape: Wilderness, Garden, City. The implicit, and frequently explicit, rationale of the application of the Machine to the Wilderness was to attain an ideal state midway between savage nature and congested city, this utopia being the Garden. But the active impulse so fervently held in the American soul could not be bridled when the Garden had been accomplished:

The objective, in theory at least, was a society of the middle landscape, a rural nation exhibiting a happy balance of art and nature. But no one . . . had been able to identify the point of arrest, the critical moment when the tilt might be expected and progress cease to be progress. As time went on, accordingly, the idea became . . . a rhetorical formula.

On the level of popular thought, there was little awareness in Atlantic City that overdevelopment might constitute a danger. It is true that the grossest kind of exploitation, the submergence of the beachfront in amusement piers, aroused strong opposition. Furthermore, an article printed in 1873 addresses itself to the question of the appropriate personality for a shore community:

One goes to the seaside not for pomp and peacock's tails, but for saltness, Nature and a bite of fresh fish. To build a city there that shall not be an insult to the sentiment of the place is a matter of difficulty. One's ideal, after all, is a canvass encampment. A range of solid stone villas like those of Newport, so far as congruity with a watering-place goes, pains the taste like a false note in music. Atlantic City pauses halfway between the stone house and the tent, and erects herself in woodwork.

We are sure it is a sincere, natural, sensible kind of life, as compared with that of other bathing-shores. Although there are brass bands at the hotels, and hops in the evening, and an unequal struggle of macassar oil with salt and stubborn locks, yet the artificiality is kept at a minimum. People really do bathe, really do take walks on the beach for the love of the ocean, really do pick up shells.

Even here, however, the author envisions a far more artificial environment than the Garden.

A much more representative sentiment than restraint of development is expressed by two photographs opposite the title page of Heston's handbook for 1894. The first shows a wild stretch of sand dunes covered by beach grass and dotted with driftwood. The second is a view of the city from the lighthouse, illustrating heavy commercial and residential development, with the Senate Hotel in the foreground. The page is captioned: "Atlantic City in 1854 and 1894." Selected by the editor to represent the best face of the town, and placed opposite the title page to serve as a favorable introduction to the visitor, the photos strikingly convey the popular idea of "progress." The presumption which in 1854 gave a trifling hamlet on a sandy waste the exalted title "Atlantic City" had been fully justified by the complete subjugation of Nature. "Atlantic" was a "City."

The active impulse of the American culture did not cease to operate in the resort once the city had been built. As we have seen, the Machine assaulted the ocean in the form of the great piers which characterized the town. A Pennsylvania Railroad pamphlet of 1883 speaks of the "big pier, which stretches a grasping hand into the ocean." A 1907 brochure of the Atlantic City Bureau of Information proudly (and rather inflatedly) extols the piers as choice examples of the industrial spirit:

> *Extending seaward from the Boardwalk are five great Ocean Piers—in all the world the greatest of Piers devoted exclusively to recreation. Nowhere will builders and engineers find more interesting examples of steel and concrete work than in these famous structures.*

It was inevitable that when all the obvious alterations which the active impulse could undertake on Nature had been accomplished, new and sometimes bizarre efforts should occur. One of the trademarks of

The Sea-Spider, or Ocean Tricycle

the resort was the sand sculptures which "artists" formed on the beach to coax nickels out of tourists. Such artwork took classical or patriotic themes, like "The Spirit of '76" and "Washington Crossing the Delaware." More ambitious and unethical sculptors added a little cement to the sand in the interest of maintenance reduction. They were interesting, they were grotesque, they were a nuisance—depending on your viewpoint. One thing they were not was untrammeled beach. On a petty entrepreneurial scale, sand sculptures paralleled the great ocean piers in the commonly held desire of the culture to assault Nature.

An extreme example of the active impulse was the invention of a man of the cloth, the Reverend Ezra B. Lake, a resident of Pleasantville, Atlantic City's retiring stepbrother on the nearby mainland. One day in 1890 he drove an astounding, lumbering monstrosity into the shallows in front of the resort in a test run of what could have been the death knell of traditional navigation. This was "The Sea Spider" or, more properly, "The Ocean Tricyclemore Sea-Wagon," and it represented a leap of the imagination. Lake's idea was to dispense with the support of water in sailing in favor of a giant self-propelled derrick which would simply drive through the waves. A passenger platform carrying a maximum of forty persons was suspended twenty-five feet above the wheels of the crane, which were powered by a steam engine. Lake hoped to use his Sea Spider to rescue the victims of shipwreck, but his efforts were in vain, and the Sea Spider faded into the nebulae of popular history. In its crackpot way it was a bit of brilliance, a bold also-ran in the thrust of the Machine into Nature.

In short, though poised by the side of Nature, Atlantic City managed to be a thoroughly urban phenomenon. Yet while urbanity prevailed, the resort supplemented its genuine (if circumscribed) natural attractions with an illusion of rusticity which was all the more strident because it lacked reality. Here is a representative sample from Heston's handbook of 1888:

> The sea, the sea, the open sea!
> The blue, the fresh, the ever free!
> I never was on the dull, tame shore,
> But I loved the great sea more and more,
> And backward flew to her billowy breast,
> Like a bird that seeketh her mother's nest.

Only a man of remarkable detachment could regard the Boardwalk as the "dull, tame shore." But pastoral poetry abounds in the advertising of the resort; Heston scattered selections from sentimental poets like Longfellow throughout his handbooks. Natural vignettes colored promotional pamphlets, inspired magazine articles, souvenirs, and the official city seal. One Boardwalk businessman found he could push his candy faster (allegedly after a high tide engulfed his stock) if he called it "salt water taffy," and a lucrative industry was born. In its own mind, Atlantic City was very big on Nature.

Because the resort was primarily urban in spirit, expressing action

rather than contemplation and the pleasures of the City more frequently than those of Nature, it is not surprising that much natural
lore had no real function beyond that of cliché. As Marx says, Nature
was reduced often to mere "rhetorical formula," from which endless
borrowings could be made. One promotional pamphlet has a cover
portrait of the water's edge, with "A Message from the Sea" traced on
the sand. A related query—"What are the wild waves saying?"—
graces advertising ephemera as early as 1885 and as late as 1910,
and seems to have been a favorite tag for souvenir material. So as not
to dwell on Nature-as-cliché at Atlantic City, let this last example
stand for the many available:

> We have perhaps, in a rather random way, dilated too much
> upon the thousand delights that crowd upon the time and atten-
> tion of the visitors and residents of this lovely place, and it may
> seem strange to the reader that we have hitherto neglected to
> call attention to some of the grander elements that Nature here
> presents in the expansive and illimitable views of the ocean, earth
> and heaven, and especially of "Atlantic's mighty storms." Dear
> reader, it is because neither pen nor pencil are adequate to convey
> a proper conception of the awful sublimity of such a scene.
>
> We will only add, by way of conclusion, that at such times,
> when our solicitude is strained to the very utmost for the safety
> of the many frail barks that we know must be out upon the deep,
> we fully realize the feebleness of mankind when pitted against
> the elements, the sublimity of Nature's power when aroused, and
> lastly, though grandest conception of all, the majesty of Him who
> is both ours and Nature's God.

Which brings us to a related purpose served by the rhetoric about
Nature. It provided an anchor for the resort's promotional and souvenir
literature. In the article from which the above quotation is taken, the
author spends all his efforts describing what is interesting to him
and to his readers: the "thousand delights" of the city. At the end
he realizes that he ought to say *something* about the ocean. After all,
Atlantic City is an ocean resort. So he ushers out the article with a
paean to Nature. Similarly, a picture book from 1897 consists chiefly
of Boardwalk views, local buildings, perspectives of the crowded beach,
and attractive girls in bathing suits. The last photo is "Moonlight on
the Beach."

A more substantial function of nature rhetoric and imagery is suggested by an undated Lehigh Valley Railroad pamphlet, whose cover
has a simulated bas-relief of a girl in a bathing suit poised on a
dolphin. An oar and a rope as a frame, some gulls, and a sailboat
plying the horizon complete the composition, a poor man's "Birth of
Venus" with local variations. In contrast to this relatively natural
tableau, the centerfold shows "Bathing Hour, Atlantic City," the wave-

lets abroil with the human throng. This juxtaposition comprises the classic City by the Sea theme, repeated endlessly in resort literature.

The actual title "City by the Sea" goes back as far as 1854, and, as homely as it seems, its constant reiteration hints at a sensuous pleasure popularly felt at the idea of living in urban comfort by the side of the ocean wilderness. The Steel Pier recommended its music hall at its ocean end, wherein "gay couples whirl in entrancing waltzes above the rolling waves of the big broad Atlantic." A Publicity Bureau pamphlet of 1909 presented a parallel appeal: "Concerts by noted bands, theaters, net hauls, bowling, and other amusements, interesting in themselves, have added zest when enjoyed over the ocean." Applegate's Pier offered a poem in this vein:

> Four spacious decks high in the air,
> 　　The old, the young, the millionaire,
> The worthy poor as well,
> 　　Seek health and rest, all find the same,
> Shielded from sun as well as rain,
> 　　A paradise to dwell.

Nature was a relish to urbanity. One businessman built a fish pond illuminated by submerged electric lights, making it possible for strollers to see the fish from the pier at night. Alfred Heston promised that Atlantic City's "piers afford an unobstructed view of the beach, the bathers, and the limitless expanse of water stretching away to the ocean's horizon. Beneath us, deep down in the clear waters, the finny inhabitants are as busy in their element as we are in ours." Furthermore, the hotels along the beachfront had glass-enclosed sun parlors luxuriously furnished, which allowed customers complete enjoyment of an ocean vista even in winter. It was fun to be in the City, but delectable to be in the City by the Sea.

Nature propaganda had a third and very important function which was akin to the second: it reflected the mock confrontation with Nature which the crowds so enjoyed. The notion of the solemn terrors of the deep was appealing to people confident that they were firmly on dry land. Heston intoned:

> There is not a mile of this beach that has not been the scene of a shipwreck at one time or another. Some places have witnessed many terrible marine tragedies during their association with human existence, and the beach has been thickly strewn with the bodies of those who have made sad landing thereon.

This message is echoed by Hall:

> The proximity of many of our hotels to the ocean where wrecked vessels of other days with valuable cargoes were driven ashore upon the sands, has robbed the deep of some of its terrors and

guaranteed to visiting thousands at all seasons all the benefits of an ocean voyage without going to the sea, and secured all the luxuries of sea-water bathing when winter winds are tossing the spray in full view of the guests' rooms.

"Terrible marine tragedies" and the "terrors" of the "deep" had a romantic quality for urban people whose lives and fortunes were safely divorced from the sea. These passages are sentimental evocations of times past, and the only fear they inspire is the imaginative but low-level variety of the children's fairy story. It is sentimental danger, because it is danger which does not apply to the audience.

It is interesting to compare these selections with the comments of an English visitor in 1896. Of course, his reaction is that of a foreigner, and thus is only indirectly relevant in understanding popular American feeling, but his sentiments are congruent with those of contemporary Americans. While he recommends a carriage ride on the sand for a pleasant summer evening, the pleasure is compounded by an exotic sense of loneliness:

The darkness, closing in around your carriage, seems to cut you off entirely from everyday life and its normal environment. An "other world" feeling, uncanny and disconcerting, gradually creeps over you. And at last the silence and the solitude grow oppressive—so oppressive that the thousand lights in the great hotels miles away are invitations strong to a life too merry to tolerate the morbid. And this is why, with new zest, you come back to the land of braying bands, brilliantly lighted ballroom, dancing folk, and the crush and clatter of the healthy happy crowd.

This venture into the Wilderness is indeed a timid one. Nature is actually "morbid," a curious association in light of traditional pastoral rhetoric, which contrasts the corruption of cities with the healthfulness of the country. But this is not a clichéd passage of nature propaganda; it is the relation of an actual experience. And when it comes to reality as opposed to ideality, "braying bands" and a "healthy happy crowd" are preferable to the Wilderness.

Such is the Englishman's reaction. Yet the history of Atlantic City's efforts to protect its bathers tends to confirm that while the American culture was inclined to sentimentalize natural danger as an abstraction, it could be extreme in the pains it took to avoid the real thing. An early innovator in lifesaving apparatus was the heroically named Captain William Tell Street, who introduced two curious angels of mercy to beleaguered bathers about 1870. His "bathing car" consisted of a wheeled wire cage mounted on floats and attached to a loop of cable running between a windlass onshore and a buoy offshore. The floats could be adjusted "to allow the car to be immersed as deep as the bather prefers." Accommodating a dozen persons, this alarming vehicle would "commend itself for the safety, pleasure and comfort of the Bather, especially to the weak and timid." Street also patented his "Life Lines for Surf Bathing," which were cables running from masts on the beach to anchors beyond the breakers. Life lines long enough to reach the water were suspended from these cables at nine-foot intervals so that—in theory—bathers could pass from line to line "with perfect confidence and safety." Congress Hall, the Seaview Excursion House, and the United States Hotel adopted Street's "Life Lines" for the protection of their guests, and an anonymous eulogist saluted the inventor:

> *The Safety Lines*
> *Behold! Along the Atlantic Coast*
>   *The cords upheld in air,*
> *See patriot flags by high winds tost;*
>   *The Safety Lines are there.*
> *Beneath them rolls the angry foam,—*
>   *The bather in his glee,*
> *Feels in the water quite at home,*
>   *From thought of danger free.*
>
> .   .   .   .
>
> *Then thanks to Street,—don't he deserve*
>   *Both praise and profit too?*
> *His happy thought will life preserve,*
>   *And bathing joys renew.*

Another grateful endorser was thankful that the "sad and sudden deaths of persons unexperienced in the mysteries of sea bathing, who were swept to swift and sudden death, with many to pity but no one to save," were a thing of the past. But few blessings are unmixed: "As for the Ladies, the majority of them prefer bathing on the 'Life Lines' to bathing with Gentlemen."

Despite Street's ingenuity, in practice the improvement of beach safety lay in a different direction. From earliest days, certain obsessions characterized Atlantic City's literature. One was the concern with establishing the town as a year-round resort. A more revealing obsession was the lifeguard service, touted in dozens of pamphlets, histories, and articles. The resort's first lifeguard, supported by the Camden and Atlantic Railroad and private subscriptions, served in front of the Seaview Excursion House in 1872 to protect the crowds of excursionists. By 1884 the resort had at least twenty-five guards, some on the police payroll and others living off fees from bathhouse keepers and occasional rewards from wealthy supplicants. One patron of lifeguards, George W. Jackson's "Popular Bathing House," was

View of the New Excursion House at Atlantic City, showing a section of Street's Patent Life Lines for Bathing and Amusement (1868)

proud to advertise itself as "The Safest Place on the Beach." A regular
paid Beach Patrol was organized in 1892.

The lifeguard service was a chief object of the resort's pride, and
reiteration of its excellence was predictable among locals and tourists.
A brochure of resort scenes featured a photograph of the guards, with
the comment: "No braver set of men live than the Atlantic City Life
Guards. . . . They are universally popular with visitors, as brave men
usually are." Another writer rhetorically asked:

> How many visitors know of the well-nigh perfect system of
> life-saving which they have at this beautiful city by the sea?
> It is there that this system has been developed to such high
> possibilities that it leads those of all other resorts in the world.

What was this "perfect system"? It was not curative, but preventive
in spirit. It was designed to keep the swimmer from running any
chances whatever. One picture book of 1897 illustrates the technique.
Lifeguards idle offshore in boats at close intervals along the beach, to
confine bathers to neck-deep water, and no one is allowed to exceed
the limit. No risk of danger here. Everyone has to conform to the level
of absolute safety. The *Inquirer* wrote on July 23, 1893:

> Although there have been no fatal accidents as yet, and al-
> though the beach is safer than ever before, the lifeguards have
> adopted extra precautions to prevent fatalities, and have received
> orders to arrest all persons who attempt to venture out to sea
> beyond the line of their boats. This is a very wise move, as fully
> 50 per cent of the drowning cases of past seasons have resulted
> from persons getting out to sea so far that they had no strength
> left with which to return.

How could it be known that "50 per cent" died in such a way? Moreover, by July 23 the summer was half over, yet no one had drowned
with the relatively lax policy. This was something more than simple
prudence.

The fact is that the crowds who came to the resort viewed the ocean
as an alien realm. Dealing with Nature was traumatic for the culture
unless it could dominate it, and the lifeguard service symbolically
dominated the ocean. Consequently, the *Inquirer* faithfully reported
the many thrilling rescues at Atlantic City, sometimes offering them as
front-page news. At the conclusion of the 1896 season, it exclaimed:
"There were upwards of three hundred rescues, many of them of a
dangerous and sensational character, made during the season now
ending, while but three drownings occurred, and in neither of these
could any blame attach to the guards." There were another three
hundred rescues recorded for 1899 (one suspects journalistic use of

round numbers) with only one drowning "during the bathing hours," and even this fatality was attributable to heart disease.

Whatever danger existed in ocean bathing was magnified by popular concern with the perils of the deep and the inclination of some to trade on that concern for public notice. Widespread interest in stories of lifesaving and the press's willingness to serve that interest had an unexpected circular effect. The *Inquirer* rather incongruously complained that "at least one-half of the rescues reported are caused by the desire of the rescued to gain a bit of cheap notoriety." It was only necessary for the publicity-conscious to flounder a bit, be retrieved, and "have the satisfaction of seeing their names in print the following day as the hero or heroine of a 'thrilling rescue.'" The city authorities were so concerned about bad advertising for their town from this cause that they contemplated an ordinance to prohibit reckless bathing, as if vanity could be made illegal.

The lifeguards' job was further complicated by the seamy tactics of barkers for rental bathing suits in the lower Boardwalk excursion area, who corralled drunken promenaders (of which there was a generous supply) into hiring suits. A skinful of booze is a bad preparation for the surf. Whatever gales prevailed externally, the internal seas were running higher still for these unfortunates, and they soon had to be plucked from the billows. The captain of the Beach Patrol, commenting on the lower Boardwalk, told the *Inquirer* in 1895 "that a majority of the rescues made by the guards stationed in that section of the city are made necessary by the fact that many of the bathers are under the influence of liquor." Human irresponsibility and incompetence did much to create the need for scrupulous supervision of bathers.

The lionization of the lifeguard service was the product not so much of the real danger inherent in the Jersey coast as of the symbolic role the service filled. At bottom, the culture wanted 100 percent protection against Nature. Man was to act on Nature; Nature was to be prevented from acting on man. The Machine—whether it was a mechanical object or an organization of humans—was man's device to effect the inequality. And the totally efficient lifeguard service— sealing off the visitor from natural danger, protecting him from his own ineptitude—reflected the wishes of the culture. To remind the public constantly of its existence was to repeat the litany of Victorian America: Nature was to be sentimentalized as an abstraction, but subjugated as a fact.

The popular tradition of Nature as a healthful refuge from the debilitating City was of great service to Atlantic City. Anyone who has experienced July in Philadelphia will appreciate the powerful attraction of an oasis for sufferers from "the dust and heat of the city, the unclouded suns and red moons, the hot winds of morning, noon, and night." English's history of the resort begins with a poem:

> *The panting City cried to the Sea,*
> *"I am faint with heat; O, breathe on me!"*
> *So, to the City, hot with flame*
> *Of the pitiless sun, the east wind came.*
> *It came from the heaving breast of the deep,*
> *Silent as dreams are, and sudden sleep.*

A Children's Sea-Shore House was opened in 1872 for invalid children suffering from noncontagious diseases or "debility incident to the hot weather and a crowded city." The Mercer Memorial Home began in 1884 to admit women "of moderate means" who could demonstrate that they were sick and of good character: "It meets a want which has often been felt by those who come in contact with the masses of workingmen in our large cities." Atlantic City, which Heston claimed had the lowest death rate of any city in the country in 1887, promoted itself with the slogan "For Health and Pleasure."

The summer heat of inland cities was not the only stimulus to the resort's health trade. Promoters of Atlantic City somewhat cynically exploited public faith in the healing powers of Nature. A commerce in invalids was invaluable as a means of maintaining local business at a survival level during the slack off season, which amounted to two thirds of the year. Thus the city repeatedly puffed itself as "the only place on the coast which is visited all the year round by health-seekers." A home-town doctor, Boardman Reed, composed a paper on the salutary effects of the resort's climate, which was disseminated in a thera-peutic spirit by local interests. The railroads distributed a number of like publications conveying the same message in different variations. A choice comment in *The New York Times* in 1878 illuminates how the medical profession, the railroads, and the resort achieved a common understanding:

> *The Winters are extremely mild, so much so that Philadelphia*
> *and Baltimore physicians have taken of late to sending patients*
> *with pulmonary complaints to these shores for the Winter months,*
> *instead of to the South. It may not be a coincidence, but I am*
> *told also, on excellent authority, not in this connection of course,*
> *but merely as an instance of the liberality of the Atlantic City*
> *railroad people, that every physician in the cities named is pro-*
> *vided annually with free passes by both competing railroads.*

Undoubtedly, fresh air, sunshine, and clean water did have real value for dwellers of dark, dirty, and crowded slums in Philadelphia and other cities. Still, the health claims made for the resort were marked by extravagance·and a convenient lack of clarity as to how cures were effected. Hall assured his readers that Atlantic City would benefit victims of consumption, catarrh, asthma, hay fever, rheumatism, chronic malaria, nervous disorders, sickliness in children, anemia and "impoverished blood," heart diseases, cardiac dropsy, bronchitis, emphysema, colds, laryngitis, pneumonia, Bright's disease, diabetes, eczema, skin troubles, digestive disorders, neurasthenia, mania, and insanity. The Camden and Atlantic Railroad advised that "little is known of the modus operandi of nature's healing process, but certain it is that many forms of phthisis, bronchitis, erysipelas, dyspepsia, valvular heart complaints, and febrile affections are mitigated and often cured by brief sojourns in this pleasant city by the sea."

Much was written of the "ozone" in Atlantic City's air, and its health benefits. "Bertha on the Board-Walk" expressed one author's reservations about this mysterious gas:

> Best of all Bertha notes the salty smell of the sea ozone, and as her train races across the meadows she opens her car window still more to breathe it in deliciously. Really it is the combined smell of rotting seaweed, derelict oyster-shells, and other marine flora, but why tell Bertha so? What's the use in letting her know that even the sea ozone is bunk? She's going to be bunked very steadily anyway during the next ten days in almost everything else.

A Pennsylvania Railroad pamphlet of 1889 credited the town's salubrity to the purity and dryness of the atmosphere, the influence of the Gulf Stream on the climate, and the mild winters. It imagined the seaside atmosphere to be magically tonic: "[The air] is light and buoyant in effect, and as it inflates the lungs of one who experiences it for the first time, the result is akin to that which would be produced by the drinking of a beaker of effervescent wine."

Though the results of marine therapy were extensive, the causes were mysterious. English was sure that "with but few exceptions all the diseases that flesh is heir to, yield to these saline effects and this particular climate." A brochure for the Marlborough-Blenheim Hotel was lyrical in its enthusiasm:

> There is here constantly an unseen, indescribable something, in the air or in the sea, on the sands or in the stream of ever-changing life, which acts as a tonic, invigorating alike to the old and to the young, to the feeble and to the strong, which robs idleness of its ennui and makes it rest indeed.

Seaside healing, obscure but potent, must have aroused poignant hopes in troubled parents, particularly when they read claims such as this:

> *The little invalid must not be forgotten. During the heated term the beach is a grand baby show. Here is the healthy, happy baby sent from the city to escape the heat and its attending dangers, and there is a poor little sufferer, far advanced in marasmus; and as a rule both are benefited. Between these two extremes are many children more or less delicate, with pale faces and thin bodies. They have had all the diseases that childhood is supposed to be heir to; or have grown too rapidly at a fearful cost to their animal economy. A few weeks in Atlantic City will change all this, and the little invalid will become a healthy, rosy-cheeked child. This is not a miracle, it is simply a natural result.*

By its vagueness, health advertising for Atlantic City traded on the culture's respect for the "healthiness" of Nature and its therapeutic value for the "unnatural" City. The tangible advantages which the resort might have to offer an invalid were greatly expanded with assurances of the intangible superiority of a "natural" environment. Everyone, not just the sick, could find the promised wholesomeness of a seaside visit an added reason for going to Atlantic City.

Besides sanctifying an urban resort with the healthy blush of Nature, nature rhetoric legitimized the urban experience. Leo Marx's study of anti-urban feeling applied largely to artistic and intellectual minorities in nineteenth-century America. The culture as a whole took pleasure in the City and had few qualms about the use of the Machine on Nature. Nevertheless, a sufficient remnant of the pastoral tradition did persist in popular thought, and necessitated the use of nature rhetoric as a means of ratifying the urban preference. Psychologically reassured by nature rhetoric, the culture went its way, creating and enjoying the City. Among aesthetes and philosophers, nature rhetoric expressed a view of the utopian society, the Garden, to which many of the intellectual elite wished to return. But the masses of Americans had no desire to recover the Garden. For them, nature rhetoric was a kind of mental ballast, a homage to tradition, serenity, and order, which did not prevent them from zestfully pursuing the extant life of the urban world. Victorian reverence for Nature does not involve rejection of the City, any more than the motto "In God We Trust" on our coins today involves cancellation of professional football games on Sunday. One in fact supports the other.

Nature rhetoric legitimized the City in terms of three ideals: order, space, and morality. Atlantic City was garish, noisy, crowded. The sentimental poetry, etchings, and prose which burbled about the sea and the untrodden shore, the eternal ebb and flow of the ocean, the hand of the Creator in the mighty deep, and suchlike themes, conveyed a sense of order and quietude which in fact did not exist at the resort, and would have driven customers away if it did. Yet the pastoral tradition exalted the serenity of Nature as superior to the clatter of the City. The crowds who came to the resort had fathers or grandfathers who had lived close to the soil themselves, and immigrants among the crowds had come to the New World from the peasant villages of Europe. Pastoralism was a memory—recent for some, distant for others —of a life which seemed romantic. Men had rejected that life, or had been forced to reject it, but time and the certainty that there was no going back made a comfortable sentimentality possible. Nature rhetoric expressed the peace, organic rhythms, and simplicity which the pastoral tradition recommended to urban folk. Nature rhetoric met the needs of pastoral memory in the culture, allowing its members to pursue the urban ways that they preferred.

Heston's handbook of 1888 has two exquisitely contradictory passages:

> The solid character of its patrons from the better elements of society, the quiet, homelike aspect of the place, the natural scenery and charms peculiar to itself, conspire to make Atlantic City the very ideal of a summer resort. Art and design have added to its attractions, beautifying it with broad avenues, with walks bordered with trees, and with gardens whose fragrance unites with the cool breeze of the ocean to delight and refresh those who seek rest and recreation at the seashore. . . .
>
> There is no monotony on the island, or if there is it keeps itself carefully concealed in some of the hotels that never advertise. There are all sorts of architecture, all sorts of life, and all sorts of people in the place—high-toned, low-toned, betwixt-and-between, fair to middling, half-and-half, black and white, old gold, turkey red, and chrome yellow. If you don't see what you want, it is because you haven't asked for it.

The first passage assures the potential visitor to Atlantic City (and the author himself) that the resort is a safe place for respectable guests. It then identifies "respectability" in resorts with calm, describing the serene aspect of this "very ideal of a summer resort." The passage is at an emotionally low level, and suggests a feeling of restraint, of disciplined order. The strategy of the passage is to promote the resort *negatively*, as a place where there is *less* of life to contend with than one usually meets. Life in Atlantic City is life minus problems, distractions, and unpleasant people. The resort is pictured largely in pastoral terms: "quiet," "homelike," "natural scenery," "trees," "gardens," "fragrance," "cool breeze," "ocean," "rest." True, there are "art and design," but they merely have made the Wilderness into the

Garden, not the City. This is the utopian situation, wherein the Machine has tilled Nature only to the desired pastoral condition. A stable paradise has been achieved.

The second passage is separated by twenty-five pages from the first, a distance sufficient to prevent the author and most readers from stumbling upon a comparison. This time the appeal is not to the pastoral tradition but to the contemporary love of dynamic city life. The prose allures the visitor with the excitement and variety of a great resort. Emotionally at a high level, the passage jettisons restraint in an outflow of feeling. In the city anything goes: "If you don't see what you want, it is because you haven't asked for it." The strategy is to promote the resort *positively*, as a place where there is *more* of life to revel in than one usually meets. The pastoral imagery is gone in favor of words and phrases suggestive of activity and excitement: "no monotony," "all sorts," "life," "people," "turkey red," "chrome yellow." Repetition of elements in the passage gives it cadence, contributing to its energetic emotional state. Thus it differs from the balanced phrases of the first passage, which suggest quiet. An artist would have made the contrast clearer; nevertheless, the different functions of the two passages are successfully achieved. The urban rhetoric expresses reality, the natural rhetoric respects tradition.

An amplified selection from the Pennsylvania Railroad's "Message from the Sea" pamphlet highlights this popular conception of Nature's comforting orderliness:

> In a concise form [in this pamphlet] he will find answered the questions, how to get there, how to go when the time comes; when the dust and heat of the city, the unclouded suns and red moons, the hot winds of morning, noon, and night, prompt a longing to shuffle off time and its concerns,—to forget who is president and who is governor, what race he belongs to, what language he speaks,—and to listen to the great liquid metronome as it beats its solemn measure, steadily singing when the solo or duet of human life began, and to swing just as steadily after the human chorus has died out, and man is a fossil on its shores.

In addition to order, Nature meant space. It appears that the susceptibility of an object to sentimentalization varies inversely with the distance in time or space of the object from the observer. Hence the sea is more likely to be sentimentalized than the land. Victorian man shaped the land to his needs, but he did not shape the sea. The land bore evidence of generations of activity, a visible testimony to its accessibility. Man used the sea, but it retained its primeval form. Thus it conveyed an impression of being more distant, timeless, and unchangeable. In the late nineteenth century, when the Machine was rapidly rendering the existence of the Garden problematic, when parts of eastern America were becoming as industrially desolate as the valleys of southern Wales, the sea provided a handy substitute for open land in the popular imagination. In Atlantic City, the Machine, having conquered the land, came to a halt only at the water's edge, the boundary of a new imaginative Garden. Even here it would scarcely rest content, but darted out piers over the water as if to conquer and urbanize the sea itself. The ocean provided psychological wide-open spaces for the urban masses, to whom the Western frontier (in truth, already vanished) had no relevance. For the crowds of Philadelphia and the smaller cities of the East, the ocean wilderness became the frontier. The popular literature intoned the pastoral ideal in a marine idiom, while the business of city living and city building continued apace.

Nature rhetoric also legitimized the City in terms of morality. To put it in crudest form, the unconscious message of resort literature said: "The sea is calm; let's join the clatter of the city. The sea is pure; let's have a hot time in town." The latter contradiction is also evident in the two passages juxtaposed above, as witness: "The solid character of its patrons from the better elements of society"; and "If you don't see what you want, it is because you haven't asked for it." The possibility of immorality is implicit in the "disorder" of urban life. City life is "disorderly" in village terms, for the close and often constricting mutual supervision of small communities is lacking. People can do what they really want, for better or for worse. Order and morality are thus closely related, so it is not surprising to see nature rhetoric in the service of both. Prose, poetry, and illustration expressing natural order encouraged the illusion of personal discipline. Victorians, while they desired pleasure, feared the relaxation of discipline. The order of the sea provided a sanctifying backdrop for the inviting disorder of the city, and the purity attributed to the sea sanctified pleasure which otherwise would have aroused guilt for breach of discipline. Discipline and pleasure could coexist.

The moral legitimation of seaside pleasure is typified in the following selection, a poem written in 1906 by a local poet:

> *The sea to our ills serves as balm and as lotion,*
> *   'Mong its buffeting waves from our cares we are free.*
> *Each day we return with a zealot's devotion*
> *   To kneel at the shrine of the god of the sea,*
> *And bow to the charms—'tis a pleasure and duty—*
> *   To the half-hidden charms of America's girls;*
> *One feels as he looks on their grace and their beauty,*
> *   The blue sea is showing its loveliest pearls.*

In eight lines of this omnibus effort, the author expresses order, piety, patriotism—and lechery.

The mermaid is interesting in this connection. In Heston's handbook for 1894 there is an innocuous tale of a mermaid and a fisherman, supposedly of local origin. The fisherman is lured to his death by this siren, leaving his devoted wife and family: "His soul, like a bark with rudder lost, / On passion's changeful tide was tossed." This uplifting morality tale is accompanied by an illustration of the mermaid, done in the lewdly blatant style of some of the sleazier romantic art of the period. Mermaids of a similarly generous breast development appear on the title page of a photograph album promoting the resort, so the incident is not isolated. At any rate, it is a surprising illustration for a Heston handbook, the Holy Bible of the Family Resort, since it is certainly the zippiest page in what is otherwise a rather sober effort. And Heston must have known he had a good thing, because he reprinted it in the edition of another year. The slender morality tale is just a gloss, as are the mermaidenly trappings of the girl. What we have is a strapping Victorian wench stark naked from the waist up. But bare breasts are fine on a mermaid: "The salt water washes away all impropriety." For Victorian Americans, the City symbolized pleasure, not excluding illicit pleasure. Nature symbolized purity and chaste amusements, amusements socially sanctioned but pallid compared to the high times associated with the City. The mermaid provided a nexus between pleasure and chastity. Obviously sensual, her sensuality nevertheless was innocent. Nature conferred her innocence, rendering the mermaid "naturally" and "innocently" sensuous. Victorian Americans sentimentalized the sea and ascribed to it an intangible purity. The fact that water can wash away dirt was abstracted to a moral analogue, whereby the sea purified pleasure. If the mermaid walked the Boardwalk she would be a strumpet, but invested with the purity of the sea, she was fit material for a family guidebook.

Urban in reality, Atlantic City surrounded itself with the aura of Nature. In so doing, it reconciled disparate needs of the culture. Urban variety and excitement attracted more visitors than pastoral order and serenity, but both had to be served. Urban pleasure drew more patrons than natural purity and personal discipline, yet each had to be secured. Though the City better suited the activities of Americans, Nature had its functions to perform. The visitor to the City by the Sea, assured that the sea conferred its wholesome benefits, turned to the city for action.

7

"Fallen Lady"

SEVERAL of the most important attributes of Atlantic City during the 1890's continued to characterize the resort in the twentieth century. Yet by the 1970's the City by the Sea could no longer be called the national resort by any but the most fervent loyalists. This concluding chapter departs from the framework of the 1890's to consider the nature and reality of Atlantic City's "decline," drawing freely on data since the turn of the century.

By the late 1960's a number of grim statistics delineated the plight of a community whose urban problems, normal for an American city at this point in history, were compounded by its resort economy. Atlantic City had stopped growing and had begun to lose population, each successive census marking the ebbing of urban vitality:

1940....64,094	1960....59,544
1950....61,657	1970....47,859

From 1960 to 1970 net outward migration amounted to 10,580 persons, of whom 8,258 were white and 2,322 black. Thus, since the city lost nearly one third of its white population in that decade, the black population comprised 45 percent of the total in 1970. The resort contained more than half the population of Atlantic County in 1940, and just over one quarter thirty years later. *Newsweek* claimed that the resort had the second-oldest population in the country, after St. Petersburg, Florida; one fourth of the permanent residents were over sixty years of age.

In 1965, 91 percent of the housing had been built before 1939. An investigation of poverty in the resort during 1965 disclosed that, according to a dozen different measurements, "Atlantic City is the poorest city in New Jersey." *Survey* magazine remarked in 1912 how tuberculosis-free the resort was, which is considered surprising in light of the poor housing for blacks. At that time, the city had the lowest infant mortality rate in New Jersey. But in 1965 Atlantic City

ranked first in the state in the incidence of tuberculosis and pneumonia deaths, and, compared with cities of its size, first in syphilis. Due to the seasonal fluctuation of jobs, unemployment rose from 4 percent to 15 percent for nearly nine months a year. One third of the permanent population received welfare assistance. The Federal Bureau of Investigation's Uniform Crime Report, released in August 1972, added to this gloomy portrait. Among 528 American cities in the 25,000 to 50,000 population group, Atlantic City had the highest total number of crimes in seven standard categories. This was due to the extraordinary number of thefts, which the resort's chief of police attributed to the difficulty of providing security in hotels and motels during the summer season.

Still, most of these statistics demonstrate depressed conditions for natives of the town, but do not necessarily show that the resort, as a resort, had grown threadbare by 1970. But such was the widely held view. "In Search of Marvin Gardens," an article appearing in *The New Yorker* in 1972, took a forlorn shuffle through the littered back alleys of the town. The motion picture *King of Marvin Gardens*, released in the same year, was pervaded by the mood of a late afternoon in winter, as it traced the collapse of a euphoric young man's world of illusion amid the peeling paint and rusty fixtures of a Boardwalk hotel. *Philadelphia Magazine*, whose literary niche might be described as muckraker-chic, reported that prostitution was rampant, the city government corrupt, and organized crime flourishing. Although this, as we have seen, is not much different from the old days, the magazine added that night clubs could draw only third-rate performers. One informant claimed: "The proof of the pudding about what's happening to this town . . . is that it can no longer support a first-rate night club, winter *or* summer."

One couple attending a librarians' conference in 1969 warned fellow professionals against eating in the hotel dining rooms, which were "like the trains of the past just before the end of the posh dining cars": "The tarnished elegance is there, the service is supposedly there, but the soul is gone, and the prices remain high." The great hotels had fallen on evil times. The Ambassador, built in 1929 at a cost of nearly eight million dollars, was sold at a federal bankruptcy court auction in 1970 for only two million. It had been closed since 1966, standing beside the Boardwalk as "a tomblike symbol of the whole city's dimming luster." In a mighty blast of masonry, the elegant but insolvent Traymore Hotel settled to the ground in May 1972, demolished despite its landmark status.

Beyond the bare facts of hard times in the resort, a remarkable

myth about the city took shape in the late 1960's. It held that Atlantic City was once a showcase of elegance, a playground of the cream of society, which lost its upper-class clientele and turned into a commercialized proletarian bazaar.

A *New York Times* article, reporting Atlantic City's celebration of the hundredth anniversary of the Boardwalk, was quite explicit: "The sedate, uppercrust promenade of 1870 . . . has become the Great Wood Way, parade site, convention favorite, and the clientele has . . . well, changed." The city has developed into a "peculiar admixture of crass vulgarity, rampant commercialism and vestigial gentility," crowded with old people, teenagers, blacks, and blue-collar families. There is a striking contrast between Boardwalk sleaziness and hotel-row opulence: "It is a barely believable experience to walk a few steps from pinball machines and foot-long hot dogs and step into the vast Turkish-carpeted silences of the Marlborough-Blenheim." These "islands of posh living" constitute "a cabin-class corner on a ship that has become all-tourist." Similarly, *Philadelphia Magazine*, claiming that "Atlantic City is living off its reputation," said that the Boardwalk had "turned" into a schlock strip of auction houses, shoddy souvenir shops, Nathan's

A LOWER
BOARDWALK FAIRY

hot dog and Gino's hamburger stands. *TV Guide* offered what it believed to be a nutshell history of resort "decline": "Fifty years ago, Atlantic City was not the proletarian playground you see today. Rich Philadelphians and New Yorkers strolled the Boardwalk in tuxedos and ball gowns or had themselves pushed about in rolling chairs." And finally, *Newsweek* spoke of the vanished "blue bloods" and the "genteel

upper class" of the "turn of the century" who disappeared "during the '30's and '40's."

The general tendency of popular explanations for Atlantic City's supposed decline was to see the resort's current situation as its own fault. Somehow, the town had ceased doing something which once made it successful, or had begun doing something which ended its success. As a result, commercialization displaced refinement, and the vulgar crowd squeezed out the gentry.

Philadelphia Magazine's revelations of corruption in the city government certainly have nothing of historical novelty about them. As we have seen, the roots of official corruption were visible at least as early as 1891. In the twentieth century, the peculiarly advantageous resort climate brought forth plant, flower, and fruit—and it proved to be a bumper crop. Louis Kuehnle, whom we met in Chapter 5 during the 1908 crisis, was imprisoned in 1911 for an interest in city contracts that proved to be more pragmatic than civic. The administrations of Mayors William Riddle (1912–16), Edward L. Bader (1920–27), and Anthony M. Ruffu, Jr. (1927–30), were particularly stormy. Other highlights of the resort's criminal history include the granting of one hundred and fifty indictments by a county grand jury in 1922 against operators of vice establishments, and the suspension of the entire city vice squad in 1930 for alleged complicity with rum runners.

Kuehnle's colorful successor was Enoch L. ("Nucky") Johnson, who ruled the city and county as Republican party boss and County Treasurer from 1911 to 1941. He profited immensely during Prohibition by shielding bootleggers and speakeasy proprietors, and after repeal forged a handsome new income from protection of numbers, horse-race betting, and prostitution. Commanding the black vote of the city, he remained untouchable in office, and it was not until the beginning of the Second World War that the federal government was able to convict him and forty associates for income-tax evasion. So tight a hold did Johnson have on the town that agents were forced to turn to such esoteric investigating techniques as counting the number of towels sent by the various brothels to the laundries to determine what amount of taxes were being evaded.

After Johnson departed the scene, Frank "Hap" Farley took over as county political boss and strong man of the Republicans. *Philadelphia Magazine* ran an exposé of him in 1971, accusing him of casual manipulation of public resources for personal benefit, sinister friendships with organized crime, and squalid administration of law enforcement. In November of the same year, he was defeated for

reelection to the State Senate, but his legacy promised to survive. In the spring of 1972, Mayor William T. Somers, former Mayor Richard S. Jackson, and City Commissioners Karlos P. LaSane and Arthur W. Ponzio were indicted for extortion in the granting of city contracts. Prior to winning the mayoralty race in 1969, Somers had worked for seventeen years in the office of the Atlantic County Treasurer (i.e., Farley), and Jackson was a Farley adviser.

More interesting, perhaps, than the careers of successive Babylonians at the seaside are Atlantic City's continuing efforts to be a national resort and the lasting conflict between its different faces as the archetypal American Pleasure Resort and Family Resort. It will be remembered that the city named its streets after the various states to promote its national aspirations at the time of its founding. "Monopoly," which became probably the most successful commercially designed board game in twentieth-century America, very suitably took its "properties" from the street names of the resort. In like manner, the great amusement entrepreneur John Lake Young built a home for himself in 1908 on the Million Dollar Pier and called it "No. 1 Atlantic Ocean." This proved a neat publicity gimmick, his address becoming so well known that the post office would deliver mail so designated.

The resort had many slogans expressing its hoped-for cultural representativeness, such as: "The Boardwalk of Atlantic City is THE Promenade of America," "Mecca for Millions," and "The world's playground welcomes you all the time." In 1926 the President Hotel was completed at a cost of five million dollars. It had a top-floor "Presidential Suite," which, so the scheme went, was to become the summer White House for the nation's chief executives. Calvin Coolidge was invited to be the first promotional patsy, but that dour and narrowly honest man declined the role, and the booster's dream bubble burst. Fantasies sprang eternal in the civic breast, and the ultimate was Atlantic City's invitation in 1946 to the United Nations to make its headquarters there. The prospectus unblushingly suggested that the resort is "located on what might well be considered an international island five miles from the mainland," and the city offered to make the one-thousand-room Chalfonte–Haddon Hall available "on satisfactory terms."

In gesture or in promise, the Family Resort bestrode the decades. "Decency" legislation was a lively fact of resort government in the post-Victorian period, as the city fathers clumsily sought to shield respectable families from corrupting displays of nudity. The celebrated "mackintosh law" of 1907, forbidding the wearing of bathing suits

without a coverall on the boardwalk, became a perennial gesture of tokenism in moral enforcement. The taboos of the Gilded Age died hard, as evidenced by a note in *The Rotarian* for 1936, advising conventioneers that women were now allowed to play golf in shorts. Together with such gestures of propriety went ongoing proclamations of Atlantic City as the Family Resort. In 1930 the reformist Mayor Harry Bacharach sought to refurbish the city's image:

> *I want to restore confidence that apparently has been considerably shaken, if not lost. It is not only our purpose to obtain patronage of a high type for short stays, but also to attract the family trade that formerly came here in large numbers.*

In 1941, in a public address in the arch-respectable *Christian Science Monitor*, Mayor Thomas D. Taggart, Jr., attempted to renew confidence once more: "This new government is pledged to provide refined wholesome relaxation and entertainment throughout the year." And in 1946 the prospectus to the United Nations encouraging it to locate on Absecon Island breezily claimed that the resort was "a city with an historically non-controversial background," a claim valid only in the realm of foreign relations. As headquarters of the U.N., what a mecca for schoolchildren Atlantic City would have been!

Of all the curiously proportioned progeny of the booster's devious loins, one of the most curious and indisputably the most successful has been the Miss America Pageant. Creature of the resort's philosophy, it became in turn the single most important manifestation of the resort to the country, and indeed to the world. Begun in 1921, it ran in its first series through 1927, when public criticism for various reasons forced its termination. It was revived temporarily in 1933, and permanently in a revised format in 1935. Adapting successfully to the changing media, an impressive accomplishment in itself, it continues today as one of the most popular television spectaculars.

At first, the idea was to bring winners of city beauty contests, sponsored by newspapers, to the resort to compete against each other. Fifty-seven cities were represented in the 1922 contest, and eighty in 1924. Atlantic City benefited by free publicity in communities throughout the country and by the national hoopla surrounding the grand finale, but more particularly, the contest brought tens of thousands of visitors to the resort in September, after the regular season had closed. Later the contest was reorganized by states, with city contests coordinated to produce state champions. The judges consisted largely of illustrators and popular painters, particularly those connected with magazines. (Norman Rockwell, destined to be the artist-laureate of the

lower middle class, helped judge the 1922 and 1923 contests, a fitting choice indeed.) While the Miss America Pageant produced a deficit from 1921 to 1927 amounting to $52,000, made up from contributions by the Chamber of Commerce, this was surely a trifling sum compared to the profits the contest made indirectly.

On the most basic level, the Pageant was a pleasure event, and although it belonged to a well-established trend in the culture, it had the nice timing to appear in a notably hedonistic decade. The *Atlantic City Daily Press* described the "Roller Chair Parade" of the second contest of 1922:

> *There were piquant jazz babies who shook the meanest kind of shoulders, pink-skinned beauties of all types who had come across the continent. . . . Tanned athletic girls, bare of limb, shapely of figure and wearing their abbreviated water togs gracefully, olive-hued and bejeweled favorites of the harem, stately colonial dames in hoop skirts, mandarin ladies, with black eyes peeping coyly from behind waving fans.*

Miss Trenton had the bad luck to be too late to enter the Pageant, but her float was a smash hit and took the prize. She was arrayed as the Queen of Sheba, borne on a golden elephant "drawn by four dusky slaves in typical costume, while two slave girls stood behind."

Besides the annual display of attractive bodies, the Pageant responded to the cultural desire for pleasure on a different level. The contest served as a vehicle for Hollywood, offering its entrants the possibility of stardom, and vicariously tantalizing spectators everywhere with daydreams of the high life which awaited one so lucky as to reach the screen. A Motion Picture Ball was held on the Steel Pier in 1922, and the Universal Film Company made test films of each entrant. That company, the Famous Players–Lasky Corporation, Florenz Ziegfeld, Lee Shubert, and the Arrow Film Company promised contracts to girls in the Pageant who had potential for stage and screen. The revived Pageant of 1936 continued in this mode, as one newspaper account shows: "To choose a girl who would 'click' in the movies, the Pageant Committee has said, was one of its aims. In that way, the spectacle may be built into a national institution, they hope." Some women objected to the connection between the contest and show business, such as a competitor in the 1925 edition, who claimed that she had been forced to sign a contract to appear in a motion picture if she won. For most, however, resisting Hollywood was furthest from their minds.

Miss America was sufficiently successful in the 1920's to arouse widespread criticism from those who were disturbed by the actual or imagined hedonism of the Pageant. The Trenton, New Jersey, Y.W.C.A.

worried about the "grave dangers from unscrupulous persons to which the girls were exposed":

> It was noticed by competent observers that the outlook in life of girls who participated was completely changed. Before the competition they were splendid examples of innocent and pure womanhood. Afterwards their heads were filled with vicious ideas.

Bishop William J. Hafey of Raleigh, North Carolina, roasted the Pageant for its "exploitation of feminine charm by money-mad men," and the Atlantic County Federation of Church Women and the Ocean City Camp Meeting Association were similarly aggrieved.

There was secular criticism, too. The *Philadelphia Bulletin* questioned the basic desirability of parading women for display and selection, as well as the "humbuggery" and general folly of the Pageant. The contest caused "mutterings and frownings in various cities of the country." Private judging of the girls in bathing suits was a principal sore point, but *The New York Times* damned the whole business as a "reprehensible way to advertise Atlantic City." A meeting of women from educational, religious, civic, and social organizations, held in Philadelphia in 1927, proclaimed a national campaign against the Pageant because it exploited young women for advertising purposes. Finally, the chairman of the judges of the 1923 contest, Penrhyn Stanlaws, was dismayed by the emphasis on body at the expense of intellect. At a time when a college-educated woman was a rarity, he maintained: "I have not seen one girl who is a real representative of the true American girl. There must be found some way to persuade the real American girl—the college type, for instance—to enter. . . ."

From the first, the promoters of Miss America, on the local level at least, had not been wholly unaware that the pleasure emphasis must be balanced by a certain amount of discipline. They tended to select girls with conservative hair styling who would not identify Miss America with flaming youth. Bobbed hair handicapped any entrant, for it was thought to be bold in tone, and judges were convinced that the traditional long hair of the Victorian woman was an essential part of "natural beauty." *The New York Times* discovered this bias as early as 1922. That year the directors of the Pageant were pleased to discover that fifty-five of fifty-seven entrants had unbobbed hair. Since these fifty-five had emerged from a national field of at least seven thousand contestants, the judges "came to the conclusion that the trend is back to normalcy insofar as the 'crowning glories' of the fair sex" were concerned. They also took courage from the fact that Margaret Gorman, winner of the 1921 Pageant, had long hair. But a disturbing inconsistency appeared. Of twenty local girls selected on the basis

of appearance to act as attendants to the court of "King Neptune" (part of the ballyhoo of the event), all but two had bobbed hair. Disturbed, the judges hurriedly inspected over a hundred photos of Atlantic City girls who were connected with the contest, and every one had short hair. The conclusion was inescapable that the selection of women to be sent to the national contest had been made with loaded dice.

But, if there had been some discipline to balance the pleasure, critical voices around the nation proved that there had not been enough. Promoters let the physical appeal of the competition speak for itself, and began to emphasize the "constructive" aspects of Miss America. In 1925 the resort's *Daily Press* declared "every vestige of the objectionable removed": "This year the carnival will be on a higher plane than ever, and its fair participants will represent pastors' daughters, school teachers, college girls and femininity generally of the most desirable type." Lois Delandor, the 1927 winner, had unbobbed hair, did not smoke, did not drink tea or coffee, did not eat pickles, and won on her parents' twentieth wedding anniversary. In 1928, in an unsuccessful attempt to keep the Pageant going, the Chamber of Commerce went so far as to eliminate the swimsuit judging altogether.

When Miss America was revived in 1935, promoters added new reforms to insulate the contest against criticism. Now sensuality would have to be justified by "talent," which each contestant would be required to demonstrate on the stage.

> [*The title*] *will be a bit more valuable, perhaps, this year, because with good looks will go exceptional talent. And while in the past good looks usually sufficed to win both the coveted trophy and perhaps a stage and screen career, this time there will be no "beautiful but dumb" Dora in a carload of young and vivacious womanhood.*

Judging henceforth was done according to an exact scheme, with beauty of face counting 25 percent, figure 25 percent, talent 25 percent, personality 15 percent, and grace of carriage 10 percent. While this 25 percent concession to the demands of female intellectuality meant singing and dancing rather than, say, organic chemistry, it was a guise sufficient to enable Mayor Charles D. White to boast at the 1936 opening ceremonies that the resort esteemed the pleasures of the mind: "We are past the time when beauty parades are in the nature of floor shows. . . . This is a cultural event seeking a high type of beauty. Atlantic City has a keen interest in the way of art, beauty and culture." This was the right note at last, and the contest was further polished in 1938 by forbidding the women to have any contact with males during the Pageant. By 1969 the annual contest

was "indeed ascetic," with official female chaperones, roommates, and hostesses. Even fathers were not allowed to meet their daughters during the event.

The struggle to be the national resort, the conflict between pleasure and discipline, corruption—these continued to characterize Atlantic City year after year, into the 1970's. It was not in these areas that major changes occurred, but in the Machine, which in turn tapped the vein of pastoral sentimentalism so destructive to the City. Ultimately, changing modes of transportation practically destroyed the resort's ability to attract patronage across class lines, threatened the physical appearance of the city, and sapped the illusion-creating potential the town once had so vigorously exploited. Atlantic City did not "fall"— it was abandoned. It persevered in formulas which had been highly successful, but though a large part of its patronage continued to respond eagerly to what it offered, an important minority left it behind, to return no more.

So long as railroad travel remained the major form of transportation, the sentiment surrounding Nature was an innocuous and even useful cultural strain, of benefit to a seaside resort which sold its urban pleasures amid reassuring, if specious, rural harmonies. Railroad travel provided the centralizing force necessary to a pleasure city, bringing hundreds of thousands of customers to a small area in which the lavish variety and excitement of concentration could profitably exist.

The ultimate in railroad transportation seemed to be at hand when the *Philadelphia Inquirer* announced in July 1900 that Lina Beecher and his American Railway Company (encountered in Chapter 3 as builders of Flip Flap amusement rides) planned to construct a spectacular monorail between Philadelphia and Atlantic City. This extraordinary innovation would reduce travel time to thirty minutes for "at least a hundred trains a day" which would scorch across the route. An illustration of the projected appearance of the train was worthy of a design prospectus for a federal railroad resuscitation scheme of the 1970's. Features included a Buck Rogers–style torpedo-shaped lead car to minimize wind resistance, an electric motor for each unit, aluminum construction, practically noiseless operation, and magnetic brakes to stop the train in three lengths at full speed. The cars would travel over a single elevated rail, with two side rails for stability and power transmission, and all weight would be placed in the center. Alas for a vain fantasy, the line was never built, but slipped into the graveyard of visionary railroad schemes which was to become so populous in the latter part of the twentieth century.

HALF AN HOUR IT WILL TAKE
TO REACH ATLANTIC CITY

New System of Transit Promised by Combination of Capitalists by Which Philadelphians May Be Whirled to the Sea in Thirty Minutes

A Car on the Proposed Single Rail Road to Atlantic City

A foreshadowing of the true course of resort transportation appeared in the *Inquirer* only thirteen days after the unveiling of Beecher's monorail. On June 29, 1900, the week-old Philadelphia Locomobile Club assembled its vehicles amid a great crowd of spectators at its headquarters on North Broad Street and wheezed away on a pioneer run to Atlantic City (using the Camden ferry). Six and a half hours later the expedition reached the resort, "slight accidents and delays for refreshments" having slowed its progress. At first a curiosity, motor vehicles steadily increased in popularity, infringing on the railroads' monopoly to the Jersey shore.

From 1896 through the 1920's, the only unimpeded access to Atlantic City was by means of a railroad bridge across the Delaware River just north of Camden, preserving a sizable competitive edge for train service in the face of rapidly increasingly automobile travel. But in 1926 the first automobile bridge was opened, bringing a sudden flood of buses and cars to Atlantic City. The Reading Railroad, seeing the handwriting on the wall, strove desperately to retard fate by issuing an ultimatum to Atlantic City. The Reading's president threatened to cut back service and cancel plans for a new terminal if the resort did not restrict bus service. Some in the city relished the suppliance of the once-mighty railroad. A local newspaper dryly replied: "If the railways enforce the ultimatum a long guess would be that somebody, somehow, will provide the service the railways refuse."

The end was not yet for the transportation medium which had given birth to the resort, but it was a matter of time. The New Jersey Turnpike and the Garden State Parkway, as well as better roads from Philadelphia, changed travel habits and also made the resort as much an outpost of New York City as of Philadelphia. The crowds that came by bus and private car brought plenty of money with them, but there was an important difference. It did not go to the hotels, and hotels were the glory of the Boardwalk. Hotels had framed the Boardwalk on the landward side, creating a stage setting for the hordes of visitors, tempting them with the heights of success which it seemed American life could offer. One did not have to be able to afford them; it was a vicarious thrill to promenade past them and to bask in the opulent aura which they engendered. When they faltered, when they were emptied, when at last they began to be pulled down, they left a vacancy as jarring as missing teeth in a beautiful woman. The more widely spaced motels which took their place sold comfort and contemporaneity, but it was not the same. They could offer the good life to the passing stroller, but they could not lift his fantasies. They told the onlooker that the sky was no longer the limit: it was more often only two stories from the ground.

The creation of suburbia was the great manifestation of an unleashed pastoral impulse. During the 1890's, Nature had largely been confined to rhetoric in the resort, and transportation had contained the centrifugal impulse which pursuit of Nature entailed. The flourishing of urban life involved a definite constraint; namely, that individuals would have to be compelled (in this case by available transportation) to live and to take their pleasure in clusters on the landscape. The genuine pleasure which Americans took in their cities was at odds with their continued sentimentalization of Nature. Nothing guaranteed that the opposing forces should stay in balance, and indeed, the evolution of transportation tipped the scale fatally. Thanks to the automobile, strip development soon blighted the Jersey coast.

The second blow came with the development of cheap, safe airplane travel. The emergence of the airplane as the most prestigious form of

the transportation machine meant that places reached by other means lost a good part of their luster, and Atlantic City, once the terminus of an exciting rail system, was just another highway resort. Now Miami Beach became available to the nouveaux bourgeois, and Europe to the upper middle class. Less sacrifice than was formerly necessary for a week on the Jersey shore took the urbanite to a distant land. And because the option of traveling infinitely further was available, the pastoral impulse made it necessary to go there. Places nearer at hand would no longer serve, if one had sufficient money to make a choice. What did it matter that Miami Beach was not the Wilderness? It was the flight to newness that counted. The Machine, once the ally of the City, now became its destroyer.

For Atlantic City, the pastoral impulse meant finally that, with air transportation, increased leisure, and higher incomes, the resort was too near Philadelphia to sustain a high popularity among people with choice. Given the recurrent American desire to escape urban life for the "Wilderness," there to ravage Nature and to re-create a City which in turn becomes unsatisfactory, there seems to be an ideal distance for a resort to lie from a center of population. In the late nineteenth century, Atlantic City was just the right distance from Philadelphia to be considered special. Gloucester, New Jersey, was too close to be regarded as more than an offscouring of the metropolis, a marginal dive suitable for the Sundays of the poor and oafish. Similarly, Atlantic City held itself superior to Coney Island, which was simply a commuter amusement park for New York City. Atlantic City was far enough away from Philadelphia to make going there a meaningful change, yet it was not too far away to serve as a vacation place for the lower middle class. Florida, for example, was too remote to fit the budgets and the week-long vacations or weekend jaunts of many. So the resort was happily placed for many decades, neither too near nor too far. The airplane destroyed this equilibrium.

It can be seen, if one looks closely, that Atlantic City carried the seeds of its own destruction. This is evident in the popularity of "foreignisms" at the end of the century. Dr. Boardman Reed, the booster-physician, in his promotional pamphlet issued by the Pennsylvania Railroad, "demonstrated" the superiority of Atlantic City to Florida, the western states, and Europe. Intended to glamorize the resort by association, this foreignism implied the superiority of the reference points. When the audience got enough money, time, and transportation, it would go to these distant places instead. On the Boardwalk in 1891 were four "Japanese" goods dealers and a seller

of "Turkish" goods, and "imported" goods of indeterminate ilk were
sold in many other stores. The "connoisseur," promised the Bureau of
Information in 1907, would be mightily attracted by the "rarest im-
portations" of "Armenia and Syria, China and Japan, Canada and
Mexico, Egypt and Turkey, India and Persia, Italy and Scandinavia,
Paris and London." Foreignisms prevailed in entertainment, too, such
as "The Venetian Lady Troubadours" at Guvernator's Mammoth
Pavilion, and the Kiramura Sisters, "Japanese Equilibrists," and the
Haidaboro Family, "Russian Peasant Dancers," both at the Steel Pier.
The Steel Pier had bands, like the "Royal Berlin Orchestra," which
performed selections such as "Turkish Patrol" and "The Wizard of the
Nile." In the "Egyptian tent" at the foot of South Carolina Avenue
could be seen a collection of artifacts and mummies, including the
remains of "King Tafnekt," "Princess Ransorma," and "Queen Tatet."

One of the jolliest purveyors of foreign hokum was the Japanese
Tea Gardens on the Boardwalk at Connecticut Avenue, a "delightful
patch of Orientalism" and a "Japanese Fairyland on a Mammoth
Scale." Anxious to accommodate itself to Occidental usage, the
Gardens offered "Japanese cake walks" and "Japanese Sacred Concerts"
for Sundays. The "Famous Neapolitan Band" was in attendance, too,
for the establishment was not culturally hidebound. Certain incidents
of general human interest, and with particular appeal to American
audiences, tended to occur at the Gardens from time to time, beginning
in August 1896:

> A tender little romance has blossomed amid the flowers and
> shade trees and oddly constructed buildings of the Japanese
> Village. Among the residents of this novel plot are Osaka Kingoro
> and Miss Yedo Nasan, both of whom came from the Flowery
> Kingdom several weeks ago to assist in illustrating the customs
> and manners of their native country. They had never met previous
> to their coming to Atlantic City and were introduced after arriv-
> ing at the Village. It was a case of love at first sight. They sought
> each other's company, and soon the attachment ripened into a
> tender affection which only the marriage bond can satisfy.
> One day this week they went to Manager Kushibiki and told
> him of their love, informing him that they intended to give up
> their engagement at the Village and return to their far-away home
> in Japan. Here was an unlooked-for predicament, but the almond-
> eyed manager was equal to the emergency and suggested that
> the wedding take place in the Village. He further agreed to defray
> all the expenses of the ceremony and to not only increase their
> salaries for the balance of the season, but to furnish the happy
> couple with transportation back to Japan in the fall. The offer
> was finally accepted, and according to the present program the
> happy event will be celebrated next Tuesday evening at 8:30

o'clock in the presence of the audience. Visitors to the Garden on Tuesday evening will, therefore, have the pleasure of witnessing the first simon-pure Japanese wedding ever occurring in this country.

Manager Kushibiki prudently advertised the forthcoming marriage in the issue of the *Inquirer* which reported the above.

"Matrimonial fever" again gripped the resort's Asians in August 1899, when two Japanese men were married to brides from Philadelphia and West Chester, Pennsylvania, in ceremonies publicly celebrated at the Gardens. The nuptials of Hano Sakuro of Nagoya and Maybelle Dion of Philadelphia a year later were "a wholly public affair, and as invitations had been sent to the hotels for distribution among guests there was a large crowd present." Atlantic City's visitors were also fortunate to witness the novel christening at the Gardens in 1898 of "a little follower of the Mikado," who was given the name "Taselyo Tokwai, which, translated into English, means Atlantic City." Thus did Nippon come to New Jersey.

The American preference for the "frontier," for the distant rather than the near at hand, was a pastoral impulse inimical to the city. Americans who had money would go as far as they could afford, and they would regard anything less as inferior. In the long run, Atlantic City was too near Philadelphia to fit the needs of the upper middle class. Even in Victorian days it suggested utopias beyond itself, in the foreignisms it peddled on the Boardwalk.

All the same, the option to pursue the "frontier" lay with those who had the necessary money. The nouveaux riches and the upper middle class left Atlantic City, but the lower middle class, who had been there all along, stayed behind. *The resort did not shift from one kind of patronage to another: part of its traditional patronage slipped away.* The lower middle class continued to crowd the Boardwalk, to favor the cheap amusement, food, and merchandise stores that had always lined the waterfront, and to fill the motels (which had replaced boardinghouses as well as hotels). But now they did not have the upper middle class and the occasional wealthy visitor to accompany them. Where once the resort had boasted of its mélange of affluent and humble in pursuit of pleasure, now there were only the humble. The possibilities for illusion further contracted.

Moreover, new faces were beginning to appear among the ranks of the lower middle class. Minorities such as the Jews had long been present, but now French Canadians arrived in large numbers, traveling south from Montreal. As a group, however, by far the most important newcomers were the blacks. In 1971, *The New York Times*

reported "scenes that would have surprised visitors a generation ago: blacks riding in motorized rolling chairs driven by whites, and sitting in cafes where they were once unwelcome." Blacks also thronged the weekend buses to the shore, taking over the excursion trade once the domain of the lower-middle-class white population of Philadelphia. Like the white urban masses of the turn of the century, they were eager for the good things of life which they believed were within their reach, and Atlantic City suited their means and taste.

The crowded, noisy, dirty, garish, and cheerfully vulgar resort of the 1970's still had marked similarities to the resort of the 1890's. It is ironic, nevertheless, that by honorably persevering in its traditional role for the urban lower middle class, Atlantic City had won the disdain of the more privileged. Confronted with a city which had remained relatively constant for a hundred years, upper-middle-class observers of the 1970's found it impossible to conceive that it expressed their predecessors' aspirations for utopia. Therefore, the city must have been different. It must have been a place of tasteful consumption and refined elegance. It was comfortable to forget the banal (if hearty) preferences of the upper middle class in Victorian society and to sneer at the tawdriness of Atlantic City. It was also comfortable to sneer at the contemporary nouveaux bourgeois who found the modern resort to their liking.

Some of this was simply racial feeling. It has been remarked that whites tend to see any sport as "ruined" once the blacks take it over, and the same is certainly true for resorts. As blacks reached toward upper-middle-class status they increasingly used Atlantic City as a transitional resort; but whites, who had passed through the process, looked down on the resort's new clientele. Yet the resort's visitors were still mostly white, so the change in upper-middle-class attitude could not be attributed completely to racism. Atlantic City was the same stage, but the old players looked down on the new cast, black and white.

It is the chiefest of ironies that Atlantic City succeeded in becoming a cultural symbol but that *the symbol had a place in time*. By the 1970's the upper middle class had long since rejected what it had to offer, and had grown impatient with its problems as well. The entertainment value of scandal in the resort had worn thin, and the shocked outrage of the *Bulletin* crusade of 1891 had yielded to the derisive and condescending muckraking of *Philadelphia Magazine*. Atlantic City appeared a perpetual bad boy, its adolescent bumptiousness turned to boorish senility. Bert Parks, master of ceremonies of the Miss America Pageant since 1955, quite rightly characterized the contest as "the biggest Cinderella story in America," the product of "the old American dream and the old frustration of wanting royalty and never having it." Yet he spoke for the lower middle class. When the Victorian lady strutted the stage each year, the upper-middle-class critic detected a whiff of formaldehyde in her wake, and the grim college-trained legionaries of women's liberation assailed the "sexism" of the event.

Though the upper middle class had abandoned Atlantic City, the lower middle class had not. Furthermore, the need of the whole culture for illusion had not diminished. From Super Bowl to Disney World to Woodstock, Americans expressed their continued taste for the extravagant and the fantastic. If one criticized Atlantic City, past and present, for trading in illusion, it was necessary to remember that it was a matter of viewpoint. After all, an illusion is a dream you don't believe in anymore.

The autumn break-up—they may
never meet again.

REFERENCES
AND INDEX

Notes

The following abbreviations have been used for frequently cited newspapers: *ACDP / Atlantic City Daily Press* (Atlantic City Public Library, Local History Collection); *ACDU / Atlantic City Daily Union* (Atlantic City Public Library, Local History Collection); *NYT / New York Times*; *PB / Philadelphia Bulletin*; *PI / Philadelphia Inquirer*.

A WASHBASIN

3   *"Whence came Atlantic City?"* Alfred M. Heston, *Illustrated Hand-Book of Atlantic City, New Jersey* (Atlantic City: A. M. Heston and Company, 1889), p. 43. Hereafter referred to as *1889.*

"rich reward" Atlantic City and County, New Jersey, Biographically Illustrated (Philadelphia: Alfred M. Slocum Company, 1899), pp. 36–37, 43. Hereafter referred to as *Atlantic City and County.*

3-4   (*Pitney's background*) John F. Hall, *The Daily Union History of Atlantic City and County, New Jersey* (Atlantic City: Daily Union Printing Company, 1900), pp. 179–81. Hereafter referred to as *Daily Union History.*

4   *"only seven houses"* A. L. English, *History of Atlantic City, New Jersey* (Philadelphia: Dickson and Gilling, 1884), p. 86. Hereafter referred to as *History.*

(*Pitney's backers*) Alfred M. Heston, *Absegami: Annals of Eyren Haven and Atlantic City, 1609 to 1904* (Camden, N.J.: By the Author, 1904), I, 10–11. Hereafter referred to as *Absegami.*

"ten thousand shares of stock" Carnesworthe, *Atlantic City: Its Early and Modern History* (Philadelphia: William C. Harris and Company, 1868), pp. 34–45. Hereafter referred to as *Early and Modern History.*

"The work-worn artisan" Richard B. Osborne, *Camden and Atlantic Railroad: Engineer's Report, June 24th, 1852* (Philadelphia: n.p., 1852), p. 11.

"lungs of Philadelphia" Atlantic City and County, p. 44.

"winter port" Hall, *Daily Union History,* p. 191.

"Wharves and a station" Atlantic City and County, pp. 38–39.

5   (*Gardner quote*) Heston, *Absegami,* I, 324.

"They organized a . . . Land Company" Carnesworthe, *Early and Modern History,* pp. 34–35.

"You will be satisfied" Charter and By-Laws of the Camden and Atlantic Land Company (Philadelphia: Inquirer Book Press, 1853), p. 8.

"$300 an acre" Hall, *Daily Union History,* p. 187.

"$800 a front-foot" Ibid., p. 315.

"The people who lived here" English, *History,* p. 85.

161

(*Surf House Association*) Hall, *Daily Union History*, p. 192.

"*Various names*" Heston, *Absegami*, I, 13.

5-6   (*Osborne's map*) *Atlantic City and County*, p. 41.

6   "*cultural symbolism*" Definitions are a melancholy necessity. I use the term "culture" in its anthropological rather than aesthetic sense, the following being a tolerable (if grammatically awkward) definition: "A culture is a set of patterns, of and for behavior, prevalent among a group of human beings at a specified time period and which, from the point of view of the research at hand of the scale on which it is being carried out presents, in relation to other such sets, observable and sharp discontinuities" (Clyde Kluckhohn, "Culture," *A Dictionary of the Social Sciences* [New York: Free Press of Glencoe, 1964], pp. 165–68).

    The use of "popular culture" is a bit more problematic. I do not employ these words in an anthropological sense, but rather as a descriptive term useful in the present case for historical analysis. The reader should be careful not to infer anthropological meaning when the term appears. Russel Nye, in his introduction to *The Unembarrassed Muse: The Popular Arts in America* (New York: The Dial Press, 1970), investigates the differences between "folk," "popular," and "elite" art, and refers to earlier elaborations of these and related terms. There is considerable difference of opinion among scholars over which words to use and whether the things referred to are good or bad for society. I shall not attempt to codify the terminology, declaring only that I join those who find popular culture on balance interesting and palatable, sometimes even moving, its bad qualities redeemed by evidence of the positive side of human personality.

    In this book, popular culture means basically the aesthetic output of the artistically untrained majority of the culture, as well as its expressions of value and belief, when these do not proceed from disciplined and informed study. Thus I add popular opinion to popular art to achieve what I mean by popular culture, in the manner of Henry Nash Smith, who refers to the latter term as "the beliefs and attitudes that most Americans took for granted, with the accepted patterns of thought and feeling" (*Popular Culture and Industrialism* [New York: New York University Press, 1967], p. v). Oscar Handlin ascribes a number of qualities to popular culture which are relevant to its meaning for this study. Describing it as it was during the first decades of the twentieth century, he finds that it "was composed of a complex of subcultures" and "differed from the defined [official] culture in the lack of an accepted set of canons or of a normative body of classics." It was "closely related to the felt needs and familiar modes of expression of the people it served," and, though "unstructured and chaotic, dealt directly with the concrete world intensely familiar to its audience." It was "closely tied to the traditions of those who consumed it," and, most important, offered to "millions of people . . . a means of communicating among themselves and the answer to certain significant questions that they were asking about the world around them" ("Comments on Mass and Popular Culture," in *Culture for Millions?* ed. by Norman Jacobs [Princeton: D. Van Nostrand Co., 1961], pp. 65–67).

    Scholars have tended to view popular culture as the stale fodder of the conforming multitude, in contrast to "superior or refined culture," which boldly explores the new (Edward Shils, "Mass Society and Its Culture," *ibid.*, p. 5). This is true in many cases. But Tom Wolfe has shown that, in fact, popular culture often

generates new styles and ideas which the educated and moneyed classes adopt in a rather lame and pathetic fashion (see the introduction to *The Kandy-Kolored Tangerine-Flake Streamline Baby* [New York: Farrar, Straus and Giroux, 1965], pp. lx–xvii). His description of Leonard Bernstein's party for the Black Panthers is celebrated, but there is a further example familiar to me. The Italian street market of South Philadelphia, once an ethnic preserve, has become a weekend recreational spot and life-style seminar for avant-garde types from the sophisticated wards of the city. On Saturdays the sidewalks are jammed not only with Italian and black housewives but with representative figures from *The New Yorker*, the *Whole Earth Catalog*, and *Ms.* magazine, who pick their way past slaughtered goats, piles of fennel, and baskets of live crabs. Similarly, in the present study Atlantic City foreshadows the growing hedonism of American society, a trend which the high culture was very timidly recognizing.

Popular culture has been distinguished from "mass culture," the critical factor being the impact of technology in massive doses: "The necessary condition of mass culture is technology, as this is the necessary condition of mass man" (Roy H. Pearce, "Mass Culture/Popular Culture: Notes for a Humanist's Primer," *College English*, XXXIII [March 1962], 417–32). At what point technological influence acquires such importance as to produce the qualitative change from popular to mass culture is naturally a highly debatable question. Scholars have held mass culture in less favor than popular culture, finding it more remote from its audience and more detached from that audience's needs. I believe that the material used in this book belongs more to popular than to mass culture. The boundary between the two is not a distinct one in any case, but I suggest that *tangentiality* is a factor to be considered in appraising the categories. For example, a snatch of rhyme in praise of seaside womanhood, tacked at the foot of a page in a resort advertising handbook, has for me less the quality of mass culture than a modern *Life* magazine cover or a portrait of a Gibson girl. The editor of the handbook is not really selling the poetry (or womanhood either): it is somewhat peripheral to his main purpose. The term "popular culture," therefore, may adhere to an element in an example of mass culture when it is tangential to the primary material of the latter, which is closely scrutinized for its ability to attract mass consumption.

On the other hand, Atlantic City is more appropriately styled a "mass" rather than a "popular" resort. The critical role of railroad transportation, widely dispersed advertising on a massive scale, and highly organized commercial services to visitors make Atlantic City qualitatively different from a popular resort. An example of the latter is Yellow Springs in Chester County, Pennsylvania. This modest mineral spa accommodated at most a couple of hundred daily visitors during its heyday in the 1840's, had only two inns, depended on word of mouth supplemented by brief notices in a few paltry county newspapers, and could be reached only by rather sketchy stage connections from Philadelphia. It is perhaps not coincidental that it folded just about the time that Atlantic City opened for business (Charles E. Funnell, unpublished research for Natural and Historic Resource Associates, 313 South Sixteenth Street, Philadelphia, Pennsylvania 19103).

There remains but to define "cultural symbol." I can imagine no more succinct nor satisfying description than that of Leo Marx, who identifies it as "an image that conveys a special meaning (thought and feeling) to a large number of those who share the

culture" (*The Machine in the Garden* [New York: Oxford University Press, 1967], p. 4).

"*I have ever claimed*" English, *History*, p. 49.

(*Richards named streets*) Hall, *Daily Union History*, p. 183.

(*Atlantic City incorporated*) English, *History*, p. 53.

"*The first train*" *Atlantic City and County*, pp. 38–39.

"*proximity of the Gulf Stream*" *Atlantic City By the Sea* (Philadelphia: Passenger Department, Pennsylvania Railroad, 1889), p. 4.

"*free of malaria*" *Atlantic City and County*, pp. 33–34.

"*straight line from Philadelphia*" Brighton, England, with which Atlantic City was often compared, is similar to the American resort in this respect. It is London's nearest point to the Channel.

(*Technology changing the countryside*) Marx, *The Machine in the Garden*, p. 32.

7   "*A casual study of the map*" *Atlantic City and County*, pp. 33–34.

"*drawbacks of Cape May*" Philadelphia, Historical Society of Pennsylvania, John Hill Martin scrapbook, "Atlantic City Sketches," 1856–85. Hereafter referred to as "Atlantic City Sketches."

(*1873 magazine article*) "A New Atlantis," *Lippincott's Magazine*, June 1873, p. 620.

"*The attractions here*" Alfred M. Heston, *Illustrated Hand-Book of Atlantic City, New Jersey* (Atlantic City: A. M. Heston and Company, 1888), p. 37. Hereafter referred to as *1888*.

"*American Brighton*" Maurice M. Howard, "Our American Brighton," *Potter's American Monthly*, November 1880, pp. 321–33.

8   "*The first editor*" Hall, *Daily Union History*, p. 323.

"*The season has been a failure!*" "Atlantic City's Season Is Over," *PI*, August 30, 1891, p. 12.

9   "*would seek the pleasures*" Ibid.

(*Population figures*) Figure for 1885, Alfred M. Heston, *Heston's Hand Book of Atlantic City* (Philadelphia: Franklin Printing Company, 1892), p. 106; for 1860, 1865, 1870, 1875, 1880, 1890, 1895, Hall, *Daily Union History*, p. 345; for 1885, Trenton, New Jersey State Library, Archives and History Bureau, "New Jersey State Census, 1885, Volume for Atlantic County"; for 1900, 1910, 1920, U.S. Department of Commerce, Bureau of the Census, *Fourteenth Census of the United States: State Compendium, New Jersey* (Washington: Government Printing Office, 1925), p. 8; for 1905, Trenton, New·Jersey State Library, Archives and History Bureau, "New Jersey State Census, 1905. Atlantic City."

"*the years of expansion were . . . over*" Sixty years later, Atlantic City had only 48,000 inhabitants.

"*Those who went away in '61*" Heston, *Absegami*, I, 325.

"*days of darkness*" *Report of the President and Managers of the Camden and Atlantic Railroad Company to the Stockholders*, January 15, 1871 (Philadelphia: Lineaweaver and Wallace, 1871), p. 15. The full statement reads: "The Company has passed through its days of darkness and depression, and is now rapidly approaching the period when it will take its place among the dividend-paying roads of the country." The 1871 report indicates that profits must have been reinvested or used to pay off interest on bonds. From 1856 to 1870, annual profit as a percentage of operating expenses ranged from nearly 70 percent down to 50 percent, an impressive statistic as far as it goes. In 1870, earnings were $334,000, expenses $167,000, and profit $166,000. The railroad's indebtedness prevented such favorable earnings from being profitable to its investors, at least through 1871.

The railroad estimated its excursion business for 1871 at 35,000 passengers. The growth of villages along its route supplemented the summer business of its terminus, Atlantic City.

"The railroad's troubles" Heston, *Absegami,* I, 25.

"The dust was . . . fierce" Atlantic City Public Library, Local History Collection, letter of E. W. C. Smith to unidentified newspaper, ca. 1900, in "Reminiscences of Absecon Beach and Atlantic City, 1795–1914. A. M. Heston, 1914." Hereafter referred to as "Reminiscences of Absecon."

11   *"High tides"* English, *History,* p. 75.

"Greenhead flies" Ibid., pp. 70–72.

"hundreds of wet places" Heston, *Absegami,* I, 23.

(Cope quote) Charles Henry Cope, *Reminiscences of Charles West Cope* (London: Richard Bentley and Son, 1891), p. 291.

"Permanent structures . . . property rights" English, *History,* pp. 152–53.

(United States Hotel) William McMahon, *So Young . . . So Gay* (Atlantic City: Atlantic City Press, 1970), p. 123. Hereafter referred to as *So Young.*

"I could not help wishing" A. G. Penn, "To Atlantic City by Way of ——— [sic]," *Lippincott's Magazine,* October 1870, p. 425.

"tiresome areas" Hall, *Daily Union History,* p. 253.

12   *"sea-water baths"* English, *History,* p. 126.

(hotels and boardinghouses) Carnesworthe, *Early and Modern History,* pp. 71–73.

"streetcars" McMahon, *So Young,* pp. 66–67.

"city hall . . . fire department" English, *History,* pp. 120–22.

"summer population . . . 34,000" *Atlantic City and County,* p. 44.

"the retired first mayor noted" Heston, *Absegami,* I, 32.

"the turning point" ACDU, July 11, 1891, p. 1.

"dull and disappointing" Hall, *Daily Union History,* p. 197.

"Michigan Pavilion" Alfred M. Heston, *Illustrated Hand-Book of Atlantic City, New Jersey* (Philadelphia: Franklin Printing House, 1887), p. 116. Hereafter referred to as *1887.*

"narrow-gauge line . . . sold" English, *History,* pp. 132–35.

"first direct rail connection" Heston, *1889,* p. 41.

(C & A sold) Harold F. Wilson, *The Jersey Shore* (New York: Lewis Historical Publishing Company, 1953), I, 474.

"Travel time . . . hour and a half" *Atlantic City By the Sea,* pp. 9–11.

"wash-basin" "A New Atlantis," p. 620.

(Excursion houses) English, *History,* p. 149.

"second boardwalk" McMahon, *So Young,* p. 74.

13   *"pier of iron"* Hall, *Daily Union History,* pp. 257–62.

(*Park Bath House*) English, *History*, p. 159.

(*Brighton Hotel*) McMahon, *So Young*, p. 22.

"*506 hotels and boardinghouses*" Gopsill's *Atlantic City Directory . . . for 1888* (Philadelphia: James Gopsill's Sons, 1888).

(*Bedford House ad*) "Atlantic City Sketches."

(*Heston succeeds English*) English, *History*, p. 137.

"*I would rather be right*" Alfred M. Heston, ed. *South Jersey: A History, 1664–1924* (New York: Lewis Historical Publishing Company, 1924), III, 20–23. Hereafter referred to as *South Jersey.*

13-14 | (*Daily Union*) Hall, *Daily Union History*, p. 323.

14 | "*a real Vanity Fair*" Letter of J. H. Martin, "Atlantic City Sketches."

"*prestidigitateur*" *Ibid.*

"*There was no Sunday*" Newspaper clipping in Heston, "Reminiscences of Absecon."

"*the nearest building*" English, *History*, p. 83.

"*policy men*" Newspaper clipping, May 1882, "Atlantic City Sketches."

"*corruption*" English, *History*, pp. 164–65.

"*work force*" A selection of 426 names of employed blacks from each of the four wards of Atlantic City, taken from the New Jersey state census of 1905, shows the kinds of jobs a large resort needed to have filled. The 201 females included 62 cooks, 32 housekeepers, 29 waitresses, 9 maids, 8 servants, and 2 nurses. The rest consisted of 14 schoolchildren, a janitress, and a keeper of a "general house" (perhaps a tavern). The males had greater job diversification. A total of 224 of them included 69 waiters, 31 laborers, 21 bellmen, 10 cooks, 9 railroad porters, 7 barbers, and 6 hod carriers. The remaining number, 47, worked at 32 assorted jobs, involving such comparatively interesting employment as fireman (railroad?), musician, furniture dealer, publisher, pipefitter, and preacher. There were 18 male schoolchildren. Thus the rather narrow range of direct service work which resort employment offered was supplemented by a modest number of more varied tasks proceeding from indirect resort services, such as construction or provision for the needs of the black community itself. Trenton, New Jersey State Library, Archives and History Bureau, "New Jersey State Census, 1905. Atlantic City."

14-15 | (*Black population figures*) Trenton, New Jersey State Library, Archives and History Bureau, "New Jersey State Census, 1885, Volume for Atlantic County"; *ibid.*, "New Jersey State Census, 1895. Volume for Atlantic County"; *ibid.*, "New Jersey State Census, 1905. Atlantic City"; U.S. Department of Commerce, Bureau of the Census, *Fourteenth Census of the United States: State Compendium, New Jersey* (Washington: Government Printing Office, 1925), pp. 30–31.

15 | "*paltry handouts*" The *Daily Union* recorded a scene in 1897 which is pertinent here: "Yesterday afternoon from 2 to 3 o'clock the overseer's office [Overseer of the Poor] . . . was nearly full all the time. All his applicants during that hour were colored, excepting one." *ACDU*, January 30, 1897, p. 1. Naturally, this could be racially selective reporting, but it does illustrate the demand for relief in the resort.

"*Blacks were housed*" Margaret L. Brett, "Atlantic City: A Study in Black and White," *Survey*, XXVIII (September 7, 1912), 724–25. Hereafter referred to as "Black and White."

"*Colored people came here*" Heston, *1888*, p. 124.

"*The railway . . . hired*" English, *History*, p. 133.

"*He was notified*" ACDU, June 14, 1893, p. 1.

16 "*James Jones*" ACDU, June 12, 1893, p. 1.

"*mixed couples . . . discouraged*" ACDU, July 18, 1901, p. 1.

"*no serious 'problem'*" ACDU, August 1, 1893, p. 4.

"*The Camden and Atlantic encouraged*" English, *History*, p. 30.

"*pipeline*" Ibid., p. 72.

"*cisterns . . . superior*" *Summer Sketches of the City By the Sea: Atlantic City for Season 1883* (N.p.: Camden and Atlantic Railroad, 1883), p. 27. Hereafter referred to as *Summer Sketches*.

17 "*an out-of-doorness*" *Atlantic City By the Sea*, p. 5.

(*Physicians' endorsement*) English, *History*, pp. 139–40.

"*The convention element*" *Atlantic City and County*, p. 72.

(*1894 conventions*) PI, July 15, 1894, p. 9.

(*A.M.A. convocation*) ACDU, June 5, 1897, p. 1.

(*President Harrison*) ACDU, July 11, 1891, p. 1.

(*Reviews of handbook*) Heston, *1888*, inside front and back covers.

(*Distribution of handbook*) Ibid., pp. 128–30.

18 "*a very easy matter*" Heston, *1887*, p. 81.

"*One hundred subscribers*" Editorial, *ACDU*, March 1, 1894, p. 4.

"*in 1900 hotelkeepers . . .*" John T. Cunningham, *The New Jersey Shore* (New Brunswick, N.J.: Rutgers University Press, 1958), p. 102.

(*Postcard messages*) New Brunswick, New Jersey, Rutgers University Library, New Jersey Collection, postcard file; author's collection.

18-19 (*Song*) Harry Williams and Egbert Van Alstyne, "Why Don't You Try, or the Rolling Chair Song" (New York: Jerome Remick and Company, 1905).

19 "*part of the definition of happiness*" In 1928, *The New York Times* said of the resort: "It has come to typify in the minds of millions of people the idea of a capitalized Good Time. . . . It is a national institution. Having become such it trundles along under its own momentum. One goes there because other people go there." R. L. Duffus, "The Big Parade on Atlantic City's Boardwalk," *NYT*, August 12, 1928, sec. IV, pp. 12–13, 20.

"*The architecture is varied*" James F. Downey, "A Queen of the Coast," *Demorest's Family Magazine*, August 1895 [no page numbers].

"*gingerbread*" Frank Ward O'Malley, "The Board-Walkers: Ten Days with Bertha at Atlantic City," *Everybody's Magazine*, August 1908, p. 236. Hereafter referred to as "Board-Walkers."

"*the town lacks*" Alfred M. Heston, *Heston's Hand Book of Atlantic City* (Philadelphia: Franklin Printing Company, 1892), p. 56. Hereafter referred to as *1892*.

20 (*Warner quote*) Charles Dudley Warner, "Their Pilgrimage," *Harper's New Monthly Magazine*, LXXII (April 1886), 677–78, 680.

"*One official begged*" ACDU, June 27, 1893, p. 1.

"*More doctors*" ACDU, July 15, 1891, p. 1.

(*Travel time sixty-eight minutes*) Heston, *1892*, p. 32.

(*Travel time fifty minutes*) *Atlantic City and County*, p. 173.

21-3 (*Philadelphia–Atlantic City train ride*) Charles S. Boyer, *Rambles Through Old Highways and Byways of West Jersey* (Camden, N.J.: Camden County Historical Society, 1967); Camden and Atlantic Railroad, Timetable, Effective 29 March 1890; Geological Survey of New Jersey, 1888, 1890, 1891, 1900; Heston, *1888*; Heston, *1892*; *Pleasant Places on the Reading Railroad* (N.p.: General Passenger Department, Philadelphia and Reading Railroad, 1895); George R. Prowell, *History of Camden County* (Philadelphia: L. J. Richards and Co., 1886).

23 "*the Brighton of Philadelphia*" Thomas M. Dale, *Atlantic City in the Twentieth Century*, speech at the Bourse, December 2, 1897, on the occasion of the presentation of Resolutions from the Hotel Men's Association of Atlantic City to the Traders' League of Philadelphia (N.p.: n.p. [1897]). Hereafter referred to as *Twentieth Century*.

"*the verdict of the people*" Heston, *1892*, p. 110.

"*eighth wonder*" "The New Baedeker: Casual Notes of an Irresponsible Traveller," *The Bookman*, XXX (September 1909), 51. Hereafter referred to as "Baedeker."

NEWPORT OF THE
NOUVEAUX BOURGEOIS

25 "*representatives of the best society*" *Atlantic City By the Sea*, p. 7.

"*A modern Appian way*" Dale, *Twentieth Century*.

"*there is hardly a family*" Hall, *Daily Union History*, p. 231.

"*Practically all*" John Steevens [*sic*], "The Charm of Eastertide at Atlantic City," *Harper's Weekly*, April 18, 1908, p. 20. Hereafter referred to as "Eastertide."

"*467 names*" ACDU, July 16, 21, 26, 28, December 1, 8, 15, 22, 29, 1890; February 22, 1892; June 3, July 24, 1893; July 2, 16, 23, December 3, 10, 17, 31, 1894; July 23, 1895; July 20, 23–25, August 6, 7, 1900. Hereafter referred to as *ACDU* Society Listings.

26 "*appropriate Social Registers*" *Social Register, Philadelphia, 1893*, VII, 3 (New York: Social Register Association, November 1892); *ibid., 1894*, VIII, 2 (New York: Social Register Association, November 1893); *ibid., 1900*, XIV, 3 (New York: Social Register Association, November 1899). The *Social Registers* for 1890–92 were not available to me, but the use of the 1893 volume (published in November 1892) probably makes little or no difference. It seems unlikely that the number of individuals listed in the *Social Register* in 1890, but not listed three years later, would be very large. Moreover, the *Social Register* had the habit of listing recently deceased members of society, so the loss of names by death would be further reduced.

"*327 distinguished visitors*" "Society at the Seaside," *PI*, July 17, 1892, p. 12; "Society at the Seaside," *PI*, July 24, 1892, p. 12; "Society," *PI*, July 31, 1892, p. 12; "Summer Resorts," *PI*, July 22, 1894, p. 9; "Beside the Bounding Billows," *PI*, July 14, 1901, Summer

Resort Section, p. 4; "Beach Costumes of Fair Bathers" and "The Social Whirl," *PI*, July 21, 1901, sec. 2, p. 11.

"14 are found" *Social Register, Philadelphia, 1893*; *Social Register, Philadelphia, 1894*; *Social Register, Philadelphia, 1901*, XV (New York: Social Register Association, November 1900).

"142 arrivals" "Beside the Bounding Billows," *PI*, July 14, 1901, Summer Resort Section, p. 4.

"763 addresses" *Social Register, Summer 1900*, XIV, 19 (New York: Social Register Association, 1900).

"brief descriptions . . . in the Daily Union" ACDU Society Listings.

27 (*Descriptions of ladies*) *Ibid.*

"The ultra-swell" O'Malley, "Board-Walkers," p. 233.

"Some of these people came" "Atlantic City," *PI*, August 5, 1894, p. 9.

28 *"These men are mainly"* "Baedeker," p. 46.

"failing to attract" Editorial, *ACDU*, January 28, 1892, p. 4.

"Chelsea" Heston, *1887*, pp. 73–74.

(*Ledlie story*) "Summer Resorts," *PI*, July 22, 1894, p. 9.

(*Hall estimate of cottages*) Hall, *Daily Union History*, pp. 227–31.

(*C & A brochure*) *Summer Sketches*, pp. 15–19.

"commutation tickets" "A Rush to the Seashore," *ACDU*, June 26, 1893, p. 1.

29 *"little historical record"* They did form a Cottagers' Association in 1889, primarily to protest the routing of train tracks through the city and to seek lower commutation rates to Philadelphia. The organization seems to have withered away after two years.

(*Geographical origins of blacks*) Trenton, New Jersey State Library, Archives and History Bureau, "New Jersey State Census, 1905. Atlantic City."

"What are we going to do . . . ?" "Down by the Sea Shore—Atlantic City," *PI*, July 23, 1893, p. 10.

30 *"could keep the blacks in their place"* *Ibid.*

"Washington Post *complained"* *ACDU*, July 23, 1900, p. 1.

"a . . . young colored lady" "Some Curious Scenes Depicted on Beach at Gay Atlantic City," *PI*, July 28, 1900, p. 3.

"criticism of a black . . . newspaper" *ACDU*, August 8, 1891, p. 1.

"black tourists" Little evidence has emerged of how such restrictions were enforced. It seems most probable that the white community had a fair consensus on how the blacks should be treated, and that a reproving word from a hosteler, waiter, or passing citizen sufficed to enlighten black offenders of the code. Moreover, a black who sought his pleasures where he was not wanted had to calculate that appeal might be made to his employer by an angry white. Atlantic City must have had certain aspects of a "company town," since the single-purpose economy precluded most alternative kinds of employment. On the other hand, there were many employers, preventing the monopoly which made the disciplinary potential of the company town so oppressive.

"five thousand blacks" *ACDU*, September 3, 1891, p. 1.

"post-season windfall" In one of Alfred Heston's scrapbooks is an undated clipping from a Bucks County (Pennsylvania) newspaper

which, from internal evidence, must have appeared about 1904. It records: "Yesterday over 6,000 negroes were here to enjoy the annual colored excursion of the first Thursday in September." Heston, "Reminiscences of Absecon."

30-1   (Inquirer *descriptions of black excursions*) "The City by the Sea," *PI*, September 6, 1896, p. 21; "Colored People Invade Atlantic," *PI*, September 2, 1897, p. 12; "Atlantic City," *PI*, September 4, 1898, p. 15.

31   (*August excursions of blacks*) "In the Merry Throng Down by the Sea," *PI*, August 18, 1897, p. 12; "Discussed Race Problem," *PI*, August 23, 1899, p. 5; New Brunswick, New Jersey, Rutgers University Library, New Jersey Collection, postcard file.

"Ten tramps" "Itinerant Visitors Warned," *ACDU*, June 21, 1893, p. 1.

32   (*Tramps in jail*) "City Jail Records," *ACDU*, January 29, 1897, p. 1.

(*Depression of 1893*) *ACDU*, June 23, 1893, p. 4.

(*Coxey's Army*) "At the Seaside—Atlantic City," *PI*, August 12, 1894, p. 9.

"There are no beggars" O'Malley, "Board-Walkers," p. 238.

(*Salvation Army, Volunteers of America*) Brett, "Black and White," pp. 725–26.

33   *"study of 225 . . . hotels"* Heston, *1887*, pp. 131–34.

(*Annual wages*) Paul L. Douglas, *Real Wages in the United States, 1890–1926* (Boston: Houghton Mifflin Company, 1930), table following p. 392.

"the lower middle class could meet the prices" Comments one newspaper: "The grand hotels serve the wealthy, but the moderate ones give entertainment to thousands." Newspaper clipping from unidentified Bucks County (Pennsylvania) newspaper, ca. 1904, in Heston, "Reminiscences of Absecon."

"newspaper clipping" "Atlantic City Sketches."

"doubling up" "Greatest and Best—Our Island City," *ACDU*, July 4, 1891, p. 1.

34   (Times *reporter*) "A Sunday Sea-Side Resort," *NYT*, August 14, 1883, p. 3.

"three fifths the annual total" In 1887, for example, Heston's handbook lists 212 "hotels," while *Gopsill's Directory* lists 443 "hotels, cottages, and boardinghouses." It is a safe bet that Heston did not omit anything worthy of the name "hotel." In fact, he included many establishments with a dozen rooms or less. Thus, 47 percent (212/443) should certainly be reduced to obtain a rough estimate of the proportion of hotels to the total number of lodging places.

(*Table*) All figures in this table except that for 1884 were compiled from *Gopsill's Atlantic City Directory for 1882–1883* (Philadelphia: James Gopsill, 1882) and *Gopsill's Atlantic City Directory* (Philadelphia: James Gopsill's Sons), volumes for 1885–1908. The figure for 1884 was compiled from *Holdzkom and Company's Atlantic City Cottage and Business Directory for 1884* (Atlantic City: Holdzkom and Company, 1884).

"hard times of the 1890's" It is possible that some might be induced to open a boardinghouse when depression struck. If, for example, an Atlantic Avenue merchant saw his trade dry up, his wife might

decide to start a boardinghouse in their home, since even marginal profit was better than none.

35   *"Nearly every branch"* "At the Summer Resorts—Atlantic City," *PI*, July 16, 1893, p. 10.

"The crowds in the city" Hall, *Daily Union History*, p. 197.

"protest meeting" Obviously, the excursion trade did not appeal equally to all business interests in the resort. Broadly speaking, there were two major economic camps in Atlantic City who were potential rivals. The first consisted of the proprietors of the large and prestigious hotels, other businessmen catering to upper-middle-class patronage, local professional and religious leaders, and citizens not directly dependent on a mass-resort economy. The second included small hotel and boardinghouse keepers, respectable saloonkeepers, the multitude of small shop and restaurant keepers, and amusement operators. On the fringes of the second group were businessmen of varying respectability and legality, such as Boardwalk hawkers, small-time entertainers like sand "sculptors," operators of unlicensed saloons and Sunday-closing violators, gamblers, brothel proprietors, and so forth. Conflict between the economic camps figures prominently in Chapter 5, "Babylonian Days," over the issue of Sunday liquor selling. Naturally, the excursion crowd was of nil (or even negative) interest to the high-class resort businessmen, even if it was the lifeblood of the others.

"astonishing sum" English, *History*, p. 154.

36   (*Hillman and Mackey*) "Atlantic City Sketches."

(*Seaview Excursion House*) "A New Atlantis," p. 620.

(*West Jersey Excursion House*) "Atlantic City Sketches."

"Ball Room . . . Billiard Room" English, *History*, p. 223.

(*Applegate's Pier*) Heston, *1887*, p. 15.

(*Heinz Pier*) Postcard, author's collection; trade card, author's collection.

37   (*Stunts of the 1890's*) "Visitors of a Day at Atlantic City," *PI*, August 12, 1898, p. 2; "Atlantic City," *PI*, August 21, 1898, p. 15; "Rain Swept the Long Boardwalk," *PI*, August 24, 1897, p. 5; "With the Merry Throng at the Seaside Resorts," *PI*, August 10, 1899, p. 5.

38   *"Single girls"* Dreiser superbly describes the pleasures of newly found social opportunity in *Sister Carrie*, when Carrie meets Drouet on the train to Chicago.

38-9   *"Mrs. Duff,"* *"four osculatory bits,"* *"Dan and Mary"* "A Sunday Stroll at Atlantic," *PI*, July 13, 1896, p. 7; "Review of the Passing Show at Atlantic City and Cape May," *PI*, August 2, 1899, p. 6; "Atlantic City's Merry Throng of Seekers After Pleasure," *PI*, August 1, 1899, p. 14.

39   *"Lover's Pavilion"* Heston, *1887*, p. 54.

"Baltimore ordinance" ACDU, June 28, 1893, p. 4.

"A noteworthy feature" "At Atlantic City: The 'Evening Bulletin's' Exposure Bears Good Fruit," *PB*, August 12, 1890, p. 1.

"Just ran across" Atlantic City, Public Library, Local History Collection, scrapbook of postcards. Hereafter referred to as "Atlantic City Postcards."

"It must be borne in mind" Hall, *Daily Union History*, p. 252.

40 | *"Such attitudes were congruent"* Yet Atlantic City, by providing the opportunity for illicit sex, could be a threat to family values. The shopgirl's dream lover might turn out to be a rake, the shopgirl might discover a bit of the tart in her own soul, or the upstanding young man might avail himself of a lady of easy virtue. But it is possible that, on a higher level, illicit sex helped the family to survive.

"The Autumn Break-Up" Heston, *1888*, p. 68.

"unmatched girls" "A New Atlantis," p. 615.

"A wedding will take place" "Atlantic City Romance," *PI*, August 23, 1893, p. 5.

"the crowd itself" Cape May to Atlantic City: A Summer Note Book (N.p.: Passenger Department, Pennsylvania Railroad Company, 1883), p. 39. Hereafter referred to as *Cape May to Atlantic City.*

"bathe in people" "The Spectator," *Outlook*, CIV (July 26, 1913), 719.

41-2 | *"Talking of love," lapel buttons* "Atlantic City Sketches"; "Atlantic City," *PI*, July 19, 1896, p. 18.

(Incense tapers, other fads) "Gay Atlantic," *PI*, August 8, 1897, p. 20; "The City by the Sea," *PI*, August 23, 1896, p. 18.

"Hello, My Baby," clothing styles, palmistry, phrenology "Atlantic City," *PI*, August 6, 1899, sec. III, p. 1.; Atlantic City, Public Library, Local History Collection, loose newspapers in folders, *Atlantic Journal*, July 30, 1890, p. 1; "Atlantic City," *PI*, July 22, 1900, sec. II, p. 8; "Atlantic City," *PI*, July 12, 1896, p. 18.

42 | *(Bathing suits, "bicycle girl," Fourth of July)* "Atlantic City," *PI*, August 14, 1898, p. 15; "Atlantic City Sands," *PI*, August 15, 1897, p. 20; "The City by the Sea," *PI*, July 5, 1896, p. 18.

"widow craze" "At the Summer Resorts—Atlantic City," *PI*, July 2, 1893, p. 10.

44 | *"the summer girl"* "Belles of the Beach at Gay Atlantic," *PI*, July 22, 1900, Half-Tone Supplement, p. 1.; "Atlantic City," *PI*, July 28, 1895, p. 14.

"everyone was potentially in on the act" Fads not only are an attempt to create community, they are also (as a corollary) the expression of a felt lack of community. The feverish pleasures of Atlantic City bespeak not only what the culture could deliver—for a price—to its members, but also what it withheld from them.

(Reed brochure) Reprinted in English, *History*, pp. 183–94.

"Academy of Music" "Don't Be Slow: A Great Rush for the Academy's Opening Bill," *ACDU*, June 22, 1893, p. 1; McMahon, *So Young*, pp. 43–44.

"Esplanade" "Atlantic City," *PI*, July 10, 1898, p. 13.

44-5 | *(Rolling-chair design)* Somers Point, New Jersey, Atlantic County Historical Society, Silas R. Morse Scrapbook, 1840–1928. Hereafter referred to as "Morse Scrapbook."

45 | *"Afterward, well wrapped up"* Hall, *Daily Union History*, p. 237.

"The Piers at Atlantic City" "Some Gowns Seen at Atlantic City," *PI*, September 3, 1899, Half-Tone Supplement, p. 7.

46 | *"Easter Parade, copied"* Steevens, "Eastertide," p. 22.

"forty thousand passengers" Hall, *Daily Union History*, pp. 247–49.

46-7 | (*Baltzell*) Edward D. Baltzell, *Philadelphia Gentlemen: The Making of a National Upper Class* (Glencoe, Ill.: Free Press, 1958).

47 | "*pocketbook . . . coat of arms*" In 1922, a visiting New Zealand woman exclaimed: "Dollars is the password here. You can have what you want if you are prepared to pay for it. Not so at Newport, where the amazing mansions of New York's Four Hundred are like a battlement along the cliff, warning off intruders." Nellie M. Scanlon, "American Cities As Seen by a New Zealand Woman," *NYT*, October 29, 1922, sec. VIII, p. 2.

"*Chicago investigated*" Special Park Commission, *Report of Investigation of Bathing Beaches* (N.p.: Chicago City Council, 1913).

"*horse show*" Hall, *Daily Union History*, p. 243.

"*St. Nicholas' Church*" "Atlantic City Sketches."

"*pile it on*" "Down by the Sea Shore—Atlantic City," *PI*, July 30, 1893, p. 9.

"*And the things that were sold!*" "The Spectator," pp. 718–19; Warner, "Their Pilgrimage," p. 682; "Acid in the Juice," *PI*, September 2, 1899, p. 3.

48 | (*Entrepreneurs' new language*) Helen C. Bennett, "Come On In— The Water's Fine!" *American Magazine*, August 1926, pp. 45, 144; *ACDU*, August 21, 1890, p. 4; "Atlantic City's Foul Blots," *PI*, August 4, 1895, Sunday Supplement, pp. 21–22; *ACDU*, August 29, 1900, p. 4.

48-9 | (*Fralinger's career*) Heston, *South Jersey*, IV, 211.

50 | (*Young's career*) Ibid., IV, 415–16; "Atlantic City," *PI*, September 3, 1899, sec. III, p. 4; "Atlantic City," *PI*, July 22, 1900, sec. II, p. 8.

"*There we find the fakir*" "At the Seaside—Atlantic City," *PI*, August 26, 1894, p. 9.

51 | (*McLean*) Albert F. McLean, *American Vaudeville as Ritual* (Lexington: University of Kentucky Press, 1965). Hereafter referred to as *American Vaudeville*.

"*Immigrants just off the boat*" Ibid., pp. 40–41.

(*Dockstader shows*) Atlantic City, Public Library, Local History Collection, Alfred M. Heston scrapbook, "Good Times Book, vol. I, Trips 1894–1895." Hereafter referred to as "Good Times Book."

51-2 | (*Analysis of vaudeville*) McLean, *American Vaudeville*, pp. 35–36, 66–83.

52 | (*Doyle's Pavilion*) *ACDU*, August 17, 1900, p. 4.

(*Young's Ocean Pier Theatre*) Atlantic City, Public Library, Local History Collection, untitled scrapbook of theater programs. Hereafter referred to as "Scrapbook of Theater Programs."

(*Iron Pier*) *ACDU*, July 23, 1894, p. 1.

(*The Empire*) *ACDU*, July 30, 1900, p. 4.

53 | "*snickering at the lowbrows*" Recall the *Times* reporter who was appalled by an Atlantic City boardinghouse.

54 | (*Rand, McNally*) William E. Meehan, *Rand, McNally and Company's Handy Guide to Philadelphia and Environs, Including Atlantic City and Cape May* (Chicago: Rand, McNally and Company, 1895), pp. 163, 168–69.

"*Four spacious decks*" *ACDU*, July 5, 1890, p. 1.

"When the curtain rises" Gaston Lichtenstein, A Visit to Young's Pier at Atlantic City, N.J., reprinted from the Tarborough Southerner, Tarborough, N.C. (Richmond, Va.: William Ellis Jones, 1908), pp. 3–5.

(Inquirer vignette) "Down by the Sea Shore—Atlantic City," PI, July 9, 1893, p. 10.

"Another reporter" "At Atlantic City: A Record of Unique Characteristics," undated clipping (from The Tribune [?]) in "Atlantic City Sketches."

(Hebrew Charity Ball) "Down by the Sea—Atlantic City," PI, July 29, 1894, p. 9.

55   "When Lent comes" Atlantic City By the Sea, p. 6.

(The Casino Girl) "Good Times Book."

"slumming" "Down by the Sea Shore—Atlantic City," PI, July 9, 1893, p. 10.

"It is almost worth a visit" "A Sunday Sea-Side Resort," NYT, August 14, 1883, p. 3.

GAMES FOR THE MAUVE PREDICAMENT

57   "learned pigs" "Atlantic City Sketches."

"escaping" PI, July 30, 1894, p. 2.

(Iron Pier) ACDU, July 14, 1893, p. 1.

(The Amphitheatre) ACDU, July 7, 1894, p. 1.

(Inlet Amusement Park) ACDU, July 12, 1894, p. 1.

(Daily Union review) ACDU, July 14, 1894, p. 1.

57-8   (The Zoo) ACDU, July 2, 1900, p. 1.

58   (Bostock and humane movement) McLean, American Vaudeville, p. 147.

"Destruction of Herculaneum" ACDU, July 23, 1894; p. 1.

59   "Scenograph" "Scrapbook of Theater Programs."

"Custer's Last Stand" McMahon, So Young, p. 158.

(She) ACDU, July 3, 1890, p. 4.

"danger by proxy" Spectacles of this kind appealed also to rural visitors to Atlantic City, but they had special meaning for city dwellers. On the other hand, most farming in the 1890's was by no means a savage battle with the wilderness. Though the automobile had not yet appeared to end rural isolation, there were such influences as urban magazines, newspapers, and mail-order merchandise, protest movements like the Grange which were intensely concerned with urban economic power, land-grant colleges, easier rail travel to an increasing number of cities, and other phenomena of the kind which brought the farmer and the town closer together than they had been before the Civil War.

60   "rather than to dominate" Domination and the inverse, the desire to be dominated, may both express a sense of frustration with the distance between one individual and another, or between a culture and an object (i.e., Nature).

(Wonderland) ACDU, August 24, 1900, p. 4.

61   "the Petrified Woman" ACDU, July 23, 1894, p. 1.

	(*Freak shows*) ACDU, July 23, 1893, p. 1; June 30, 1893, p. 1; July 6, 1893, p. 1; June 26, 1897, p. 1.
	"*the new carrousel*" ACDU, July 5, 1890, p. 1.
62	"*$300 a week more*" ACDU, July 22, 1890, p. 1.
	"*building another merry-go-round*" ACDU, June 2, 1893, p. 1.
	(*Dentzel*) Frederick Fried, *A Pictorial History of the Carousel* (New York: A. S. Barnes and Company, 1964), pp. 52–58.
	"*other carrousels*" Gopsill's Atlantic City Directory . . . for 1891 (Philadelphia: James Gopsill's Sons, 1891).
	"*first ferris wheel*" "Morse Scrapbook."
	"*in front of the Seaview Excursion House*" Ibid.
	"*credit Somers*" McMahon, *So Young*, pp. 83–84.
	"*constructed . . . at Kentucky Avenue*" ACDU, August 8, 1891, p. 1.
	"*wheel was made double*" McMahon, *So Young*, pp. 83–84.
	(*Crystal Palace Carrousel*) ACDU, July 1, 1890, p. 1.
	(*Enterprise wheel*) ACDU, June 10, 1893, p. 1.
62-3	(*Smith wheel*) ACDU, July 27, 1893, p. 1.
63	"*Mt. Washington Toboggan Slide*" ACDU, July 15, 1889, p. 1.
	(*Casino Toboggan Slide*) ACDU, July 3, 1890, p. 4.
	"*intriguing hybrid*" ACDU, May 31, 1893, p. 1.
	"*photograph of a switchback*" "A Queen of the Coast" [no page numbers].
	"*Scenic Railway*" William F. Mangels, *The Outdoor Amusement Industry* (New York: Vantage Press, 1952), pp. 81–93.
	(*Photograph of "Flip Flap Railway"*) "Good Times Book."
64	(*Horseshoe Curve*) "New Jersey News," PI, August 20, 1897, p. 2.
	"*Flying Bicycles*" Gopsill's Atlantic City Directory . . . for 1891, pp. 229–30, 245–46.
	"*suspended from above*" ACDU, July 28, 1893, p. 1.
	"*1,400-foot track*" ACDU, July 29, 1893, p. 1.
	(*Lake's career*) "Jesse S. Lake," *National Cyclopaedia of American Biography*, 1929, XX, 228–29.
64-5	(*Revolving Towers*) McMahon, *So Young*, p. 107.
65	(*meaning of "merry-go-round"*) The *Oxford English Dictionary* is of little help in discovering the origin of "merry-go-round," though it notes the use of the term as early as 1729. To "go round" had long been employed as a phrase, but how "merry" and "go round" were first joined together is a matter of my speculation. *Oxford English Dictionary*, VI, 364.
	(*Corliss engine*) Henry Nash Smith, in *Popular Culture and Industrialism*, p. 71, says of the Corliss engine that "the very monumentality of the machine, with its thirty-foot flywheel, its twenty-seven-foot walking beams, and its towering height of thirty-nine feet above the main floor of the building, lent itself to the kind of statistical boasting that was often noted in this period as an American trait." In *Centennial: American Life in 1876* (Philadelphia: Chilton Book Company, 1969), p. 304, William Peirce Randel notes that "the Corliss engine always attracted a dazed and reverent crowd."

66   *"Debs's mother"* Ray Ginger, *Eugene Debs: The Making of an American Radical* (New York: Collier Books, 1962), p. 32.

    (*1896 train wreck*) "Atlantic City's Story of Death," *PI*, August 1, 1896, p. 1.

    (*1906 train wreck and poem*) Wilson, *The Jersey Shore*, II, 848–49.

66-7   (*Newton testimony*) Smith, *Popular Culture and Industrialism*, pp. 323–24.

67   (*Beard quote*) *Ibid.*, pp. 57–58.

68   *"The new merry-go-round"* ACDU, July 10, 1890, p. 1.

    "Charles Pugh" ACDU, June 10, 1893, p. 1.

69   (*Casino Toboggan Slide*) ACDU, July 3, 1890, p. 4.

    "cog railway" "Pikes Peak," *Encyclopaedia Britannica*, 1972, XVII, 1075.

    "great tunnel" "Saint Gotthard Pass," *Encyclopaedia Britannica*, 1972, XIX, 901.

    "The tunnel has been pronounced" "Switzerland," *Appleton's Annual Cyclopaedia and Register of Important Events of the Year 1881*, New Series, VI, 819.

70   (*History of the merry-go-round*) Mangels, *The Outdoor Amusement Industry*, pp. 52–56.

70-1   (*History of the Ferris wheel*) *Ibid.*, pp. 105–15.

71-2   (*History of the roller coaster*) *Ibid.*, pp. 81–93.

72   (*History of the "Flip Flap"*) *Ibid.*, pp. 99–102.

74   *"old as Methuselah"* ACDU, August 28, 1891, p. 1.

    "rotary swing . . . unpatentable" Mangels, *The Outdoor Amusement Industry*, pp. 105–15.

    "placed a sign" Somers Point, New Jersey, Atlantic County Historical Society, framed photograph.

    "tried . . . to sue" ACDU, June 16, 1893, p. 1.

    "no mention of the home-town boy" ACDU, June 22, 1893, p. 1.

    "This scenic railway" ACDU, August 26, 1891, p. 4.

THE PERSPECTIVES OF JANUS

    I have been influenced in my interpretation of the role of the family in American life by Jules Henry's *Culture Against Man* (New York: Random House, 1963), particularly Chapters 2 and 5.

78   *"front-page articles"* The *Bulletin* began to devote attention to the Atlantic City affair on August 2 and lost interest only after October 7.

79   *"I would like Atlantic City"* "At Atlantic City: The 'Evening Bulletin's' Exposure Bears Good Fruit," *PB*, August 12, 1890, p. 1.

    "The solid character" Heston, *1887*, pp. 46–47.

    (*Winter Ocean Parlor, Seaside Parlor*) *Ibid.*, p. 115.

    (*Park Baths*) *Ibid.*

    (*1904 brochure*) Somers Point, New Jersey, Atlantic County Historical Society, *To the American Bankers' Association Is Hereby Cordially Extended an Earnest Invitation* . . . (Atlantic City Board of Trade, 1904).

80   *"There is this difference"* Steevens, "Eastertide," p. 22.

"none but the better class" Heston, *1887*, p. 79.

"What bosh . . . !" "Atlantic City: The Town by the Sea on the Eve of a Big Sensation," *PB*, August 2, 1890, p. 2.

81   (*Description of Sunday family outing*) "A Merry-Go-Round: Atlantic City and Its Queer Sunday Laws," *PB*, August 6, 1890, p. 7.

82   *"You have no friends"* "At Atlantic City: Some of the Queer Things at the City by the Sea," *PB*, August 16, 1890, p. 1.

(*Schaufler's Garden*) *ACDU*, July 9, 1891, p. 1.

(*Fred Albrecht*) "Daring Feats on a Tight Rope," *ACDU*, June 27, 1893, p. 1.

"A feature of Atlantic" English, *History*, p. 175.

(*Guvernator's "strict order"*) *Ibid.*, p. 227.

"every civilized nation" Hall, *Daily Union History*, pp. 255–57.

(*Fortescue Pavilion*) "Twentieth Season—Nearly Two Decades of Successful Boardwalk Attractions," *ACDU*, June. 18, 1897, p. 1.

83   *"not repulsive"* *ACDU*, July 13, 1891, p. 1.

"Minnie Lee" *ACDU*, July 5, 1893, p. 1.

"the Zartinis" "Chaste and Artistic—The Beautiful Act of the Zartinis at Fortescue Pavilion," *ACDU*, June 24, 1897, p. 1.

(*Mrs. Williams*) English, *History*, p. 168.

(*Applegate's Pier*) Heston, *1887*, p. 15.

(*Ocean Pier*) "Singing on the Pier," *ACDU*, July 8, 1893, p. 1.

"services . . . at the merry-go-round" "Against Sunday Opening," *ACDU*, July 17, 1891.

(*Ministerial Union*) "Object to Circus on Sunday," *NYT*, May 6, 1927, p. 6.

"There are many delightful" "Atlantic City Sketches."

84   *"Shock-headed youths"* "Baedeker," pp. 42–43.

"The Baltimore police" *ACDU*, June 28, 1893, p. 4.

"Lover's Pavilion" Heston, *1887*, p. 54.

"Thus it is that women" "Baedeker," pp. 46–47.

(*James North*) Hall, *Daily Union History*, p. 139.

85   *"Here crowned with light"* Dr. James North, *Atlantic City in Picture and Poem* (Camden, N.J.: By the Author, 1906).

86   *"Bevies of girls"* Heston, *1887*, p. 48.

"This latter will become" "At Gay Atlantic," *ACDU*, July 4, 1897, p. 24.

"where the 'Peeping Tom's' " Dale, *Twentieth Century*.

"Black Patti Troubadours" *ACDU*, August 7, 1900, p. 4.

"trade cards" "Atlantic City Sketches."

87   *"postcards"* "Atlantic City Postcards."

88   *"Dear Brother"* Author's collection.

"No Place For a Minister's Son" "The Spectator," pp. 718–19.

"The quietude of Lent" "Atlantic City Sketches."

89   *"The sublime majesty"* Hall, *Daily Union History*, p. 252.

"When the sun shines forth" *Ibid.*, p. 245.

"Aside from the attractions" Heston, *1887*, p. 111.

"buy all the beer" "Seeking Comfort Down by the Sea," *PI*, July 10, 1893, p. 2.

90   *"One queer thing"* "Atlantic City Sketches."

"services in the skating rink" Ibid.

"a pagan metropolis" "Sunday Observance—Where Draw the Line?" *ACDU*, July 20, 1891, p. 1.

"This paper concedes" "At Atlantic City: Some of the Queer Things at the City by the Sea," *PB*, August 14, 1890, p. 1.

91   *"The Squire is a good deal"* "At Atlantic City: The 'Evening Bulletin's' Exposure Bears Good Fruit," *PB*, August 12, 1890, p. 1.

"Now I advise" Ibid.

"We can't stop" Ibid.

"coat of arms" Hall, *Daily Union History*, p. 139.

92   *"The industrious glass blower"* "It's a Queer Law!" *PB*, August 4, 1890, p. 1.

"All appreciate" ACDU, July 13, 1891, p. 4.

BABYLONIAN DAYS

Note: During its 1890 series on Atlantic City, the *Philadelphia Bulletin* repeated certain titles several times in its daily coverage of events.

93   (*Population of the resort*) Figures for 1890, 1900, 1910, Wilson, *The Jersey Shore*, II, 1127; figure for 1895, Trenton, New Jersey State Library, Archives and History Bureau, "New Jersey State Census, 1895. Volume for Atlantic County."

(*6,000 and 4,000 passengers*) ACDU, June 10, 1893, p. 1.

94   (*20,000 passengers*) "Just Before the Fourth," ACDU, July 3, 1893, p. 1.

(*46,680 passengers*) "The Opening Rush—The Glorious Fourth," ACDU, July 6, 1891, p. 1.

(*75,000 people*) "Atlantic City," PI, August 5, 1894, p. 9.

(*100,000 people*) "Down by the Sea Shore—Atlantic City," PI, August 27, 1893, p. 9.

(*Number of beer gardens and saloons*) U. S. Department of Interior, Census Office, *Eleventh Census, 1890. Report on the Social Statistics of Cities in the United States* (Washington: Government Printing Office, 1895), pp. 114–15. The population of the respective cities in 1890 was Atlantic City (13,055), Philadelphia (1,046,964), and New York City (1,515,301). The city limits of New York had not yet been extended to include Brooklyn.

"so wonderfully prolific" Kellow Chesney gives a marvelous picture of the English criminal class of this era in *The Anti-Society: An Account of the Victorian Underworld* (Boston: Gambit, 1970).

"We have had an inroad" Undated letter to "The Times" [?] in "Atlantic City Sketches." Newly arrived criminals were themselves liable to exploitation by sophisticated semilegal parasites. The *Philadelphia Bulletin* reported that several "real estate agents" made their living in Atlantic City by renting cottages to disreputable women, collecting the rent in advance. In a short time they

threatened the women with legal action for running a brothel, and when their tenants fled they were free to rent again. "At Atlantic City: The License Outrages Create a Big Sensation," *PB*, August 28, 1890, p. 1.

"The criminal repertoire" Atlantic City, Public Library, Local History Collection, loose newspapers in folders, *Atlantic Journal*, August 27, 1890, p. 1; "Acid in the Juice," *PI*, September 2, 1899, p. 3; "Atlantic Thinning Out," *PI*, August 27, 1895, p. 2; "Atlantic City's Foul Blots," *PI*, August 4, 1895, Sunday Supplement, pp. 21–22; "Stole a Bather's Watch," *PI*, July 1, 1895, p. 2.

94-5   (*Lewis Jerome fleeced*) "Big Fish Got Away," *ACDU*, July 20, 1893. The gamblers had in fact rented a house belonging to the brother of the chief of police, but the *Atlantic City Daily Union* represented the landlord as ignorant of the character of his tenants. The sharpsters' quick exit from town puts their claim to protection in doubt. Still, the presence of many criminal exiles from Philadelphia indicates an indulgent attitude among city officials, and possibly protection.

95   (*Pickpockets*) "Atlantic City," *PI*, August 11, 1895, p. 14; "To Guard Atlantic City Visitors from Light-Fingered Gentry," *PI*, July 25, 1900, p. 5.

"waiter . . . fell prey," "badger game," "knockout game" "Her Little Game," *ACDU*, July 29, 1893, p. 1; "Atlantic City's Foul Blots," *PI*, August 4, 1895, Sunday Supplement, pp. 21–22.

(*"Dutchy" Muhlrod*) "At Atlantic City: Open Violations of the Law in the City by the Sea," *PB*, August 7, 1890, p. 1.

"resort madams" "At Atlantic City: Some of the Queer Things at the City by the Sea," *PB*, August 14, 1890, p. 1.

"low saloon on Atlantic Avenue" "Atlantic City's Season Is Over," *PI*, August 30, 1891, p. 12.

"They brought with them the scum" "At Atlantic City: 'Dutchy,' the Gambler, Still Holds the Fort," *PB*, August 8, 1890, p. 1.

96   *"Officer Retzbach"* "Police News," *ACDU*, June 24, 1897, p. 1.

"no one made any complaint" "Atlantic City Wet; Governor Defied," *PB*, August 24, 1908, p. 3.

97   *"The consensus of opinion"* "Atlantic Faces Big Liquor Fight," *PB*, August 4, 1908, p. 8.

"90 per cent of them" Ibid.

"commended the Bulletin" "At Atlantic City: Soiled Doves Are Now on the Wing for Safety!" *PB*, August 22, 1890, p. 1.

"Not a word of commendation" Quoted in "At Atlantic City: Some of the Queer Things at the City by the Sea," *PB*, August 14, 1890, p. 1.

"interfere with the selling" "At Atlantic City: Some of the Queer Things at the City by the Sea," *PB*, August 18, 1890, p. 1.

"Shaner . . . threatened" "At Atlantic City: The 'Evening Bulletin's' Exposure Bears Good Fruit," *PB*, August 12, 1890, p. 1.

"It is time a halt" "The Gambling Dens Are Now Wide Open," *ACDU*, July 17, 1900, p. 1.

98   (*Stoy "demurred"*) "Atlantic City's Sunday Can't Be Made Dry," *PB*, August 3, 1908, pp. 1, 14.

"Roulette, faro and poker" "List of Gambling Joints Given Out in Atlantic City," *PB*, August 12, 1908, pp. 1–2.

"Would that the Review" *ACDU*, July 28, 1893, p. 4.

99   *"There are just about half"* "The Move Is Made to Arrest Crime," *ACDU*, July 20, 1900, p. 1.

"tenderloin" "Mayor's Stand is Commendable," *ACDU*, July 24, 1900, p. 1.

"for the first time in years" "Atlantic City's Tenderloin Was Closed All Night," *PB*, August 28, 1900, p. 2. It appears that the tenderloin was literally the "wrong side of the tracks," centering along Arctic and Baltic avenues and mainly to the east of the West Jersey and Seashore main line into the city.

"As a result of the raid" "Atlantic City Notes," *Philadelphia Public Ledger*, August 29, 1900, p. 5.

"sleeping dog" Let an exception be recorded. On July 17, 1900, the *Daily Union* exclaimed: "Vice stalks brazenly abroad by night rubbing raiment with virtue . . . and immorality elbows innocence upon the Boardwalk." ("The Gambling Dens Are Now Wide Open," *ACDU*, July 17, 1900, p. 1.) Aside from the rhetorical quality of this statement, the burden of evidence points to districted vice as the fundamental situation in 1900. No doubt there were many free-lance prostitutes who operated outside the district if the authorities for some exceptional reason tolerated or failed to apprehend them.

"signs of . . . public discontent" For 1893, see *ACDU* for July 27–29.

100   *(Liquor-license irregularities)* "At Atlantic City: Things Down There Begin to Grow Interesting," *PB*, August 25, 1890, p. 1.

"They are run from away down" "At Atlantic City: Open Violations of the Law in the City by the Sea," *PB*, August 7, 1890, p. 1.

(Levy's) "At Atlantic City: The 'Evening Bulletin's' Exposure Bears Good Fruit," *PB*, August 12, 1890, p. 1.

"the little man could find" "At Atlantic City: Strange Things Done in the Fair City by the Sea," *PB*, August 13, 1890, p. 1.

"What community would hail" "At Atlantic City: Some of the Queer Things at the City by the Sea," *PB*, August 14, 1890, p. 1.

"listed the names" "At Atlantic City: The Work of the 'Evening Bulletin' Shows Itself," *PB*, August 9, 1890, p. 1.

101   *"ladies' entrance"* "At Atlantic City: A Few Spasms of Fictitious Virtue May Be Expected!" *PB*, August 16, 1890, p. 1.

102   *"Bella Thomas' place"* "At Atlantic City: Some of the Queer Things at the City by the Sea," *PB*, August 16, 1890, p. 1.

"There is a notorious . . . house" "At Atlantic City: Some of the Queer Things at the City by the Sea," *PB*, August 14, 1890, p. 1. An interesting cross-reference to the madam's distribution of her business cards "in the gardens" is this awkwardly phrased apology in English's history of Atlantic City: "The standard at which they [the open-air concert gardens] are held elsewhere, must not be judged by what they may be regarded here. They are conducted with order and decorum." English, *History*, p. 175.

(Charles Coleman's gambling house) "At Atlantic City: Some of the Queer Things at the City by the Sea," *PB*, August 19, 1890, p. 1.

("disorderly saloon," Harry Smith's saloon) "At Atlantic City: Things Down There Begin to Grow Interesting," *PB*, August 23, 1890, p. 1.

"interracial house of prostitution" "At Atlantic City: The Work of the 'Evening Bulletin' Shows Itself," *PB*, August 9, 1890, p. 1.

"*low negro resort*" "At Atlantic City: Halt Is Cried to Individual Police Protection," *PB*, August 27, 1890, p. 1.

103   "*Next summer*" "At Atlantic City: The Wave of Reform Is Rolling to the Land," *PB*, September 6, 1890, p. 1.

"*Commission had reported unfavorably*" "Split over Fort's Policy," *PB*, August 28, 1908, p. 2.

"*Goldenberg made public*" "Gambling Dens Run Openly in Atlantic City," *PI*, August 13, 1908, pp. 1, 4.

"*Fort . . . demanding*" "Stoy Comes Out for Wet Sunday in Atlantic City," *PB*, August 15, 1908, pp. 1–2.

"*To the People*" "Fort Threatens to Send Troops to Clap Lid on Atlantic City," *PB*, August 27, 1908, pp. 1–2.

104   "*castigated Fort*" Editorial, *PB*, August 28, 1908, p. 6.

105   "*political boss*" "Atlantic City Officials Admit Town's Wide Open," *PI*, August 4, 1908, pp. 1, 4.

"*jailed for contract frauds*" See "Cleaning Up Atlantic City," *Literary Digest*, June 29, 1912, pp. 1332–33, and "The Rise and Fall of Kuehnle," *Literary Digest*, December 27, 1913, pp. 1285–93.

(*Donnelly and Westcott*) "Atlantic City Officials Admit Town's Wide Open," *PI*, August 4, 1908, pp. 1, 4.

(*Graff and Stafford*) "Fort Threatens to Send Troops to Clap Lid on Atlantic City," *PB*, August 27, 1908, pp. 1–2.

"*Ruffu . . . in 1930*" "Ruffu Asks Speedy Trial," *NYT*, March 25, 1930, p. 22.

"*Muhlrod . . . catered*" "List of Gambling Joints Given Out in Atlantic City," *PB*, August 12, 1908, pp. 1–2.

"*conferring with Dutchy*" "At Atlantic City: The 'Evening Bulletin's' Exposure Bears Good Fruit," *PB*, August 12, 1890, p. 1; "At Atlantic City: 'Dutchy,' the Gambler, Still Holds the Fort," *PB*, August 8, 1890, p. 1.

"*a mysterious tip*" "At Atlantic City: Some of the Queer Things at the City by the Sea," *PB*, August 18, 1890, p. 1.

"*officer No. 66*," "*at Mabel Haines's*" "At Atlantic City: The Story of a Much Annoyed Resident," *PB*, September 1, 1890, p. 1.

"*Mrs. Haines complained*" "At Atlantic City: A Few Spasms of Fictitious Virtue May Be Expected!" *PB*, August 11, 1890, p. 1.

"Bulletin . . . *wanted to know*" "At Atlantic City: Some of the Queer Things at the City by the Sea," *PB*, August 16, 1890, p. 1.

106   "*O'Neill . . . retorted*" (Italics mine.) "At Atlantic City: The 'Evening Bulletin's' Exposure Bears Good Fruit," *PB*, August 12, 1890, p. 1.

"*The Council . . . supported*" A similar unintentionally revealing incident took place three years later. During a meeting of the City Council, one councilman criticized the chief of police for "catching rather small fish," and suggested that he start cleaning up the dollar gambling machines. A motion was made to close all the gambling places in town, but it "was lost from the fact that when the roll was called there was not a quorum on the floor, a sufficient number having retired to the anteroom to have this effect." "Council's Doings," *ACDU*, July 11, 1893, p. 1.

106-7   "*There is no doubt*" "After Sunday Saloons in Atlantic City," *PI*, August 9, 1900, p. 2.

107 | (*Goldenberg and Bacharach*) "Atlantic's Sunday Can't Be Made Dry," *PB*, August 3, 1908, pp. 1, 14.

(*Higbee*) *Ibid*. Disorderly houses were defined as places "licensed for the sale of liquors, where sales are habitually made to minors of both sexes, and where drunken and disorderly persons are allowed to congregate, and . . . [places] not licensed for the sale of liquor, where intoxicants are sold and where women solicit from the windows." "Indict Gamblers and Liquor Men, Is Court's Order," *PB*, August 21, 1908, p. 1.

(*Mayor Stoy*) "Atlantic's Sunday Can't Be Made Dry," *PB*, August 3, 1908, pp. 1, 14.

"*run exclusively for visitors*" "Gambling Dens Run Openly in Atlantic City," *PI*, August 13, 1908, pp. 1, 4.

"*only men who are wealthy*" "List of Gambling Joints Given Out in Atlantic City," *PB*, August 12, 1908, pp. 1–2.

107-8 | (*Speidel's testimony*) "Atlantic City Officials Admit Town's Wide Open," *PI*, August 4, 1908, pp. 1, 4.

108 | (*Goodman*) "Stoy Comes Out for Wet Sunday in Atlantic City," *PB*, August 15, 1908, pp. 1–2.

"*laws should be adjusted*" "Atlantic City Not a Village, Says Clergyman," *PI*, August 15, 1908, pp. 1–2.

"*continental Sunday*" "Gardner May End Atlantic City War," *PB*, August 25, 1908, p. 12.

109 | (*Johnson quote*) "Saloon Owners in Atlantic City Decide to Close," *PB*, August 29, 1908, p. 1.

"*forced the Royal Arch*" "Atlantic City Yields; Will be Dry on Sunday," *PB*, August 28, 1908, p. 1.

"*Speidel . . . was able to pressure*" "Dry Sunday Again at Atlantic City," *PB*, September 5, 1908, p. 1.

"*grand jury . . . indicted*" "Split over Fort's Policy," *PB*, August 28, 1908, p. 2.

"*police raided*" "Atlantic City Men Free Until Grand Jury Acts," *PB*, August 18, 1908, p. 2.

"*And maybe the gambling fraternity*" "Lid to Stay Off in Atlantic City Until Fort Acts," *PB*, August 17, 1908, pp. 1–2.

"*the gamblers believe*" "Dry Sunday Again at Atlantic City," *PB*, September 5, 1908, p. 1.

(*Goodman sermon*) "Atlantic City Not a Village, Says Clergyman," *PI*, August 15, 1908, pp. 1–2.

109-10 | (Bulletin *editorial*) *PB*, August 28, 1908, p. 6.

110 | "*a sinner above*" *Ibid*.

("*Manifesto*" *quotes*) "Atlantic Men Reply to Fort," *PB*, September 8, 1908, p. 11.

113 | "*No Admission to the Laboratory*" "At Atlantic City: Some of the Queer Things at the City by the Sea," *PB*, August 19, 1890, p. 1.

113-14 | (*Boardwalk attractions in 1895*) "Atlantic City's Gay Throng," *PI*, July 30, 1895, p. 2; "Ready for Business," *PI*, July 3, 1895, p. 2; "Atlantic City's Foul Blots," *PI*, August 4, 1895, Sunday Supplement, pp. 21–22; "Atlantic City," *PI*, August 11, 1895, p. 14.

114 | "*those despicable scoundrels*" "At Atlantic City: Some of the Queer Things at the City by the Sea," *PB*, August 20, 1890, p. 1.

"*citizen of Reading*" "At Atlantic City: Things Down There Begin to Grow Interesting," *PB*, August 25, 1890, p. 1.

"*Beardless boys*" "At Atlantic City: The 'Evening Bulletin's' Exposure Bears Good Fruit," *PB*, August 12, 1890, p. 1.

(*Mrs. Thompson's brothel*) "At Atlantic City: Things Down There Begin to Grow Interesting," *PB*, August 23, 1890, p. 1.

(*Minnie Mason*) "Police News," *ACDU*, June 28, 1897, p. 1.

115   "*makes her heart sore*" "At Atlantic City: Things Down There Begin to Grow Interesting," *PB*, August 23, 1890, p. 1.

"*gambling men of New York*" "Atlantic Men Reply to Fort," *PB*, September 8, 1908, p. 11.

"*jealous of Atlantic City's prosperity*" "Atlantic Faces Big Liquor Fight," *PB*, August 4, 1908, p. 8.

"*abbreviated bathing suits*" "Mayor's Stand Is Commendable," *ACDU*, July 24, 1900, p. 1.

"*the coons and gamblers*" *ACDU*, March 9, 1892, p. 1.

"Daily Union *sneered*" "The Police Crusade," *ACDU*, July 20, 1900, p. 1.

"*protected white places*" "Fort's Raids Rile Atlantic Citizens," *PB*, September 14, 1908, p. 2.

116   "*desire of the culture to protect the family*" The shortcomings of family life are so taken for granted today by many of our contemporaries, particularly college-educated young people, that Victorian respect for the institution is facilely dismissed as cheap sentimentality further evidencing the smug conceit of the late nineteenth century. Victorians, of course, had good reason for cherishing the family as a source of emotional support in a society threatened by the depersonalizing forces that accompany urbanization and industrialization. Nevertheless, contemporary anti-family convictions having the guise of scientific objectivity are difficult to sustain empirically. Men and women continue to attempt to create families, and to date no widely imitable and stable alternative has emerged. The probability that our generation is having an unusually hard time achieving a viable adulthood is not prima facie evidence that the result will be more satisfactory than what previous generations achieved with far less pain, or that the family will be supplanted by some "superior" form of social organization. On the other hand, it is a historical fact that many Victorians established and preserved families and avowed themselves happy in the process. In short, a disposition for or against the family appears to depend on subjective opinion far more than on such dubiously "objective" data as appeals to "inevitable" social evolution and to the necessity of "progressive" behavior for a successful society.

In this connection, Charles E. Rosenberg's "Sexuality, Class, and Role in Nineteenth Century America" (Mimeographed. Philadelphia: University of Pennsylvania, n.d.) notes: "Even in the self-consciously liberated 1970's, when the expression of sexuality is sometimes seen as a moral imperative, we seem not to have produced a generation of psychically fulfilled and sexually adequate citizens." Rosenberg believes that "the social and sexual values of mid-and-late nineteenth century were probably no more inimical to human potential than those of any other period. Or . . . if they were, it remains still to be demonstrated."

Although the weight of evidence in the present study points to the family as the critical factor in understanding Atlantic City's vice problems, it is necessary to record the existence of a numerous "bachelor culture" during the Victorian period, a portrait of which is given in Ned Polsky's *Hustlers, Beats, and Others* (Chicago: Aldine Publishing Company, 1967). It would be very difficult or impossible to determine what proportion of Atlantic City's vice woes were due to confirmed bachelors as opposed to errant family males or males not yet entered into marriage. Common sense suggests that while the "sporting crowd" contributed to the resort vice industry, they had plenty of company from elements that bore some closer relationship to the family, such as young males on a spree, promiscuous single women, respectable married people (no doubt largely males) letting go for a few hours, and so forth. However, the question of the bachelor culture's role in Atlantic City, while interesting in itself, is not of essential importance here. No matter who generated the moral problems of the resort, the culture felt them to be a threat to the family. Secondly, though the culture might tend to wink at bachelor practices, it appears that in its most sober mood it did not have two distinct moral demands for members of its families and its bachelors (the sexual double standard always being remembered). Had this been the case, then stories of resort vice might be expected to have taken scrupulous note if bachelors were involved, for, by so doing, the blame or threat would have been removed from the family. But this did not occur.

"The flaunting, brazen women" "At Atlantic City: 'Dutchy,' the Gambler, Still Holds the Fort," *PB*, August 8, 1890, p. 1.

"A halt must be cried" "It's a Queer Law!" *PB*, August 5, 1890, p. 1.

"Hotel men . . . say" "Atlantic's Night: City Council and the Question of Regulating Liquor," *PB*, September 22, 1890, p. 2.

"Surely the women and children" "Atlantic City Must Obey Law, Says Gov. Fort," *PB*, August 14, 1908, pp. 1–2.

"Innocent children" "It's a Queer Law!" *PB*, August 5, 1890, p. 1.

'The near-sighted" "At Atlantic City: Some of the Queer Things at the City by the Sea," *PB*, August 20, 1890, p. 1.

117-18   (*Peter's Beach, Oceanic Dancing Pavilion*) "Atlantic City's Foul Blots," *PI*, August 4, 1895, Sunday Supplement, pp. 21–22.

118   *"policeman . . . rebuffed"* "At Atlantic City: Some of the Queer Things at the City by the Sea," *PB*, August 14, 1890, p. 1.

"Galatea" "At Atlantic City: Mayor Hoffman Compelled to Enforce the Laws," *PB*, August 30, 1890, p. 1.

"a moral cleansing" "Atlantic Reform: Atlantic City Clergymen Endorse the Evening Bulletin," *PB*, September 14, 1890, p. 1.

"the sanctity of the family" A notably cynical exception occurred on June 13, 1893, when Hattie White, "one of the 'five sisters' on New Jersey avenue," was brought before a city judge on a charge of operating a "disorderly house." The complainant dropped the charge after the judge admonished him to tell the truth because he was "making serious charges against a woman." The *Daily Union* concluded that Hattie was "free again to catch others in her magical trap." ("It Pleased the Court," *ACDU*, June 13, 1893, p. 1.) This kind of conscious perversion of cultural values is rare indeed.

THE MADDING CROWD

119   *"population . . . 18,000"* Trenton, New Jersey State Library, Archives and History Bureau, "New Jersey State Census, 1895. Volume for Atlantic County."

120   *"The minute Bertha"* O'Malley, "Board-Walkers," p. 234.

"ten thousand people" "Down by the Sea Shore—Atlantic City," *PI*, July 23, 1893, p. 10.

"Between the Boardwalk" "Baedeker," p. 42.

"carriage rides" Undated illustration in "Atlantic City Sketches."

"mayor prohibited driving" "At the Seaside," *PI*, July 17, 1892, p. 12.

"the spinal cord" McMahon, *So Young*, pp. 74–78.

121   *"A big roller skating rink"* "At Atlantic City: A Record of Unique Characteristics," undated newspaper clipping (from *The Tribune*[?]) in "Atlantic City Sketches."

(*History of the piers*) Frank M. Butler, *Book of the Boardwalk* (Atlantic City: The 1954 Association, 1953), pp. 15–20; McMahon, *So Young*, pp. 61–62; English, *History*, p. 162; Atlantic City, Public Library, Local History Collection, loose newspapers in folders, *Atlantic Journal*, August 13, 1890, p. 1.

121-2   (*Controversy over beach development*) McMahon, *So Young*, pp. 59–60, 76–78, 173; Atlantic City, Public Library, Local History Collection, loose newspapers in folders, *Atlantic Journal*, July 23, 1890, p. 1; "Atlantic City," *PI*, August 6, 1899, sec. III, p. 1; "Atlantic City," *PI*, August 14, 1898, p. 15.

122-3   (*Hotels and commercial enterprises on the Boardwalk*) Gopsill's *Atlantic City Directory . . . for 1891.*

123   *"The effect was extraordinary"* Robert Venturi's *Learning from Las Vegas* (Cambridge: M.I.T. Press, 1972) is an architectural study of a modern suburbanized analogue of Atlantic City. His emphasis on the attraction value of the façade recalls the Boardwalk strip, which, considered as a collectivity, was a vast façade for the whole of the resort. The factor limiting the analogy of Las Vegas to Atlantic City can be stated in one word: automobile. In today's Las Vegas, the automobile is the basic unit around which the resort is structured. In Atlantic City of the 1890's, city structure was oriented to the pedestrian, and the Boardwalk was a pedestrian avenue.

"city people seek" Jane Jacobs, *The Death and Life of Great American Cities* (New York: Vintage Books, 1961), p. 37.

(*Steel Pier*) Heston, "Good Times Book."

(*Postcards*) "Atlantic City Postcards."

"Fairly good attendance" "Down by the Sea Shore—Atlantic City," *PI*, July 23, 1893, p. 10.

"As far as the lure" Quoted in McMahon, *So Young*, p. 80.

124   *"oddities," "tragedies," "comedies"* "Chinatown in the Surf," *PI*, August 27, 1899, sec. III, p. 1; postcard, author's collection; "In the Merry Throng Down by the Sea," *PI*, August 18, 1897, p. 12.

125   *"The objective"* Marx, *The Machine in the Garden*, p. 226.

"On the level of popular thought" Attention is called to the definitions I have given in the Preface.

"One goes to the seaside" "A New Atlantis," p. 615. By "canvass encampment," the author probably means the tent clusters such as might be found at seaside religious retreats.

"Atlantic City in 1854 and 1894" Alfred M. Heston, *Heston's Hand Book of Atlantic City* (Philadelphia: Franklin Printing Company, 1894).

126   *"a grasping hand"* Cape May to Atlantic City, p. 39.

"Extending seaward" *Atlantic City, New Jersey: America's Greatest Resort* (Atlantic City: Bureau of Information and Publicity, 1907), p. 23. Hereafter referred to as *America's Greatest Resort* (1907).

"sand sculptures" "The Sand Artist at Atlantic City," NYT, June 11, 1911, Picture Section, p. 4.

127   *"Sea Spider"* Leslie Dorsey and Janice Devine, *Fare Thee Well* (New York: Crown Publishers, 1964), p. 296.

"The sea, the sea" Heston, *1888*, p. 25.

"salt water taffy" McMahon, *So Young*, pp. 103–04.

128   *"A Message from the Sea"* Cape May to Atlantic City.

"A related query" "Atlantic City Sketches"; "Atlantic City Postcards."

"We have perhaps" Howard, "Our American Brighton," p. 333.

"picture book" J. Murray Jordan, *Atlantic City* (Philadelphia: By the Author, 1897).

128-9   *(Lehigh Valley pamphlet)* *Atlantic City Reached Via the Lehigh Valley Railroad System* (Boston: John A. Lowell and Company, n.d.).

129   *"The actual title"* English, *History*, p. 63.

"gay couples" *Steel Pier, Atlantic City, 1907* (N.p.: n.p. [1907]).

"Concerts by noted bands" *Atlantic City, New Jersey: America's Greatest Resort* (5th ed.; Atlantic City Publicity Bureau, 1909), p. 15.

"Four spacious decks" ACDU, July 15, 1890, p. 1.

"fish pond" ACDU, June 2, 1893, p. 1.

"piers afford" Heston, *1887*, p. 55.

"sun parlors" Hall, *Daily Union History*, p. 235.

"There is not a mile" Heston, *1887*, p. 130.

"The proximity" Hall, *Daily Union History*, p. 235.

130   *"The darkness"* Francis H. Hardy, "Seaside Life in America," *Cornhill Magazine*, New Series, I (November 1896), 610.

130-1   *(Street's apparatus)* Captain William Tell Street, *Life Lines for Sea Bathing* (Frankford, Pa.: By the Author [ca. 1870]).

131-3   *(Early lifeguards)* English, *History*, pp. 119, 218.

133   *(Praise of lifeguards)* J. Murray Jordan, *Atlantic City* (N.p.: By the Author, 1903) (no page numbers); Walter B. Peet, "Where Life-Saving Is an Expert Science," *Harper's Weekly*, September 5, 1908, p. 25.

"picture book" Jordan, *Atlantic City*.

"Although . . . no fatal accidents" "Down by the Sea Shore—Atlantic City," PI, July 23, 1893, p. 10.

"*rescues*" "Life-Saving Record," *PI*, September 2, 1896, p. 7; "Season Is Closing," *PI*, August 31, 1899, p. 5.

134 "*at least one-half*" "August Days at the Leading Seashore Resort," *PI*, August 20, 1899, sec. IIJ, p. 1.

"*a majority of the rescues*" "Everything Goes at Atlantic City," *PI*, August 14, 1895, p. 2.

"*Nature as a . . . refuge*" Charles Rosenberg's *The Cholera Years* (Chicago: University of Chicago Press, 1962), pp. 6 and 28, examines a particular health problem and its relation to urban life. He notes that "in 1832, most Americans regarded the United States as a land of health, virtue, and rustic simplicity. Cities seemed often unnatural . . . excrescences in an otherwise green and pleasant realm." When cholera struck in that year, "almost everyone who could afford to left the city. Farm houses and country houses within a thirty-mile radius were completely filled." Great progress in urban sanitation during the nineteenth century did not eradicate popular belief in the superior healthfulness of "country" living, as may be seen in the success of Atlantic City. Indeed, a lively concern with air pollution has once again made city dwelling seem a risk-filled choice.

135 "*the dust and heat*" *Cape May to Atlantic City*, p. vi.

"*The panting City*" English, *History*, p. 3.

(*Children's Sea-Shore House, Mercer Memorial Home*) Heston, 1887, pp. 68–71.

"*lowest death rate*" *Ibid.*, pp. 66–67.

"*For Health and Pleasure*" McMahon, *So Young*, p. 57.

"*the only place on the coast*" English, *History*, p. 324.

(*Reed's paper*) Boardman Reed, *Atlantic City as a Winter Health Resort* (2nd ed.; Philadelphia: Allen, Lane and Scott [ca. 1881]).

(*Railroad publications*) For example, *Atlantic City By the Sea.*

"*The Winters are . . . mild*" "Cape May's Attractions," *NYT*, June 16, 1878, pp. 1–2.

136 "*Hall assured his readers*" Hall, *Daily Union History*, pp. 203–11, 355–56.

"*little is known of*" *Summer Sketches*, p. 19.

"*Best of all*" O'Malley, "Board-Walkers," p. 234.

"*light and buoyant*" *Atlantic City By the Sea*, p. 4.

"*with but few exceptions*" English, *History*, pp. 176–77.

"*There is here constantly*" *Marlborough-Blenheim, Atlantic City, N.J.* (N.p.: n.p., n.d.).

137 "*The little invalid*" Hall, *Daily Union History*, pp. 209–11.

"*Marx's study*" Peter J. Schmitt's *Back to Nature: The Arcadian Myth in Urban America* (New York: Oxford University Press, 1969) relates both to Marx's book and to the present study, but there are important differences. He takes most of his data from the period 1900–30, during which time the automobile exerted a profound change in American life. Secondly, many of the attitudes he presents come from men of wealth, or at least from the economically upper middle class. A number of these people were intellectual and social leaders of their day. Schmitt sees not a conflict between urban preference and rural sentiment, but a conscious fondness for "Arcadia," which consists of urban amenities and cultural opportunities plus the spiritual advantages supposedly afforded by the countryside. This self-aware pursuit of Arcadia appears, at least at the turn of the century, to have been the domain of relatively sophisticated and privileged people, as compared to the lower-middle-class crowds who frequented Atlantic City.

138   *"The solid character"* Heston, *1888*, p. 63.

        "There is no monotony" Ibid., p. 38.

139   *"In a concise form"* Cape May to Atlantic City, p. vi.

140   *"The sea to our ills"* North, *Atlantic City in Picture and Poem*, p. 13.

141   *"His soul, like a bark"* Heston, *1894*, pp. 21–23.

"FALLEN LADY"

142   (*Population, 1940–70*) Edward C. Burks, "Atlantic City Watches County Grow," *NYT*, May 21, 1972, p. 84.

        (*Outward migration*) *Ibid*. Net outward migration comprises people actually leaving the city. In addition, there were 3,440 *more white deaths than births* and 2,335 (my calculation) *more black births than deaths*.
1) Total population loss (1960–70) = whites leaving + blacks leaving + white (deaths − births) − black (births − deaths)
2) $11,685 = 8,258 + 2,322 + 3,440 - x$
3) $x = 2,335$ more black births than deaths

        "half the population" Ibid.

        "second-oldest population" "A Dowager's Decline," *Newsweek*, June 18, 1970, p. 87.

        "one fourth . . . over sixty" Elwood G. Davis, *Poverty in Atlantic City and Atlantic County* (Atlantic City: Atlantic Human Resources, Inc., 1965) (no page numbers). Hereafter referred to as *Poverty in Atlantic City.*

        "poorest city" Ibid.

        (*1912 health conditions*) Brett, "Black and White," p. 726.

143   *"unemployment"* Poverty in Atlantic City.

        "welfare assistance" James F. Clarity, "Atlantic City's Better Half Is All Most Tourists See," *NYT*, August 4, 1971, p. 35.

        "crimes" "Atlantic City Leads Nation in Crime in Its Population Class," *PI*, September 3, 1972, New Jersey Section, pp. 1, 5.

        "a forlorn shuffle" John McPhee, "A Reporter at Large: The Search for Marvin Gardens," *The New Yorker*, September 9, 1972, pp. 45 ff.

        "The proof of the pudding" Gaeton Fonzi and Bernard McCormick, "Bust-Out Town," *Philadelphia Magazine*, August 1970, p. 117.

        "The tarnished elegance" Bob Pearce and Sue Pearce, "Snow Cones and Frankfurters," *Library Journal*, LXXXIV, No. 12 (1969), p. 2415.

        "a tomblike symbol" "Hotels: Return of a $1 Guest," *Newsweek*, November 16, 1970, p. 89.

144   *"The sedate . . . promenade"* Wade Greene, "On the Boardwalk: What a Difference a Century Makes!" *NYT*, July 12, 1970, sec. X, p. 7.

        "living off its reputation" Fonzi and McCormick, "Bust-Out Town," p. 58.

"*Fifty years ago*" Neil Hickey, "There She Is: Or, Through the Years with Bert Parks and Miss America," *TV Guide*, September 5, 1970, pp. 11–12. Hereafter referred to as "Bert Parks and Miss America."

"*blue bloods*" "A Dowager's Decline," p. 86.

145   (*Kuehnle*) See "The Rise and Fall of Kuehnle," *Literary Digest*, December 27, 1913, pp. 1285–93.

"*indictments*" "Jewels Sparkle in 'Vice' Round-Up," *NYT*, September 3, 1922, p. 12.

"*suspension of . . . vice squad*" "Ruffu Asks Speedy Trial," *NYT*, March 25, 1930, p. 22.

(*Johnson*) A most interesting account of Johnson's career is contained in William E. Frank and Joseph W. Burns, *The Case of Enoch L. Johnson*, A Complete Report of the Atlantic City Investigation Conducted Jointly by the Treasury Department and the Department of Justice (N.p.: n.p.: 1943).

(*Farley exposé*) Greg Walter, "The Only Game in Town," *Philadelphia Magazine*, August 1971, pp. 50–55, 88–92.

146   "*indicted for extortion*" "Atlantic City Mayor Indicted in Extortion," *NYT*, May 5, 1972, pp. 1, 11.

(*Young*) McMahon, *So Young*, p. 165.

"*THE Promenade*" *America's Greatest Resort* (1907), pp. 23–25.

"*Mecca*," "*The world's playground*" R. L. Duffus, "The Big Parade on Atlantic City's Boardwalk," *NYT*, August 12, 1928, pp. 12–13, 20.

(*President Hotel*) McMahon, *So Young*, pp. 148–49.

(*U.N. invitation*) *To the United Nations Organization: An Invitation from the State of New Jersey and the City of Atlantic City* (N.p.: n.p., 1946). Hereafter referred to as *United Nations*.

"*mackintosh law*" McMahon, *So Young*, p. 95.

147   "*golf in shorts*" C. Edgar Dreher, "Atlantic City Has It!" *The Rotarian*, May 1936, p. 27.

"*I want to restore*" "New York Police Aid A.C.," *NYT*, August 21, 1930, p. 21.

"*This new government*" Leavitt F. Morris, "Atlantic City Sand in Your Shoes," *Christian Science Monitor*, May 10, 1941, Weekly Magazine Section, pp. 8–9, 13.

"*a city with*" *United Nations*.

"*Fifty-seven . . . in . . . 1922*" "Scores of Beauties Headed for Pageant," *NYT*, September 5, 1922, p. 19.

"*eighty in 1924*" "Philadelphia Girl Gets Beauty Crown," *NYT*, September 7, 1924, p. 9.

147-8   (*Norman Rockwell*) "King Neptune Opens Seashore Pageant," *NYT*, September 7, 1922, p. 36; "Floats Parade at Atlantic City," *NYT*, September 7, 1923, p. 24.

148   "*deficit . . . made up*" "To Decide on Beauty Pageant," *NYT*, February 19, 1928, p. 14.

"*There were piquant*" "Snappy Revue of Beauty and Carnival of Color Features Chair Parade," *ACDP*, September 8, 1922, pp. 1, 5.

(*Miss Trenton*) *Ibid.*

(*Motion Picture Ball*, "*contracts to girls*") "Big Pageant Ball," *ACDP*, September 9, 1922, p. 2.

"*To choose a girl*" "Miss America Is Eager for Public Career," *ACDP*, September 14, 1936, p. 1.

"*forced to sign*" "Two More Spurn Beauty Pageant," *NYT*, September 10, 1925, p. 29.

149 | "*grave dangers*" "YWCA Opens War on Beauty Contest," *NYT*, April 10, 1925, p. 21.

(*Bishop Hafey*) "Bishop Condemns Beauty Pageant," *NYT*, November, 30, 1927, p. 10.

(*Federation of Church Women*) "Women Open Fight on Beauty Pageant," *NYT*, November 18, 1927, p. 12.

"*Camp Meeting Association*" "Attacks Bathing Review," *NYT*, September 11, 1923, p. 15.

"*mutterings and frownings*" "An Unbeautiful Show," *PB*, September 12, 1925, p. 8.

"*reprehensible way*" "Criticism Well Deserved," *NYT*, April 21, 1924, p. 16.

"*A meeting of women*" "Attack Beauty Pageant," *NYT*, March 1, 1927, p. 3.

"*I have not seen one*" "Saw No American Beauty," *NYT*, September 9, 1923, sec. I, part 2, p. 8.

149-50 | (*Long vs. short hair*) "Pageant Directors and Judges Make Discovery That Starts Something," *ACDP*, September 4, 1922, pp. 1, 6.

150 | "*every vestige*" "Some Behind-Time Knocking," *ACDP*, September 1, 1925, p. 13.

(*Lois Delandor*) "Beauty Show Victor Is Not a Smoker," *NYT*, September 11, 1927, p. 31.

"*eliminate . . . swimsuit judging*" "Atlantic City to Drop Its Outdoor Pageant," *NYT*, March 12, 1928, p. 13.

"*a bit more valuable*" Editorial, *ACDP*, September 3, 1935, p. 8.

"*exact scheme*" "Storm Mars Beauty Meet; Defers Parade," *ACDP*, September 6, 1935, pp. 1, 18.

"*We are past*" "Miss California Captures First Talent Contest," *ACDP*, September 9, 1936, pp. 1, 8.

"*forbidding . . . contact with males*" Hickey, "Bert Parks and Miss America," p. 12.

151 | "*fathers . . . not allowed*" Chandler Brossard, "Place of the Month: Atlantic City," *Holiday*, September 1969, p. 90.

151-2 | (*Monorail*) "Half an Hour It Will Take to Reach Atlantic City," *PI*, July 16, 1900, p. 5.

152 | "*slight accidents*" "Enthusiastic Locomobilists Speed in Silent Vehicles to the Shore," *PI*, July 29, 1900, p. 3.

"*only unimpeded access*" Wilson, *The Jersey Shore*, I, 474.

"*first automobile bridge*" "Traffic Sweeps over New Delaware Bridge," *ACDP*, July 2, 1926, pp. 1, 19.

152-3 | (*Reading ultimatum*) "Cut Buses or Trains—R.R. Ultimatum," *ACDP*, July 24, 1926, pp. 1, 7.

153 | "*If the railways enforce*" "What Can They Do About It?" *ACDP*, July 26, 1926, p. 11.

"*changed travel habits*" Cunningham, *The New Jersey Shore*, p. 30.

154 | (*Gloucester*) "How Our City Grows," *ACDU*, October 4, 1891, p. 1.

(*Coney Island*) *ACDU*, July 28, 1893, p. 4.

(*Reed pamphlet*) English, *History*, pp. 183–94. English notes that Reed's pamphlet was "issued by the Pennsylvania Railroad Company."

154-5   (*"Japanese," "Turkish" goods*) *Gopsill's Atlantic City Directory . . . for 1891*, pp. 265–89.

155   "*rarest importations*" *America's Greatest Resort* (1907), p. 21.

"*Venetian Lady Troubadours*" *ACDU*, July 3, 1890, p. 4.

(*Kiramura Sisters, Haidaboro Family*) *ACDU*, August 17, 1900, p. 4.

"*Royal Berlin Orchestra*" *Steel Pier, Atlantic City, 1907*.

"*Egyptian tent*" "Petrified Man," *ACDU*, July 27, 1893, p. 1.

155-6   (*The Japanese Tea Gardens*) "Atlantic City," *PI*, July 12, 1896, p. 18; "Atlantic City," *PI*, July 24, 1898, p. 22; "Atlantic City," *PI*, August 2, 1896, p. 18; "Crowds Still Find Enjoyment Down by the Sounding Sea," *PI*, August 16, 1899, p. 5; "Gov. Roosevelt Given an Ovation at New Jersey's Popular Resort," *PI*, July 24, 1900, p. 12; "Some Curious Scenes Depicted on Beach at Gay Atlantic City," *PI*, July 28, 1900, p. 3; "Jersey News," *PI*, July 29, 1898, p. 2.

157   "*scenes that would have surprised*" James F. Clarity, "Atlantic City's Better Half Is All Most Tourists See," *NYT*, August 4, 1971, p. 35.

"*Blacks . . . thronged*" Fonzi and McCormick, "Bust-Out Town," p. 58.

" '*ruined' once the blacks take it over*" Eldridge Cleaver, *Soul on Ice* (New York: Dell Publishing Company, 1968), p. 92.

158   "*biggest Cinderella story*" Hickey, "Bert Parks and Miss America," p. 12.

"*When the Victorian lady*" See Frank Deford, *There She Is: The Life and Times of Miss America* (New York: The Viking Press, 1971), pp. 255–62.

Selected Bibliography

Alexander, Jack, "That's How They Got Nucky Johnson." *Reader's Digest,* May 1942, pp. 79–87.

Atlantic City. Public Library, Local History Collection. Alfred M. Heston scrapbook, "Good Times Book, vol. I, Trips 1894–1895."

——. Chandler Stewart scrapbook, 1906–12.

——. Minute book of the Cottagers' Association of Atlantic City.

——. "News Clippings, 1895–1910, A. M. Heston, Local History."

——. "Reminiscences of Absecon Beach and Atlantic City, 1795–1914. A. M. Heston, 1914."

——. Scrapbook of postcards.

——. Untitled scrapbook of theater programs.

Atlantic City and County, New Jersey, Biographically Illustrated. Philadelphia: Alfred M. Slocum Company, 1899.

Atlantic City By the Sea. Philadelphia: Passenger Department, Pennsylvania Railroad, 1889.

Atlantic City Daily Press, September 4, 7, 8, 1922; September 8, 1923; September 1, 2, 7, 1925; July 1, 2, 7, 8, 20–22, 24, 26, 28, 31, August 2, 4, 5, 9, 19, 23, 28, 1926; September 3, 6, 9, 1935; September 9, 14, 1936.

Atlantic City Daily Union, July 15, 17, 1889; March 6, 8, 12, July 1, 3, 5, 16, 20–22, 25, 26, 28, August 21, December 1, 8, 15, 22, 29, 1890; July 4, 6, 9–11, 13–17, 20, August 8, 10–12, 20, 26, 28, September 3, October 14, 1891; January 8, 28, February 11, 17, 18, 22, 1892; May 30, 31, June 1–30, July 3–29, August 1, 1893; March 1, 5, 10, 14, July 7, 12, 14, 16, 23, December 3, 10, 17, 31, 1894; July 2, 23, 1895; February 27, March 11, 1896; January 29, 30, February 6, 9, 26, June 5, 18, 19, 24, 26, 28, 1897; March 5, 7, 9, 1898; March 14, July 2, 17, 18, 20, 23–25, 30, 31, August 6, 7, 17, 24, 29, 31, 1900.

Atlantic City, New Jersey: America's Greatest Resort. Atlantic City: Bureau of Information and Publicity, 1906.

Atlantic City, New Jersey: America's Greatest Resort. Atlantic City: Bureau of Information and Publicity, 1907.

Atlantic City, New Jersey: America's Greatest Resort. 5th ed. Atlantic City Publicity Bureau, 1909.

Atlantic City Reached Via the Lehigh Valley Railroad System. Boston: John A. Lowell and Company, n.d.

"Atlantic City Turns Over a New Leaf." *Survey,* XXXVI (May 27, 1916), 216.

Atlantic City, the World's Greatest Resort. 7th ed. Atlantic City Publicity Bureau, 1912.

Baltzell, Edward D. *Philadelphia Gentlemen: The Making of a National Upper Class.* Glencoe, Ill.: Free Press, 1958.

Bennett, Helen C. "Come On In—The Water's Fine!" *American Magazine*, August 1926, pp. 42–45, 144.

Bliven, Bruce. "The American Utopia: Atlantic City." *New Republic*, December 29, 1920, pp. 126–27.

Blundon, B. A. *Atlantic City As a Winter Health Resort*. Philadelphia: Lineaweaver and Wallace, 1885.

Brett, Margaret L. "Atlantic City: A Study in Black and White." *Survey*, XXVIII (September 7, 1912), 723–26.

Brossard, Chandler. "Place of the Month: Atlantic City." *Holiday*, September 1969, pp. 90–91, 94.

Cape May, 1623–1903. Philadelphia: Cape May Real Estate Company, 1903.

Cape May to Atlantic City: A Summer Note Book. N.p.: Passenger Department, Pennsylvania Railroad Company, 1883.

Carnesworthe. *Atlantic City: Its Early and Modern History*. Philadelphia: William C. Harris and Company, 1868.

Charter and By-Laws of the Camden and Atlantic Land Company. Philadelphia: Inquirer Book Press, 1853.

Chesney, Kellow. *The Anti-Society: An Account of the Victorian Underworld*. Boston: Gambit, 1970.

"Cleaning Up Atlantic City." *Literary Digest*, June 29, 1912, pp. 1332–33.

Cleaver, Eldridge. *Soul On Ice*. New York: McGraw-Hill, 1968; Dell Publishing Company, 1968.

Cope, Charles Henry, M.A. *Reminiscences of Charles West Cope*. London: Richard Bentley and Son, 1891.

Cunningham, John T. *The New Jersey Shore*. New Brunswick, N.J.: Rutgers University Press, 1958.

Dale, Thomas M. *Atlantic City in the Twentieth Century*. Speech at the Bourse, December 2, 1897, on the occasion of the presentation of Resolutions from the Hotel Men's Association of Atlantic City to the Traders' League of Philadelphia. N.p.: n.p. [1897].

Davis, Elwood G. *Poverty in Atlantic City and Atlantic County*. Atlantic City: Atlantic Human Resources, Inc., 1965.

Deford, Frank. *There She Is: The Life and Times of Miss America*. New York: The Viking Press, 1971.

Dorsey, Leslie, and Janice Devine. *Fare Thee Well*. New York: Crown Publishers, 1964.

Douglas, Paul L. *Real Wages in the United States, 1890–1926*. Boston: Houghton Mifflin Company, 1930.

"A Dowager's Decline." *Newsweek*, June 8, 1970, pp. 86–87.

Downey, James F. "A Queen of the Coast." *Demorest's Family Magazine*, 1895 (pages not numbered; contained in an untitled scrapbook compiled by Alfred M. Heston in the Local History Collection of the Atlantic City Public Library).

Dreher, C. Edgar. "Atlantic City Has It!" *The Rotarian*, May 1936, pp. 26–29.

English, A. L. *History of Atlantic City, New Jersey*. Philadelphia: Dickson and Gilling, 1884.

Fonzi, Gaeton, and Bernard McCormick. "Bust-Out Town." *Philadelphia Magazine*, August 1970, pp. 56–65, 115–24.

Frank, William E., and Joseph W. Burns. *The Case of Enoch L. Johnson*. A Complete Report of the Atlantic City Investigation Conducted Jointly

by the Treasury Department and the Department of Justice. N.p.: n.p., 1943.

Fried, Frederick. *A Pictorial History of the Carousel.* New York: A. S. Barnes and Company, 1964.

Funnell, Charles E. Unpublished research for Natural and Historic Resource Associates, 313 South Sixteenth Street, Philadelphia, Pennsylvania, 1973.

Garrison, C. G. *Publication of the Results of the Investigation into the Affairs of Atlantic City. September 1, 1884.* N.p.: n.p. [1884].

George A. Crawford's Atlantic City Directory, 1900. Atlantic City: G. A. Crawford and Company, 1900.

Ginger, Ray. *Eugene Debs: The Making of an American Radical.* New York: Collier Books, 1962.

Gopsill's Atlantic City Directory for 1882–1883. Philadelphia: James Gopsill, 1882.

Gopsill's Atlantic City Directory. Philadelphia: James Gopsill's Sons, 1885–1908.

Grand Atlantic Hotel, Atlantic City, N.J. New York: South Publishing Company [1897].

Hall, John F. *The Daily Union History of Atlantic City and County, New Jersey.* Atlantic City: Daily Union Printing Company, 1900.

Hardy, Francis H. "Seaside Life in America." *Cornhill Magazine,* New Series, I (November 1896), 605–19.

Henry, Jules. *Culture Against Man.* New York: Random House, 1963.

Heston, Alfred M. *Absegami: Annals of Eyren Haven and Atlantic City, 1609 to 1904.* 2 vols. Camden, N.J.: By the Author, 1904.

————. *Illustrated Hand-Book of Atlantic City, New Jersey.* Philadelphia: Franklin Printing House, 1887.

————. *Illustrated Hand-Book of Atlantic City, New Jersey.* Atlantic City: A. M. Heston and Company, 1888.

————. *Illustrated Hand-Book of Atlantic City, New Jersey.* Atlantic City: A. M. Heston and Company, 1889.

————. *Heston's Hand Book of Atlantic City.* Philadelphia: Franklin Printing Company, 1892.

————. *Heston's Hand Book of Atlantic City.* Philadelphia: Franklin Printing Company, 1894.

————. *Heston's Hand Book of Atlantic City.* Atlantic City: A. M. Heston, 1899.

————. *Heston's Hand-Book of Atlantic City: Twentieth Century Souvenir Edition.* Atlantic City: Alfred M. Heston, 1901.

Hickey, Neil. "There She Is: Or, Through the Years with Bert Parks and Miss America." *TV Guide,* September 5, 1970, pp. 11–13.

Holdzkom and Company's Atlantic City Cottage and Business Directory for 1884. Atlantic City: Holdzkom and Company, 1884.

"Hotels: Return of a $1 Guest." *Newsweek,* November 16, 1970, pp. 89–90.

Howard, Maurice M. "Our American Brighton." *Potter's American Monthly,* November 1880, pp. 321–33.

Jacobs, Jane. *The Death and Life of Great American Cities.* New York: Random House, 1961; Vintage Books, 1961.

Jacobs, Norman, ed. *Culture for Millions?* Princeton: D. Van Nostrand Co., 1961.

Jordan, J. Murray. *Atlantic City*. Philadelphia: By the Author, 1897.

Kirkland, Edward C. *Dream and Thought in the Business Community, 1860–1900*. Chicago: Quadrangle Paperbacks, 1964.

Kluckhohn, Clyde. "Culture." *Dictionary of the Social Sciences*. 1964.

Lee, Elisha. *Atlantic City and the Railroads*. Address by Elisha Lee, Vice-President, Pennsylvania Railroad System, before the Kiwanis Club, Rotary Club and Chamber of Commerce of Atlantic City, May 15, 1923.

Lichtenstein, Gaston. *A Visit to Young's Pier at Atlantic City, N.J.* Reprinted from the *Tarborough Southerner*, Tarborough, N.C. Richmond, Va.: William Ellis Jones, 1908.

McLean, Albert F. *American Vaudeville as Ritual*. Lexington: University of Kentucky Press, 1965.

McMahon, William. *So Young . . . So Gay*. Atlantic City: Atlantic City Press, 1970.

McPhee, John. "A Reporter at Large: The Search for Marvin Gardens." *The New Yorker*, September 9, 1972, pp. 45 ff.

Mangels, William F. *The Outdoor Amusement Industry*. New York: Vantage Press, 1952.

Marlborough-Blenheim, Atlantic City, N.J. N.p.: n.p., n.d.

Marx, Leo. *The Machine in the Garden*. New York: Oxford University Press, 1967.

Meehan, William E. *Rand, McNally and Company's Handy Guide to Philadelphia and Environs, Including Atlantic City and Cape May*. Chicago: Rand, McNally and Company, 1895.

Morris, Leavitt F. "Atlantic City Sand in Your Shoes." *Christian Science Monitor*, May 10, 1941, Weekly Magazine Section, pp. 8–9, 13.

"A New Atlantis." *Lippincott's Magazine*, June 1873, pp. 609–20.

"The New Baedeker: Casual Notes of an Irresponsible Traveller." *The Bookman*, XXX (September 1909), 41–51.

New Jersey and the Negro: A Bibliography, 1715–1966. Trenton: New Jersey Library Association, 1967.

New Jersey Supreme Court. *Charles S. Baker vs. The Camden and Atlantic Railroad Company*. N.p.: Camden Democrat, 1877.

New York City. New York Public Library. Wilhelm Benignus, "Collection of Post Cards from Atlantic City, N.J., 1902–1908."

The New York Times, June 16, 1878; August 14, 1883; June 11, 1911; September 3, 5, 7, October 29, 1922; September 7, 9, 11, 1923; April 18, 21, September 7, 1924; September 10, 1925; March 1, May 6, September 11, November 18, 30, 1927; February 19, March 12, August 12, 1928; March 25, August 21, 1930; July 12, 1970; August 4, 1971; May 21, 1972.

North, Dr. James. *Atlantic City in Picture and Poem*. Camden, N.J.: By the Author, 1906.

"Nucky's Nemesis." *Newsweek*, November 3, 1941, pp. 16–17.

Nye, Russel. *The Unembarrassed Muse: The Popular Arts in America*. New York: The Dial Press, 1970.

O'Malley, Frank Ward. "The Board-Walkers: Ten Days with Bertha at Atlantic City." *Everybody's Magazine*, August 1908, pp. 233–43.

Osborne, Richard B. *Camden and Atlantic Railroad: Engineer's Report, June 24th, 1852*. Philadelphia: n.p., 1852.

Oxford English Dictionary. Vol. VI. Oxford: Clarendon Press, 1933.

Pearce, Bob, and Sue Pearce. "Snow Cones and Frankfurters." *Library Journal*, LXXXIV, No. 12 (1969), 2415–18.

Pearce, Roy H. "Mass Culture/Popular Culture: Notes for a Humanist's Primer." *College English*, XXXIII (March 1962), 417–32.

Peet, Walter B., M.D. "Where Life-Saving Is an Expert Science." *Harper's Weekly*, September 5, 1908, p. 25.

Penn, A. G. "To Atlantic City by Way of ——— [*sic*]." *Lippincott's Magazine*, October 1870, pp. 420–26.

Perry, Doris M. *This Is New Jersey: A Tercentenary Bibliography.* Trenton: Roscoe L. West Library, 1963.

Philadelphia. Historical Society of Pennsylvania. John Hill Martin scrapbook, "Atlantic City Sketches," 1856–85.

Philadelphia Bulletin, August 2, 5–9, 11–16, 18, 23, 25–30, September 1–6, 15, 16, 22, 23, 30, October 7, 1890; August 4, 28, 1900; August 3, 4, 7, 12, 14, 15, 17, 18, 21, 24, 25, 27–29, 31, September 5, 8, 14, 1908; September 12, 1925; September 9, 1926; September 9, 1927.

Philadelphia Inquirer, August 30, 1891; July 17, 24, 31, August 7, 28, 1892; July 2, 9, 10, 16, 23, 30, August 6, 13, 23, 27, 28, 1893; July 8, 15, 22, 29, 30, August 5, 12, 26, 1894; July 1, 3, 28, 30, August 4, 11, 14, 27, 1895; July 5, 12–13, 19, August 2, 23, September 2, 6, 1896; August 8, 15, 18, 20, 24, September 2, 1897; July 10, 24, 29, August 12, 14, 21, September 4, 1898; August 1–2, 6, 10, 14, 16, 20, 23, 27, 31, September 2–3, 1899; July 16, 22, 24, 28–29, August 9, 23, 1900; July 14, 21, 28, 1901; August 4, 13, 15, 24, 1908; May 5, September 3, 1972.

Philadelphia Public Ledger, August 29, 1900.

"Pikes Peak." *Encyclopaedia Britannica.* 1972. Vol. XVII.

Polsky, Ned. *Hustlers, Beats, and Others.* Chicago: Aldine Publishing Company, 1967.

Public Ordinances of Atlantic City from September 8th, 1854 to August 25th, 1903. Atlantic City: Board of Commissioners, 1913.

Randel, William Peirce. *Centennial: American Life in 1876.* Philadelphia: Chilton Book Company, 1969.

Reed, Boardman, M.D. *Atlantic City as a Winter Health Resort.* 2nd ed. Philadelphia: Allen, Lane and Scott [ca. 1881].

Report of the President and Managers of the Camden and Atlantic Railroad Company to the Stockholders. January 15, 1871. Philadelphia: Lineaweaver and Wallace, 1871.

Richards, Horace G. *One Hundred South Jersey Novels: A Bibliography of Fiction with a South Jersey Setting.* Trenton: New Jersey Folklore Society, 1947.

"The Rise and Fall of Kuehnle." *Literary Digest*, December 27, 1913, pp. 1285–93.

The Ritz-Carlton, Atlantic City, N.J. N.p.: Gilbert T. Washburn and Company, n.d.

Rood, Henry E. "The Vacation City by the Sea: A Resort Where It is Always Seasonable." *Harper's Weekly*, April 24, 1909, p. 28.

Rosenberg, Charles E. "Sexuality, Class, and Role in Nineteenth Century America." Mimeographed. Philadelphia: University of Pennsylvania, Department of History, n.d.

——— *The Cholera Years.* Chicago: University of Chicago Press, 1962.

"Saint Gotthard Pass." *Encyclopaedia Britannica.* 1972. Vol. XIX.

Sea-Side Views of the City by the Sea, Atlantic City. Philadelphia: J. B. Lippincott and Company, 1875.

Smith, Henry Nash. *Popular Culture and Industrialism.* New York: New York University Press, 1967.

————. *Virgin Land.* Cambridge: Harvard University Press, 1950; New York: Vintage Books, 1950.

Social Register, Philadelphia, 1893. VII, 3 (November 1892). New York: Social Register Association, 1892.

Social Register, Philadelphia, 1894. VIII, 2 (November 1893). New York: Social Register Association, 1893.

Social Register, Philadelphia, 1900. XIV, 3 (November 1899). New York: Social Register Association, 1899.

Social Register, Philadelphia, 1901. XV (November 1900). New York: Social Register Association, 1900.

Social Register, Summer 1900. XIV, 19. New York: Social Register Association, 1900.

Somers Point, New Jersey. Atlantic County Historical Society. Collection.

————. Hotel Dennis register, 1901.

————. Kuehnle's Hotel register, 1881–84.

————. Kuehnle's Hotel register, 1890–91.

————. Silas R. Morse Scrapbook, 1840–1928.

————. *To the American Bankers' Association Is Hereby Cordially Extended an Earnest Invitation . . .* Atlantic City Board of Trade, 1904.

Souvenir Program of the Semi-Centennial Celebration, Atlantic City, N.J. Philadelphia: Alfred M. Slocum, 1904.

Special Park Commission. *Report of Investigation of Bathing Beaches.* N.p.: Chicago City Council, 1913.

"The Spectator." *Outlook,* CIV (July 26, 1913), 718–19.

The Standard Guide of Atlantic City, New Jersey. Atlantic City: Standard Guide Publishing Company, 1909.

Steel Pier, Atlantic City, 1907. N.p.: n.p. [1907].

Steel Pier, Atlantic City, 1915. N.p.: n.p. [1915].

Steevens [*sic*], John. "The Charm of Eastertide at Atlantic City." *Harper's Weekly,* April 18, 1908, pp. 20–22.

Summer Sketches of the City By the Sea: Atlantic City for Season 1883. N.p.: Camden and Atlantic Railroad, 1883.

"Switzerland." *Appleton's Annual Cyclopaedia and Register of Important Events of the Year 1881.* New Series. Vol. VI.

To the United Nations Organization: An Invitation from the State of New Jersey and the City of Atlantic City. N.p.: n.p., 1946.

Trenton. New Jersey State Library, Archives and History Bureau. "New Jersey State Census, 1885. Volume for Atlantic County."

————. "New Jersey State Census, 1895. Volume for Atlantic County."

————. "New Jersey State Census, 1905. Atlantic City."

————. "New Jersey State Census, 1905. Supervisor's Report."

U.S. Department of Commerce. Bureau of the Census. *Fourteenth Census of the United States: State Compendium, New Jersey.* Washington: Government Printing Office, 1925.

U.S. Department of the Interior. Census Office. *Compendium of the Tenth Census, 1880,* pt. 1. Washington: Government Printing Office, 1885.

——. *Eleventh Census, 1890: Population of the United States by Minor Civil Divisions.* Washington: U.S. Census Printing Office, 1891.

——. *Eleventh Census, 1890: Report on the Social Statistics of Cities in the United States.* Washington: Government Printing Office, 1895.

——. *Vital Statistics of New York City and Brooklyn: Covering a Period of Six Years Ending May 31, 1890.* Washington: Government Printing Office, 1894.

Venturi, Robert, Denise S. Brown, and Steve Izenour. *Learning from Las Vegas.* Cambridge: M.I.T. Press, 1972.

Walter, Greg. "The Only Game in Town." *Philadelphia Magazine,* August 1971, pp. 50–55, 88–92.

Wilson, Harold F. *The Jersey Shore.* 2 vols. New York: Lewis Historical Publishing Company, 1953.

——. "Victorian Vacations at the Jersey Shore." *Proceedings of the New Jersey Historical Society,* LXXVII, No. 4 (1959), 267–71.

Wolfe, Tom. *Radical Chic & Mau-Mauing the Flak Catchers.* New York: Farrar, Straus and Giroux, 1970; Bantam Books, 1971.

——. *The Kandy-Kolored Tangerine-Flake Streamline Baby.* New York: Farrar, Straus and Giroux, 1965; Noonday Press, 1965.

Index

Illustration Credits

A PHOTOGRAPHIC ALBUM

Page ii, *top*, Atlantic County Historical Society; *bottom*, The Library of Congress. iii, *top and bottom*, The Library of Congress. iv, *top and bottom*, The Library of Congress. v, *top*, Atlantic County Historical Society; *bottom*, The Library of Congress. vi, Atlantic County Historical Society. vii, *top*, The Library of Congress; *bottom*, Atlantic County Historical Society. viii, *top*, author's collection; *bottom*, The Library of Congress. ix, *top*, Atlantic County Historical Society; *bottom*, author's collection. x—xi, The Library of Congress. xii, *top and bottom left*, author's collection; *bottom right*, The Library of Congress. xiii, *top, middle, and bottom*, author's collection. xiv, *top*, Atlantic County Historical Society; *bottom*, The Library of Congress. xv, *top*, author's collection; *bottom*, The Library of Congress. xvi, *top*, Atlantic County Historical Society; *middle*, The Library of Congress; *bottom*, author's collection. xvii, *top*, The Library of Congress; *bottom*, author's collection. xviii, *top and bottom*, author's collection. xix, *top*, author's collection; *bottom*, The Library of Congress. xx, *top and bottom*, Atlantic County Historical Society. xxi, *top*, Atlantic County Historical Society; *bottom*, author's collection. xxii, *top*, Atlantic County Historical Society; *bottom*, author's collection. xxiii, *top*, Atlantic County Historical Society; *bottom*, The Library of Congress. xxiv, *top left*, author's collection; *top right and bottom*, The Library of Congress. xxv, *top*, The Library of Congress; *bottom*, author's collection. xxvi, *top and bottom*, The Library of Congress; *middle*, author's collection. xxvii, The Library of Congress. xxviii, *top*, The Library of Congress; *bottom*, Atlantic County Historical Society. xxix, *top and bottom*, Atlantic County Historical Society. xxx, Atlantic County Historical Society. xxxi, The Library of Congress. xxxii, *top*, William McMahon Collection; *bottom*, author's collection.

ILLUSTRATIONS IN TEXT

Page 2 from *Harper's Weekly* (xxxiv, 9 August 1890, p. 613), Courtesy The New York Public Library. 126 from *Harper's Weekly* (xxxii, 25 August 1888, p. 637). Courtesy The New York Public Library. Pages 85, 117, 132, 158. Courtesy Atlantic City Public Library.

With the exception of those noted above, all line drawings reproduced in the text are from the Philadelphia *Inquirer*, 1894–1900. Courtesy University of Pennsylvania.

About the Author

CHARLES FUNNELL was born and raised in Southampton, New York. After attending public schools there, he studied history at Cornell, and later obtained his master's and doctorate in history from the University of Pennsylvania. He now lives in Philadelphia.

About the Type

THE TEXT of this book was set on the Linotype in a new face called Primer, designed by Rudolph Ruzicka, who was earlier responsible for the design of Fairfield and Fairfield Medium, Linotype faces whose virtues have for some time now been accorded wide recognition.

The complete range of sizes of Primer was first made available in 1954, although the pilot size of 12 point was ready as early as 1951. The design of the face makes general reference to Linotype Century—long a serviceable type, totally lacking in manner or frills of any kind—but brilliantly corrects its characterless quality.

This book was composed by Maryland Linotype Composition Co., Baltimore Maryland. It was printed and bound by Haddon Craftsmen, Inc., Scranton, Pennsylvania.

Chapter-opening decoration by Jane Sterrett. Design by Stephanie Tevonian.